David Maule
with Madeleine du Vivier

FOOD under

STUDENT'S BOOK

The Complete English Course

Contents

Grammar	Vocabulary	Exam Practice — Workbook
• Present Simple, Present Continuous • Future forms	• Guessing the meaning of unknown words • Travel and holidays • Negative prefixes	Writing 1 Use of English 1 Speaking 1
• Past Simple, Past Continuous • Nouns: countable and uncountable	• The law/Crimes and punishments • Suffixes • Phrasal verbs/expressions with *come*	Writing 2 Listening 4 Speaking 2
• Modal and logical deduction • Zero and first conditionals • Order of adjectives	• Compound adjectives • Word transformation	Reading 2 Writing 2 Use of English 3
• *used to* and *would* • *used to* and *be/get used to* • Present Perfect, Past Simple • *ago, already, for, since* and *yet* • *could, might, have to*	• Borrowed words • Confusing words (*say/speak/tell/talk*) • Compound nouns • Ways of speaking	Use of English 4 Listening 2 Speaking 4
• Past Simple, Past Perfect • The passive, impersonal passive • Articles: zero, definite and indefinite	• Adjectives and noun collocations • Clothes and accessories • Phrasal verbs/expressions for clothes/dressing	Writing 2 Listening 1 Speaking 2
• Present Perfect, Present Perfect Continuous • Comparatives and superlatives	• Health and fitness • Adjectives with prepositions • Phrasal verbs/expressions with *give* • Sports equipment and venues, sports	Reading 4 Writing 2 Use of English 1
• Second conditionals • *if only, it's time, 'd rather, suppose* and *imagine* • Modals • Past tenses and past modals	• Nouns and adjectives for feelings • *-ing/-ed* adjectives • Phrasal verbs/expressions with *go* • Sleep • Senses • *make* or *do*?	Use of English 2 Listening 3 Speaking 3
• Third conditionals • Modals + Present Perfect • Expressing purpose, result and contrast	• Phrasal verbs/expressions for relationships • Adjective and preposition collocations • Adjectives to describe people and character • Homographs	Reading 2 Writing 2 Speaking 1
• Reported speech (1) • *someone, anyone, everybody, nobody*, etc.	• Town and country • Phrasal verbs/expressions with *have* • Phrasal verbs/expressions for housing	Reading 1 Use of English 4 Listening 1
• Summary of conditionals and non-conditional *if*-sentences • Alternatives to *if*	• Phrasal verbs/expressions with *turn* • Science and technology • Prepositional phrases • Cars and driving	Writing 2 Use of English 5 Listening 2
• Verb patterns: *-ing* or infinitive? • Expressing preferences	• Food and cooking • Adjectives for taste • Phrasal verbs/expressions with *put* • Confusing words: *raise/rise/lie/lay/lie*	Reading 1 Writing 1 Speaking 4
• Verbs and *that* clauses • *allow/permit/let* • Verbs/adjectives and prepositions	• Environment • Word transformation • Weather • Phrasal verbs/expressions with *bring*	Reading 3 Writing 2 Use of English 2
• *-ing* forms • Causatives: *have/get* + object + past participle	• Newspapers, magazines and televison/Entertainment • Shops and shopping ← • Phrasal verbs/expressions with *fall* *Problems/Complaints*	Reading 4 Writing 2 Use of English 3
• Relative pronouns and clauses	• Education/Employment • Adjective and noun collocations • Phrasal verbs for education	Reading 3 Listening 3 Speaking 3
• Reported speeech (2) • Reporting verbs	• Money • Phrasal verbs/expressions with *look* • Prepositional phrases • American and British English • Verb and noun collocation	Writing 2 Use of English 5 Listening 4

* References such as **R1** are to parts of the exam e.g. **R**eading Part **1**.

Exam map

The University of Cambridge First Certificate in English

PAPER 1
Reading
1 hour 15 minutes
Parts 1 2 3 4

PAPER 2
Writing
1 hour 30 minutes
Parts 1 2

PAPER 3
Use of English
1 hour 15 minutes
Parts 1 2 3 4 5

PAPER 4
Listening
about 40 minutes
Parts 1 2 3 4

PAPER 5
Speaking
14 minutes
Parts 1 2 3 4

Reading, Part 1	Choosing summaries	Exam Practice Units 1/9/11

You have an article divided into 7 or 8 paragraphs and a set of headings or summary sentences, which you have to match with the paragraphs in the article. The first one is done for you and there is an extra heading or summary which you don't need to use.
Focus: identifying main points.

marks: 2 per question

Reading, Part 2	4 x multiple choice	Exam Practice Units 3/5/8/10

The text is followed by 7 or 8 multiple-choice questions, each with four possible answers. Questions may relate to: opinions or attitudes expressed in the text; the meaning of particular phrases; particular references; or to the writer's purpose or point of view. The questions follow the order of the text.
Focus: understanding detail, opinion and gist, deducing meaning.

marks: 2 per question

Reading, Part 3	Replacing sentences/paragraphs	Exam Practice Units 2/7/12/14

You have a text with 7 or 8 sentences or paragraphs removed. You have to put these back in the correct place in the text. The first one is done for you and there is an extra one which you don't need to use.
Focus: understanding the development of ideas, opinions and events in a text.

marks: 2 per question

Reading, Part 4	Choosing people or places	Exam Practice Units 4/6/13/15

This text is either continuous or, more commonly, made up of 5 or 6 sections. You also have a list of opinions, attitudes, facts, etc., which you have to connect with people or places in the text. Some of these can connect with 2 people or places. The total number is either 13 or 14.
Focus: identifying specific information and detail.
Note: the number of questions in the different parts can vary but the total is always the same.

marks: 1 per question

— Total Reading Marks: 35
Adjusted to: 40

Writing, Part 1	Compulsory letter	Exam Practice Units 1/7/11

This part is compulsory. You are given an advert, a notice, a letter, etc., and some notes that 'you' have written about it. You have to write a 120-180 word letter to accept an invitation, make a complaint, give information, etc. Marks are awarded in two areas: accuracy of language, including spelling and punctuation; and completion of the task, which is assessed on **content**, **organisation** and **cohesion**, **range** of structures and vocabulary, **register** and **format**, and **target reader** indicated in the task.
Focus: transactional writing.

marks: 20

Writing, Part 2	Choice of writing task	Exam Practice Units 2/3/4/5/6/8/9/10/12/13/14/15

Questions 2-4 provide a choice of writing tasks, which might include a composition giving your opinion, an article, a report, a letter of application, an informal letter, or a short story. You can choose to do one of these, or to answer question 5: a general question on one of the two set books. You have to write 120-180 words. Note that if you choose to write a letter in Writing Paper 2, you don't have to include an address.
Focus: writing for a specific situation.

marks: 20

— Total Writing Marks: 40

Use of English, Part 1	Gap-filling, 4 x multiple choice	Exam Practice Units 1/6/11

You read a text with 15 numbered spaces in it. In each case you have to choose the best word to fill the space from a choice of 4 possible words. This tests your knowledge of the meaning of words and their grammar, and of fixed phrases, phrasal verbs, collocations and linking words.
Focus: vocabulary and word grammar.

marks: 1 per question

Use of English, Part 2	Gap-filling, free choice	Exam Practice Units 2/7/12

The text has 15 missing words, but this time you have to think of a word to fill each of the spaces. The words needed are mainly structural, such as adverbs, prepositions, pronouns and auxiliaries. The wrong use of capitals and other punctuation doesn't lose you marks, but you must spell the words correctly.
Focus: vocabulary and structural forms.

marks: 1 per question

Use of English, Part 3	Sentence transformations	Exam Practice Units 3/5/8

You are given 10 sentences. For each one you have to complete a second sentence so that it has a similar meaning to the first. You are given the beginning and end of the sentence and you have to use a word which is given. You can't change the word given and you must use between two and five words including this word.
Focus: sentence grammar and vocabulary.

marks: 2 per question

Use of English, Part 4	Identifying extra words	Exam Practice Units 4/9/14

You have a text with 15 lines, which is similar to something that a student at your level would write. In most of the lines there is an unnecessary word, which you have to find. Most of these are functional words like auxiliaries, prepositions, pronouns or articles. Not all the lines of the text contain errors.
Focus: sentence grammar.

marks: 1 per question

Use of English, Part 5

Word building

Exam Practice Units 5/10/15

The text has 10 spaces in it. For each of these, you are given a word at the end of the line which will fill the space correctly if you change its form. This might involve adding a prefix or suffix, making it into a noun, adjective, adverb etc., or adding another element to make a compound word.

Focus: vocabulary in context.

marks: 1 per question

——— Total Use of English Marks: 75
Adjusted to: 40

Listening, Part 1

3 x multiple choice

Exam Practice Units 1/5/9

You hear one or more people talking in 8 different situations. You have to choose the correct answer from 3 options for the question given. Questions may ask where the conversation is taking place, its subject, who the speakers are, the relationship between the speakers, what happened, and also a speaker's emotion, attitude, feelings or opinion.

Focus: general understanding, main points, detail, function, location, relationships, mood, attitude, intention, feeling or opinion.

marks: 1 per question

Listening, Part 2

Gap filling

Exam Practice Units 4/10/13

You hear a talk, an interview, or a lecture, or similar. You have ten questions in the form of incomplete sentences or notes. You have to pick out information, usually up to a maximum of three words to complete the spaces. The questions are in the same order as the information you hear. Minor spelling errors aren't penalised, unless the word has been spelt out for you.

Focus: general understanding, main points, detail or specific information.

marks: 1 per question

Listening, Part 3

Matching statements to speakers

Exam Practice Units 3/7/11/14

You hear 5 short recordings with different people talking. They might be talking about a similar subject or the link might be functional — all of them asking for information, or apologising. You have to match each speaker to one of 6 statements which summarise what that person says. There is one extra statement which you don't need to use.

Focus: summarising.

marks: 1 per question

Listening, Part 4

Selecting from possible answers

Exam Practice Units 2/6/8/12/15

You hear one or more speakers talking and you have 7 questions. These come in different formats. You might have to: decide if each statement is true or false, or if an idea was stated or not; identify which of 3 speakers said what, or what was said about 3 subjects. The questions are in the same order as the information you hear.

Focus: general understanding, main points, detail or specific information.

marks: 1 per question

——— Total Listening Marks: 30
Adjusted to: 40

Speaking

You take the Speaking test with another student. If there are three candidates, they do the test together. It lasts 14 minutes. There are two examiners in the room. One of them, the interlocutor, talks with you and your partner(s). The other one doesn't take part in the discussion, but listens to what you say. You are assessed by both the examiner and the interlocutor on grammar and vocabulary, your ability to manage the discussion and interact with the other student(s), and your pronunciation.

Speaking Part 1

Interview (3 minutes)

Exam Practice Units 1/8/11/13/14

The interlocutor will ask you and your partner some questions about, for example, who you are, your family, where you live, what you do every day, what you like and dislike. You are expected to give full answers and listen to your partner.

Focus: giving personal information, talking about present circumstances, talking about past experiences, talking about future plans.

Speaking Part 2

Individual talk (4 minutes)

Exam Practice Units 1/2/5/12

The interlocutor will give you two photographs and ask you to let your partner see them. You will then be asked to talk about them for about a minute. You will have to compare and contrast the photos and give your views about a specific point, for example, to say how you think the people in the photos are feeling. Then the interlocutor will ask your partner a question connected with the photos. Your partner will also be asked to talk about a different pair of photographs and then the interlocutor will ask you a question.

Focus: giving information, comparing and contrasting, expressing opinions, personal reactions.

Speaking Part 3

Discussion with partner (3 minutes)

Exam Practice Units 2/3/5/6/7/9/10/13/14

You and your partner are shown a diagram, a plan, drawings, or photographs which illustrate a situation and a number of possibilities. The interlocutor will describe the situation to you and ask you and your partner to suggest a solution or comment on the situation, or both. The important point is the discussion between you and your partner. You don't have to reach an agreement.

Focus: exchanging information and opinions, expressing and justifying opinions, agreeing and/or disagreeing, suggesting, speculating.

Speaking Part 4

Guided discussion (4 minutes)

Exam Practice Units 2/4/5/6/7/10/11/12/14/15

The interlocutor will ask you and your partner questions relating to the situation in Part 3 in order to discuss the topic in more detail. You have more freedom in this part of the test to express your ideas, and it gives you a final chance to show what you are capable of.

Focus: exchanging information and opinions, expressing and justifying opinions, agreeing and/or disagreeing.

——— Total Speaking marks: 40

Grading and results

There is no minimum pass mark for each paper. Your results in all five papers are put together for the final mark. FCE has three pass grades (A, B and C) and two fail grades (D and E). You need about 60% of the total marks for a C grade. Candidates will receive their results approximately 2 months after taking the exam. The results include a graphic display of how the candidate did in each paper.

UNIT 1
Lifestyles

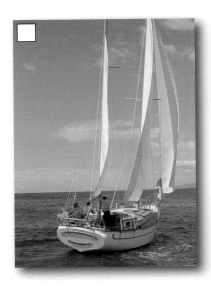

FCE Paper 5, Part 2

❶ What kind of lifestyle does each picture show? Which do you prefer? Number the boxes from 1-4 in order of preference.

❷ Now discuss your preferences with another student. What kind of lifestyle do you have?

❸ Fill in this form about your lifestyle.

Marlow Market Research into Leisure Interests

We are conducting a survey about leisure activities. Can you fill in this form?
Tick the boxes below to show how often you take part in the following activities:

1 General exercise/individual sports (swimming, squash, jogging, multi-gym)
☐ often ☐ sometimes
☐ never ☐ hardly ever

2 Extreme sports (bungee jumping, paragliding, abseiling)
☐ often ☐ sometimes
☐ never ☐ hardly ever

3 Cultural activities (theatre, cinema, ballet, reading)
☐ often ☐ sometimes
☐ never ☐ hardly ever

4 Rock music/dance (rock concerts, raves, clubbing)
☐ often ☐ sometimes
☐ never ☐ hardly ever

5 General socialising (cafés, bars, parties)
☐ often ☐ sometimes
☐ never ☐ hardly ever

6 Relaxing in the country (hiking, walking in the hills)
☐ often ☐ sometimes
☐ never ☐ hardly ever

❹ Work with other students. *Don't show the others your form* but tell them about your choices. Find a student who likes different things to you and find out *three* more things about their leisure activities.

Vocabulary

Guessing the meaning of unknown words

1 *We are conducting a survey.* Do you know the word *conducting*? It's easy to guess the meaning because of the words which are used with it. It means something like *doing*. Underline the words in the form you did not know. Was it necessary to know them to fill in the form?

It's important to learn how to work out the meanings of new words. When you see a new word, here are some questions to ask yourself:

1 **What meanings are possible for this word?** *Fill in* is a phrasal verb, but look at the words around it. *Fill in* means *complete... the form.* Here's another phrasal verb, *take part in...* What does it mean? It means something like *do, play* or *join.*

2 **Do I know this word as a different part of speech?** *Socialising.* You may know *social* as an adjective. The verb is *to socialise.*

3 **Is this word similar to another word I know?** *Paragliding.* This comes from *parachute* and *gliding.* If you know either of these words, you can guess the meaning.

4 **Is there a similar word in my language, or is the word international like bungee jumping?** This word is the same in many languages.

5 **Do I need to know the meaning of this word to do the activity?** You could complete the form without knowing the meaning of all these words.

Reading

1 You are going to read about growing coffee in Tanzania. Look at these sentences from the article. Match each word in bold with one of the definitions (A-J).

A going down

B piece of work

C treated unfairly

D freed from wild plants

E outside area near a house

F grown without chemicals

G check while others work

H side of a mountain or hill

I chemicals to kill insects

J the amount produced

1 ...to make coffee, the most important **task** to start the day.

2 I live on the **slopes** of Kilimanjaro, surrounded by fields of coffee.

3 ...I am still farming coffee — **organic** coffee.

4 ...the way farmers here have traditionally grown coffee — without **insecticides**.

5 The crops always need to be **weeded**...

6 At the farm, I **oversee** that the flesh of the cherry is separated from the bean.

7 ...wash the coffee cherries and put them on tables or concrete **patios** to dry in the sun.

8 ...the farm that used insecticides had an increased **yield**...

9 ...we felt that for years we had been **exploited** by private buyers...

10 I go home when the sun is **setting**.

2 Look at the photograph of Philip Tesha and read the introduction to the article. What things will you read about? Tell another student.

3 Read the article and check your ideas. What two things surprised you about his life?

1 ....
....
....
....
....

2 ....
....
....
....
....

FCE Paper 1, Part 1

4 This article has been divided into eight paragraphs. Choose from the list (A-I) the sentence which best summarises each paragraph (1-7). There is one extra sentence which you do not need to use.

A The coffee plants need a lot of attention.

B Coffee is a declining industry.

C Coffee comes before breakfast.

D Innovation came unexpectedly.

E Coffee has always been part of his life.

F Keeping in touch is important.

G A change might make a difference.

H The process of producing coffee is quite complex.

I Picking coffee is a family activity.

Guarantees
a **better deal**
for Third World
Producers

FAIRTRADE

A Life in the Day of Philip Tesha

Philip Tesha, 84, grows coffee on his farm on the slopes of Mount Kilimanjaro, 4,700ft above the town of Moshi, Tanzania. He and his wife, Jovithayes, have seven children and 25 grandchildren.

0   **C**

At 6am I wake with the sun, and my wife and I get out of bed. Before I go outside to feed the goats and chickens, I get dressed and put on enough water to make coffee, the most important task to start the day.

1 ⬚

I live on the slopes of Kilimanjaro, surrounded by fields of coffee. Although I am now 84, here I am still farming coffee – organic coffee. They say that Kilimanjaro coffee is the best in the world, because of the climate and the rich soil, and the way farmers here have traditionally grown coffee – without insecticides.

2 ⬚

After breakfast, I set out to climb to the coffee fields. Some of the coffee plants are 100 years old. When people know that a tree can survive so long, they think that means it is easy to grow coffee – but that is not so. The crops always need to be weeded and today we understand that we must replace old stems by planting new seedlings.

3 ⬚

I weed and pick the coffee cherries from the plants. Men, women and children work together. We have no segregation – we want to be friendly and equal. We pay people by the amount of coffee they pick. Often you see women with babies on their backs. In Africa we don't have baby-sitters. As soon as the oldest child is big enough, they will look after the younger children.

4 ⬚

The women carry the coffee back to our farm on their heads in sisal sacks. At the farm, I oversee that the flesh of the cherry is separated from the bean. Then we wash the coffee cherries and put them on tables or concrete patios to dry in the sun. After that, we bring the sacks of coffee in a lorry to the Native Farmers' Union in Moshi.

5 ⬚

In the 1950s Africans were encouraged to use insecticides, but most could not afford it. For years you might have two farmers next to each other: one used insecticides, and the other did not. Initially, the farm that used insecticides had an increased yield; but after some years we noticed that the untreated coffee plants had a better yield. We were growing organic coffee – it was a new idea – and we didn't know it!

6 ⬚

Then we spoke to Cafédirect, which works according to principles of the Fairtrade Foundation. They told us they would sell our coffee direct to supermarkets in the UK. Certainly we felt that for years we had been exploited by private buyers, because the price we used to be paid did not meet our costs. Now Cafédirect has arranged to trade with us.

7 ⬚

I stop working at about 5 or 5.30, and then I might go to a bar where I will have a glass of Kilimanjaro beer with some other farmers. I go home when the sun is setting. I don't like to go to bed late, but first I listen to the news on the World Service. I like to know what is happening in the world.

Grammar

Present Simple/Present Continuous

❶ Read the first paragraph of the text again:

At 6am I wake with the sun, and my wife and I get out of bed. Before I go outside to feed the goats and chickens, I get dressed and put on enough water to make coffee, the most important task to start the day.

**Philip Tesha is describing what he does every day, so of course he uses the Present Simple.
In the picture on page 8 we can see Philip Tesha. He's drinking a cup of coffee — and we use the Present Continuous because it's what we see *now*.**

❷ Sometimes the choice between these two tenses is not so simple. Look at the text below. Decide whether you prefer the Present Simple or the Present Continuous for questions 1-6.

Forest fires are a global problem. In Europe alone forest fires **1** *destroy/are destroying* more than half a million hectares each year. People **2** *start/are starting* most forest fires, and lightning **3** *causes/is causing* the rest. Some climatologists believe we **4** *see/are seeing* more forest fires because of changing weather patterns. Forest fires have started much earlier in the western states of the US this year due to shortage of rainfall. The ground **5** *has/is having* only about 20% of the moisture it would normally hold at this time of the year. Rivers **6** *run/are running* dry and the mountains are bare because they have only had a quarter of their usual snowfall during the winter.

❸ Work with another student and explain your choices. Then read the Theory Box.

Theory Box

Present Simple or Present Continuous?

Q1 We use the **Present Simple** when the situation is **long-lasting** or **permanent** and the **Present Continuous** when it is **limited** or **changing**. The writer thinks that the situation is unlikely to change. Another writer could use the Present Continuous in the same situation. If you chose *are destroying*, you aren't wrong — just optimistic and think the situation can change.

Q2/3 These facts are unlikely to change, so the **Present Simple** is the better choice.

Q4 This is a changing situation — so use the **Present Continuous**.

Q5 When *have* is used to mean possession it is a state verb and isn't used in the continuous. The amount of moisture in the ground is a fact and there is no need to say that the situation is temporary.

Q6 This is a changing, temporary situation — rivers can run dry quite quickly.

Remember: sometimes you have a choice between the Present Simple and the Present Continuous. It depends on the message you want to give.

❹ Look at the sentences below about Philip Tesha's daily routine. Now write some sentences about your own daily life. There are two examples to get you started.

1   He wakes up very early.
   I don't. I get up as late as possible.
2   He starts the day with coffee.
   I prefer tea in the morning.
3   He walks to work.
   I ....
4   He works outside.
   I ....
5   He works with men, women and children.
   I ....

6   He stops working at about 5 or 5.30.
   I ....
7   He might go for a drink on the way home.
   I ....
8   He listens to the radio before he goes to bed.
   I ....
9   He doesn't like to go to bed late.
   I ....

❺ Work in groups. Tell each other about your daily routine. Do you all have similar routines or do you do very different things?

🎧 Listening

❶ You will hear people talking about events in the future. Answer these questions about the conversations. What did they say which helped you answer the question? Compare your ideas with another student.

Conversation...

1 What time is their appointment?
2 What has the weather been like this week?
3 What activity are they talking about?
4 What's on at the theatre?
5 What's wrong with the woman?
6 What does the man want to do now?

FCE Paper 4, Part 1

❷ Listen again and for questions 1-6, choose the best answer A, B or C. You will hear each recording twice.

1 You overhear two men talking about a sports event. When is it?

A today
B tonight
C later this week

2 You hear the weather forecast. What will the weather be like tomorrow?

A getting colder
B getting wetter
C getting sunnier

3 You overhear a woman talking on the phone. Who is she talking to?

A her husband
B her daughter
C her son

4 You overhear a man and woman talking. What does the woman want to do tonight?

A go to the theatre
B go to the cinema
C stay at home

5 You overhear a woman talking to a friend. What does she want to do?

A to apologise
B to discuss
C to request

6 You overhear a man talking about an exam. How does he feel about it?

A pessimistic
B confident
C terrified

Grammar

Future forms

❶ Decide if you think these phrases are about the present or future. For each question, tick a box. Talk about your answers with another student.

	present time	future time
1 ...she'll be in the swimming pool...	☐	☐
2 ...the pool opens at 7.30...	☐	☐
3 ...she's getting up very early...	☐	☐

❷ Now read this phone call.

Sorry – Helen's out. She'll be in the swimming pool now. Yes, I know it's early but the pool opens at 7.30, some people like a swim before work. She's getting up very early at the moment. You could phone her tonight before 7.30 because after that she'll be in the swimming pool again. Yes, the pool opens at 7.30 tonight for an evening session. Tomorrow? She's getting up very early because she's off to Milan for a meeting. I don't see her very often these days. Maybe you could send her an e-mail. I do sometimes.

Theory Box

The future

The **Present Simple** and **Continuous** can work either in the present or future. The sections in red are in the present; the blue ones are in the future. We know the difference because of the other information in the text.

There are a number of ways of referring to the future in English — the **Present Simple**, the **Present Continuous**, and *will* and *going to*. Both of these have more than one meaning:

will
I'll do it later. **intention** I'm going to do it later. · She'll lose her job. **judgement** She's going to lose her job.
going to

However, there is a difference in meaning when we use *will* and *going to* for **intention**, or for **judgement**. Let's see if you can tell the difference. Look at the situations on the opposite page.

3 For each situation, choose the correct response, a, b or c. The responses include *will*, *going to*, the Present Simple and Present Continuous. Discuss each sentence with another student.

1 I want to see you in my office at 4 o'clock.
   a Sorry, I meet Daniel at 4.00.
   b Sorry, I'm meeting Daniel at 4.00.
   c Sorry, I'll meet Daniel at 4.00.

2 Waiter! I want to complain about this chicken.
   a I'm getting the manager.
   b I'll get the manager.
   c I'm going to get the manager.

3 Cristina — you look pale. Are you feeling OK?
   a No, I don't feel well. I think I'm being sick.
   b No, I don't feel well. I think I'll be sick.
   c No, I don't feel well. I think I'm going to be sick.

4 It's City's match today — they're winning with ten minutes to go.
   a But I've a feeling United score soon.
   b But I've a feeling United are scoring soon.
   c But I've a feeling United will score soon.

5 Emily — I'm in a hurry. Can you ask the boss to sign this?
   a OK, when she gets back from lunch.
   b OK, when she's getting back from lunch.
   c OK, when she'll get back from lunch.

6 Hi, Angie. What are you doing?
   a I'm getting ready. I see Ben in half an hour.
   b I'm getting ready. I'll see Ben in half an hour.
   c I'm getting ready. I'm going to see Ben in half an hour.

4 Write either Present Simple, Present Continuous, *will* or *going to* next to its function in the future. You will have to write two forms twice.

1 a future fact ....

2 an intention, starting from now ....

3 an intention, starting from before now ....
....

4 personal judgement, based on feelings ....
....

5 personal judgement, based on evidence ....
....

6 an arrangement made for the future ....
....

5 Read these extracts again. Write 1 to 6 in each box to show the use in the future.

a ...I'm meeting Daniel at 4.00... ☐

b ...I'll get the manager. ☐

c I think I'm going to be sick. ☐

d I've a feeling United will score soon. ☐

e ...when she gets back from lunch. ☐

f I'm going to see Ben... ☐

11 ⟩⟩⟩

6 Read Emma's diary. She's thinking of leaving Harry because she's just met Tom.

15 Tuesday	Went to club with the girls. Met Tom. Had great time. Think I may be in love with him!
16 Wednesday	Tom phoned. Wants to take me out. Problem – still seeing Harry.
17 Thursday	Harry phoned – wants to see me. Difficult – made lots of excuses.
18 Friday	Jane's birthday. Restaurant booked for 8.00.
19 Saturday	
20 Sunday	
21 Monday	

7 Harry phones on Thursday night. He wants to see Emma and makes different suggestions. Emma doesn't want to see him and makes excuses. Work with another student, and continue the conversation.

Harry So when can we meet? What about tonight?

Emma Oh, I can't. I've got my Italian class tonight.

Harry OK, tomorrow night.

Emma No, it's my sister's birthday tomorrow. We're going to a restaurant in the evening.

Harry Well, are you going to go shopping on Saturday? We could go together.

Emma No. In fact on Saturday, ¹ ....

Harry ² ....?

Emma ³ ....

Harry ⁴ ....?

Emma ⁵ ....

Use of English

1 You are going to read about Lucy Watson who joined an expedition to Borneo and was bitten by a tarantula. Have you ever had an accident on holiday? What happened? Tell another student.

FCE Paper 3, Part 1

2 Read the first sentence of the text below. There is one missing word — and below are four possible answers. Which is the correct word?

O A save B keep C rescue D conserve

3 Read the text and decide which answer (A, B, C or D) best fits each space for questions 1-10. Compare your answers with another student.

> **How cool! I've been bitten by a tarantula**
>
> A student's trip to the rainforests of Borneo ended in a race to (**0**) ...... her life after she was bitten by a tarantula – an experience she described as 'cool'. Lucy Watson, 20, was four weeks (**1**) ...... a conservation expedition when the (**2**) ...... spider bit her on the arm. Other group (**3**) ...... carried the Durham University student for nine hours through the jungle. The difficult (**4**) ...... was followed by a three-hour drive to a hospital, where Lucy was treated (**5**) ...... antibiotics. Later, she was able to (**6**) ...... the bright side – her first words over the phone to her anxious parents were: 'How cool! I've been bitten by a tarantula.' She was (**7**) ...... the next day and immediately returned to the expedition. Lucy's parents were told of the accident by the tour organiser, Trekforce Expeditions, which (**8**) ...... them at home in England. Mrs Watson said: 'When she  (**9**) ...... to the hospital, she was covered in mud and she had her first good shower (**10**) ...... four weeks.' Lucy, who has just completed the second year of her physics degree, decided to go on the expedition at the last minute.

1	A at	B through	C in	D into
2	A toxic	B poisonous	C mortal	D fatal
3	A colleagues	B leaders	C members	D comrades
4	A trek	B stroll	C bite	D ramble
5	A to	B with	C by	D for
6	A look	B understand	C know	D see
7	A expelled	B discharged	C evacuated	D detained
8	A contacted	B spoke	C said	D reported
9	A arrived	B entered	C got	D reached
10	A after	B of	C from	D in

Writing

1 Read the advert below, which appears on the Internet. Trekforce Expeditions is the organisation that sent Lucy Watson to Borneo. Before you go on an expedition you have to find the money by getting people to sponsor you.

FCE Paper 2, Part 1

2 You are going to write a letter asking for more information about Trekforce Expeditions and you have made some notes. Looking at your notes, what do you want to know? Are there any other questions you would like to ask Trekforce?

Where? In the UK?

How much?

Where do they go?

How long?

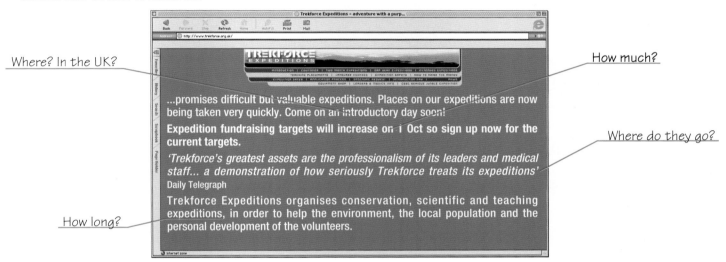

...promises difficult but valuable expeditions. Places on our expeditions are now being taken very quickly. Come on an introductory day soon!

Expedition fundraising targets will increase on 1 Oct so sign up now for the current targets.

'Trekforce's greatest assets are the professionalism of its leaders and medical staff... a demonstration of how seriously Trekforce treats its expeditions'
Daily Telegraph

Trekforce Expeditions organises conservation, scientific and teaching expeditions, in order to help the environment, the local population and the personal development of the volunteers.

3 When you write a letter, you need to use an appropriate style. Look at the two letters below. Each letter is in a different style: letter A is informal and B is formal. Fill in each space in the two letters with the most appropriate word from the box. Remember to choose words according to the style of the letter.

A

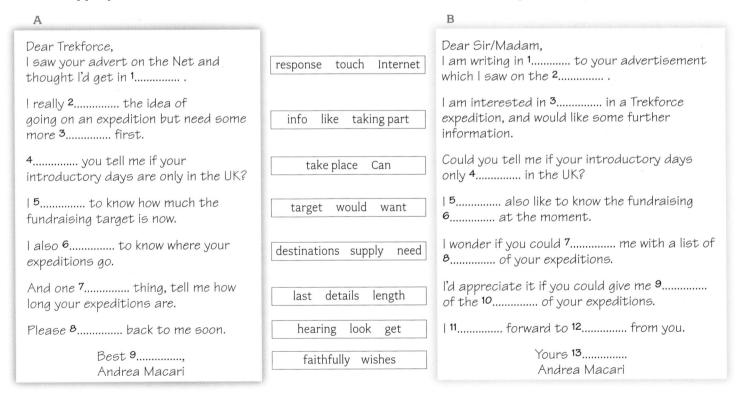

Dear Trekforce,
I saw your advert on the Net and thought I'd get in 1............... .

I really 2............... the idea of going on an expedition but need some more 3............... first.

4............... you tell me if your introductory days are only in the UK?

I 5............... to know how much the fundraising target is now.

I also 6............... to know where your expeditions go.

And one 7............... thing, tell me how long your expeditions are.

Please 8............... back to me soon.

Best 9...............,
Andrea Macari

| response | touch | Internet |

| info | like | taking part |

| take place | Can |

| target | would | want |

| destinations | supply | need |

| last | details | length |

| hearing | look | get |

| faithfully | wishes |

B

Dear Sir/Madam,
I am writing in 1............. to your advertisement which I saw on the 2............... .

I am interested in 3............... in a Trekforce expedition, and would like some further information.

Could you tell me if your introductory days only 4............... in the UK?

I 5............... also like to know the fundraising 6............... at the moment.

I wonder if you could 7............... me with a list of 8............... of your expeditions.

I'd appreciate it if you could give me 9............... of the 10............... of your expeditions.

I 11............... forward to 12............... from you.

Yours 13...............
Andrea Macari

4 What would be the correct style for your letter to Trekforce?

5 Now write a letter of between 120 and 180 words to Trekforce. You can use ideas from the formal letter, but expand each point, adding more details of your own.

Speaking

FCE Paper 5, Part 2

1 What type of holiday do you like? Where would you like to go? Would you prefer to do an extreme sport or relax on the beach?

Vocabulary

Travel and holidays

1 Tick [✔] the correct space on the table for the words that go together.

	travel	journey	trip	voyage	excursion	tour	cruise	crossing
make a		✔						
take a								
go on a								
a long								
a day								
an overland								

2 Indicate the correct answer.

1 Which flight goes at the same time all year?
charter/scheduled

2 Which ticket can't you book in advance?
standby/return

3 Which place is for holiday makers?
a marina/a resort

4 Which holiday includes flight/accommodation/meals in the price?
a package/a sightseeing

5 Which one do you look at before your holiday?
a souvenir/a brochure

6 Which one is for an aeroplane?
a track/a runway

7 Which one hurts when you sunbathe?
suntan/sunburn

8 Which holiday involves no cooking?
self-catering/full board

3 Underline the phrasal verbs in each sentence in question 4 and replace them with the correct form of the verb in the box.

to leave	to be delayed	to collect (x2)
to meet	to search	to wait
to leave	to arrive	to land
to register	to pass	

4 Read the account of a flight to Lisbon. Put the sentences in the correct order.

1 ☐ We met up with our friends in the arrivals hall.

2 ☐ The plane took off on time.

3 ☐ It took a long time to check in our luggage.

4 ☐ We picked up our luggage from the luggage reclaim.

5 ☐ However, we made it to the airport with plenty of time.

6 ☐ We touched down in Lisbon twenty minutes late.

7 ☐ 1 We set off from home at 8 o'clock.

8 ☐ We went through the Portuguese passport control.

9 ☐ Then, we got held up in a traffic jam for half an hour.

10 ☐ The security guard went through all our luggage, eight cases in all!

11 ☐ We hung around in the departure lounge until our flight was called.

12 ☐ Next, we stopped to pick up James and Isabel.

Speaking

Life, experiences and future plans

`FCE` Paper 5, Part 1

1 Work with another student. Imagine you don't know each other. What five things do you want to learn about them? Ask your five questions.

2 Now look at the questions below. Tick [✔] the ones that are the same or similar to your questions.

		topic
a	How do you normally travel to work/school?	....
b	What's your typical day like?	....
c	What kind of books do you like to read?	....
d	Do you live in a house or a flat? What's it like?	....
e	How do you think you will use your English in the future?	....
f	Where do you spend your holidays?	....
g	Where do you live? How long have you lived there?	home town
h	What do you normally do at the weekend?	....
i	What do you like about your town?	....
j	Can you tell me something about your neighbourhood?	....
k	What is/was your school like?	....

3 Look at the topics below. Write one after each question, a-k above. The first one is done for you.

> home town   house and home
> daily life   education   languages
> hobbies/likes and dislikes   travel

4 Now have a conversation with your partner. Ask and answer the questions above and think of others on the same topics.

Vocabulary

Negative prefixes

1 Underline the adjectives in these sentences.

1 It's illegal to smoke on the street in the USA.
2 He's impolite and immature sometimes.
3 He can often be irrational.

2 What do the prefixes *il-*, *im-*, *im-*, *ir* do to the adjectives? Which other negative prefixes do you know?

3 Complete the rule below for using the prefixes *il-*, *im-* and *ir-*.

Theory Box

Negative prefixes

Il- is often used with words which begin with the letter ....

Im- is often used with words which begin with the letters ....

Ir- is often used with words which begin with the letter ....

Unfortunately, there are no rules for the use of **un-**, **in-**, and **dis-**.

Un- is the most common negative prefix.

4 Write the opposite adjective using the negative prefixes. Be careful: the rules don't always work!

	adjective	opposite	stress pattern
1	moral	......immoral......	o●o [✔]
2	responsible	....	●oooo [✗] oo●oo
3	expensive	....	oo●o [ ]
4	reliable	....	o●ooo [ ]
5	logical	....	o●oo [ ]
6	pleasant	....	oo● [ ]
7	loyal	....	●oo [ ]
8	polite	....	oo● [ ]
9	efficient	....	o●oo [ ]
10	respectful	....	oo●o [ ]
11	literate	....	●ooo [ ]
12	relevant	....	oo●o [ ]

5 We do not usually put the main stress on the prefix. Look at the stress pattern next to the negative adjectives. Put a tick [✔] if the pattern is correct. Put a [✗] if the pattern is incorrect and write the correct pattern.

6 Write one more adjective for each of the negative prefixes, *dis-*, *il-*, *im-*, *in-*, *ir-* and *un-* .

7 Now test another student. Take it in turns to say an adjective. Give one point if your partner says the correct opposite adjective and one point if the stress is correct. For example:

A: Obedient

B: Disob●edient

A: 2 marks!

UNIT 2
Crime and Punishment

arrested   away   charge   charged
commit   community   convicted
court   dangerous   defended   fine
guilty   innocent   jury   lawyer
prosecuted   questioned   robbery
sentenced   serve   witnesses

The law

1 Do you know the words in the box? Work in a group to complete each space on the diagram with one of the words.

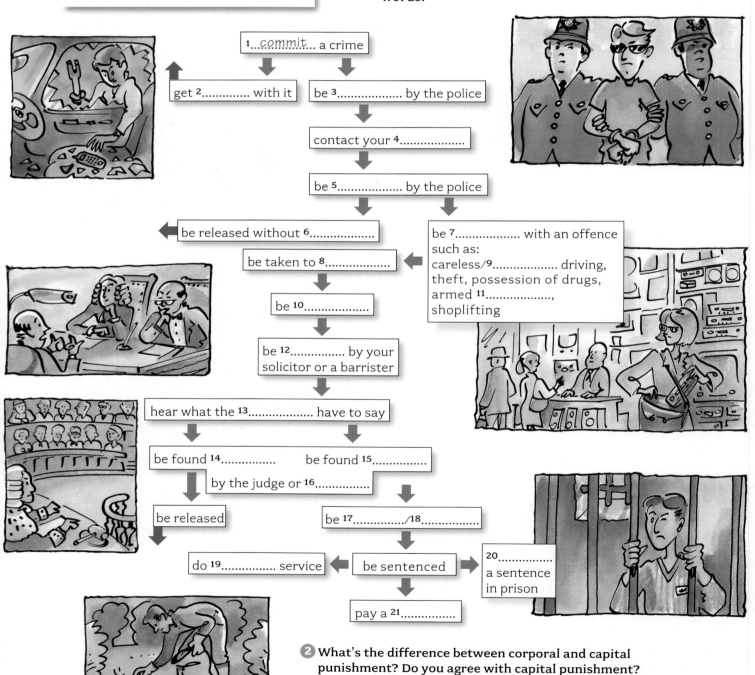

1 ...commit... a crime

get 2.............. with it   be 3.................... by the police

contact your 4...................

be 5.................... by the police

be released without 6...................   be 7.................... with an offence such as: careless/9.................... driving, theft, possession of drugs, armed 11...................., shoplifting

be taken to 8...................

be 10...................

be 12.............. by your solicitor or a barrister

hear what the 13.................... have to say

be found 14...............   be found 15...............

by the judge or 16...............

be released   be 17.............../18....................

do 19.............. service   be sentenced   20............... a sentence in prison

pay a 21...............

2 What's the difference between corporal and capital punishment? Do you agree with capital punishment? Do you think there are any crimes for which it's the appropriate punishment? Talk about your answers in a group.

Listening

1 You will hear an interview with a man who is writing a book about crime. Before you listen, check the meaning of these words and phrases in your dictionary and use them to fill in the spaces in the article below. Work with another student.

> accomplices   armed   arrest
> automatically locked   getaway car   hold-up
> make a run for it   run someone over
> security windows

If someone is planning to rob a bank, they may try to do it alone or work with one or more **1**.................. . Most bank robbers carry guns, and the crime is then called **2**.................. robbery. Usually, the robbers go to a cashier's window and say, 'This is a **3**..................' or something similar. However, many banks today have **4**.................., which begin to close when a robbery starts, and doors which can be **5**.................. . Sometimes the robbers panic and just **6**.................. . The driver may also stall the **7**.................., or even **8**.................. while trying to escape. This can make it easier for the police to catch and **9**.................. the robbers.

FCE Paper 4, Part 4

2 Now listen to the radio interview with John O'Brien, the writer. For questions 1-5, choose the best answer, A, B or C.

1 What is John O'Brien writing?
  A A crime novel.
  B A collection of short stories.
  C A non-fiction book.

2 The gang in Durham were arrested because
  A there was a problem with the car.
  B the driver was inexperienced.
  C none of them could drive.

3 The second English robber was
  A arrested as he left the bank.
  B involved in a road accident.
  C attacked by his accomplice.

4 The robber in Boston
  A tried to rob an FBI office.
  B prepared everything thoroughly.
  C missed one important detail.

5 Why was the robber in Birmingham caught?
  A He panicked.
  B He chose the wrong door.
  C The door locked automatically.

Vocabulary

rob or *steal*?

1 What's the difference between *rob* and *steal*? Write *rob* or *steal* under each picture. Then write each of the words below in one, or both, of the boxes.

> bank car house radio safe shop
> train TV video aeroplane

1 ....

2 ....

rob	steal

Grammar

Past Simple or Past Continuous

1 Read this extract from the listening. Which form, the Past Simple or the Past Continuous, is used for the longer actions?

A gang *was planning* to rob a bank, and they *hired* a man to drive the getaway car. But as they *were running* out of the bank with the bags of money, he *panicked* and the car *stopped*. He *was trying* to start it when the police *arrived* and *arrested* them.

2 Now read these sentences and put them in order, from the longest to the shortest action.

1 They *were running* out of the bank.
2 The gang *lived* in Durham in the north of England.
3 He *was trying* to get the car to start.
4 The gang *spent* the next few years in prison.

Theory Box

Here, the actions in the **Past Simple** are longer. Actions in the **Past Simple** can last a long time: *Jesse James grew up in Missouri.* **But** they can also last a short time: *He was shot in 1892.*

3 Read these sentences. What difference does changing them into the Past Continuous make?

1a He *tried* to get the car to start when the police arrived.
 b He *was trying* to get the car to start when the police arrived.
2a The gang *lived* in Durham.
 b The gang *were living* in Durham.

Theory Box

We can use the **Past Continuous** to:

1 make short actions longer. ⬅▮▮▮ TRY ▮▮➡

2 make long actions shorter. ▮▮➡ LIVE ⬅▮▮

4 Nigel is reporting a crime to the police. Read the conversation and change the verbs in brackets to the Past Simple or Past Continuous.

Nigel: Yesterday afternoon I **1**................. (*wait*) at the bus stop in Arnott Street. It's my son's birthday tomorrow and I'd just bought him a present.

Policeman: And?

Nigel: Well, three police cars **2**................. (*pull* up) outside a shop across the street and a lot of policemen **3**................. (*get out*). They **4**................. (*carry*) guns and they **5**................. (*surround*) the entrance to the shop. Then this guy **6**................. (*walk*) out and one of the policemen **7**................. (*shout*), 'Armed police! Put your hands up!' ...just like in the films...

Policeman: Go on, sir, please.

Nigel: He **8**................. (*put*) his hands up, but he **9**................. (*carry*) a plastic bag, and he looked a bit silly. Anyway, he wasn't the one they wanted and they just **10**................. (*move*) him away. Two policemen **11**................. (*run*) into the shop and a few seconds later they **12**................. (*come*) out with a guy who **13**................. (*wear*) a black ski hat and a black nylon jacket...

Policeman: Yes, sir. And what **14**................. (*happen*) next?

Nigel: My bus **15**................. (*arrive*).

Policeman: Sorry?

Nigel: Yes, while all this **16**................. (*happen*), my bus arrived.

Policeman: Very good, sir. Actually, we know all about this matter. In fact, we'd like to forget about it.

Nigel: I see. Was the man charged with armed robbery?

Policeman: No. In fact, it was a mistake. The shop sold toy guns and he **17**................. (*hold*) one of them. Someone **18**................. (*think*) he was going to rob the shop and **19**................. (*call*) the police.

Nigel: Oh... so it was a toy gun? It **20**................. (*look*) real to me.

Speaking

FCE Paper 5, Parts 3/4

1 Look at the most common criminal offences in England and Wales. Match each crime to a picture. Work in a group, number the offences from 1 to 8, starting with 1 for the most serious to 8 for the least serious.

- [ ] burglary
- [ ] robbery
- [ ] drug offences
- [ ] criminal damage
- [ ] fraud and forgery
- [ ] motoring offences
- [ ] assault
- [ ] theft and handling of stolen goods

2 Work in a group. How do you think the crimes in question 1 should be punished? Choose from the punishments in the box.

> community service
> fine of £100
> 2-year prison sentence
> 5-year prison sentence
> 10-year prison sentence
> life imprisonment

3 How do you think criminals should be punished? What are the advantages and disadvantages of putting criminals in prison?

Writing

FCE Paper 2, Part 2

1 Imagine you were a witness to one of these offences. Write a report of what you saw, in 120-180 words. Use the Past Simple and Past Continuous, linking words and time expressions. But first think of what happened and tell another student. Make sure your report answers the following questions:

- Where and when did the incident take place?
- Where were you?
- What actually happened?
- Was anyone hurt?
- When did the police arrive?
- What happened afterwards?

19 >>>

Reading

Zero tolerance

1 *Zero tolerance* means that the police do not tolerate minor crimes like dropping litter or writing graffiti. This policy has also been applied in US schools, leading to severe punishments for minor offences by students. Read these comments on zero tolerance policing.

Zero tolerance has been credited with reducing the number of shootings in New York. However, violent deaths have been declining there since 1992, when they reached a record number of 2,262.

The number of school shootings was also falling before zero tolerance was introduced. In 1993 there were 44 violent school deaths. In 2001 there were 15. The number of deaths in road accidents is much higher than by shooting. Perhaps schools should stop worrying about children who play war games and suspend those who play at driving.

Sometimes zero tolerance can lead to extreme results, like the 6-year-old child in Colorado Springs who was suspended for half a day after a teacher saw him give sweets to another child. School officials told the boy's mother that a child who brings sweets to school is comparable to a teenager who takes a gun to school.

2 Do you think the policy of zero tolerance of minor crimes is successful? Do you think it should be applied in schools? Talk about your opinions in a group.

FCE Paper 1, Part 3

3 Read the article below on the policy of zero tolerance in a school in America. Five paragraphs have been removed. Choose from the paragraphs A-F the one which fits each gap (1-4). There is one extra paragraph which you do not need. There is an example at the beginning (0).

Zero tolerance takes its toll on pupils
CENTENNIAL, Colorado

When Nepata Godec received a call from Dry Creek Elementary School last month telling her that her son and his friends were being sent home from school, she prepared herself for the worst. 'I thought somebody was in the hospital,' said Mrs Godec. [0] [D]

'So I thought, "Yes? Then what happened?"' she said. 'But that was it. We needed to come to school to pick up our son. I couldn't believe it.' That wasn't all. As the stunned parents later discovered, the principal, Darci Mickle, also questioned the boys on whether their families owned guns. [1] [ ]

Faced with the choice of obeying his parents or obeying the principal, he chose his parents. 'I asked Connor about it, and he told me he lied to Mrs Mickle and answered "no". He was afraid that the family would get in trouble,' Mr Andrew said. [2] [ ] That day, the

Dry Creek seven joined a growing number of students who have learned the hard way about 'zero tolerance'. A popular policy for schools which are worried about guns, drugs and alcohol, the no-second-chances policy has resulted in serious punishment, sometimes including arrest, for what was once seen as normal rough play.

[3] [ ] Many would question whether such an extreme reaction to a playground game is sensible. And critics also argue that the strict policies have made children feel guilty about generally acceptable behaviour. They also ask whether zero tolerance actually makes schools safer. [4] [ ]

Other examples of the crazy zero tolerance policy taken from newspapers include:

Sayreville, New Jersey:
Four kindergarten students playing cops-and-robbers are given three-day suspensions.

Jonesboro, Arkansas:
An 8-year-old boy is suspended for three days after pointing a piece of chicken at a teacher and saying, 'Pow, pow, pow.' Jonesboro was the site of a 1998 school shooting that left two dead.

Also in New Jersey:
Two kids playing cops-and-robbers are charged with making terrorist threats.

The incidents have become so widespread that they now appear on several Web sites.

A Connor may have had some reason to feel this way. Dry Creek is only about 20 miles from Columbine High School, where a shooting in 1999 left 15 dead. It is a community with reason to be nervous. However, this was no isolated incident.

B For 10-year-old Connor Andrew, whose father had worked as a licensed hunting guide, the question put him in an impossible position. He had been warned not to discuss his father's guns at school.

C Even those in favour of gun-control aren't convinced by the policy. John Head, founder of SAFE/Colorado, said the Dry Creek incident sounded harmless enough to him. 'What I have a problem with is when children have guns and point them at each other,' he said.

D But she was even more shocked when she discovered the real reason. It turned out that 10-year-old Aaron Godec and six of his class mates were being sent home from school for pointing their fingers like guns during a game of 'army-and-aliens' in the playground.

E Even without the school policy, zero tolerance is the law in Colorado, where students who carry a gun or replica gun to school are expelled. Nowhere does the law mention fingers, but Mrs Mickle said, 'We can't predict what every student is going to do.'

F At the Cherry Creek School District here, officials insist the Dry Creek incident was handled properly. 'Our handling of this incident is in line with district policy and common sense,' said district spokeswoman Tustin Amole.

Vocabulary

Crime and punishment

1 Read the descriptions of the crimes. Are they true or false? Correct the ones that are false.

1 *Manslaughter* is when you kill someone on purpose. *False. It is when you kill someone by accident.*

2 *Blackmail* is when you get money from a person by threatening to tell their secrets.

3 *Assault* is when you attack someone.

4 *Vandalism* is when you damage a building by accident.

5 *Mugging* is when you attack a person to steal something.

6 *Arson* is when you set fire to a building by accident.

7 *Smuggling* is when you take something from one country to another one and show it to the customs officers when you arrive.

8 *Slander* is when you write something false about someone.

2 Complete the table below with the correct form of the word.

criminal	crime	verb
thief	theft	-
		to rob
burglar		
	murder	
		to shoplift
kidnapper		
	terrorism	-
	pickpocketing	
hijacker		

3 Which of the crimes in questions 1 and 2 apply to the following people or things? Discuss your ideas with another student.

- A thousand packets of cigarettes
- A millionaire's son
- A shop
- A house
- A diamond bracelet
- A plane

Use of English

FCE Paper 3, Part 2

1 You are going to read about a robbery. Look at the pictures. What do you think happened? Talk about it with another student.

2 Read the passage below. Can you think of the word which best fits each space? There is an example at the beginning.

In the year 2000, a gang tried **0** ......to...... steal the 12 De Beers millennium jewels, estimated to **1**.............. worth £200 million, from **2**.............. Millennium Dome in London. The robbers smashed the gates **3**.............. the Dome to reach the Money Zone, where the De Beers diamonds **4**.............. usually kept in a secure vault. **5**.............., they attacked the display case containing the jewels **6**.............. heavy hammers.
But police officers were waiting for the gang, disguised **7**.............. cleaners and **8**.............. their guns hidden in rubbish bags. When the police arrived, **9**.............. gang set off smoke bombs. But the police overpowered **10**.............. arrested them. '**11**.............. was an overwhelming number of officers there to ensure this raid was unsuccessful,' a police spokesperson said. 'If they had succeeded, it would have **12**.............. the largest robbery in the world.'
13.............. the police struck, officers arrested a man in a boat on the River Thames. Another man, **14**.............. was listening **15**.............. police radio conversations, was arrested on the north bank of the Thames opposite the Dome.
However, even if the raid **16**.............. succeeded, the gang wouldn't have got away **17**.............. anything valuable. Liz Lynch, **18**.............. spoke for De Beers, said 'The jewels had **19**.............. replaced with replicas before the robbery. They will **20**.............. put back on display again soon.'
In February 2002, the gang members were jailed for a total **21**.............. 71 years.

3 Check your answers with another student. Your teacher will give you the missing words.

Grammar

Theory Box

Countable and uncountable nouns
Words, like **apple**, **orange**, **carrot**, **tomato** and **banana**, are countable. Others, like **bread**, **butter** and **milk** are usually uncountable. We must use another word to count **milk** like **some milk**, **two litres of milk** or **three bottles of milk**.

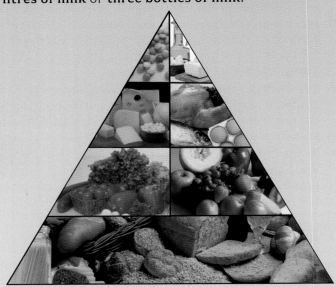

However, lots of words can be either countable or uncountable. We can say **some cake** or **a cake**, I'd like **some coffee** or **a coffee**.
Words change their meaning, depending on how we use them:

He bought a paper to read on the train.

I need some paper for the photocopier.

1 In each pair of sentences below, the first sentence needs a countable form, the second an uncountable one. Choose one of the words from the list to complete each pair of sentences. Do you know all these words?

> action   business   conflict   examination   pepper   sport

1a Can you get a green .... and an aubergine?

 b Why did you put so much .... in the soup?

2a Is fishing really a ....?

 b We need to encourage children to play ....

3a The students want to discuss the results of the .... with her.

 b We'll continue with this subject next week. It needs further ....

4a The .... is over — they've signed the peace treaty.

 b There's growing .... between Bob and Edna. One of them will have to quit.

5a We use this form for an .... in the past at a specific time.

 b If we don't take some .... the problem will just get worse.

6a Sarah took over as manager of the ....

 b It's hard to do .... in the current economic climate.

2 Choose the correct form for each of these sentences.

1 They don't keep **much/many** equipment here — they hire it.

2 I'm only looking for **a few/a little** information. Don't be so unhelpful.

3 That's a lot of money for **a/a piece of** furniture. Is it worth it?

4 There isn't **an/much** accommodation available at this time of year. The city's busy.

5 I always take **less/fewer** luggage than most other people. I like to travel light.

6 I'll give you **an/some** advice — don't get involved with him.

3 Draw a line or lines from each of the words below to either or both boxes. The first one has been done for you.

used with countable nouns	some less a/an fewer many few much a little a piece of	**used with uncountable nouns**

Speaking

❶ Look at the pictures and complete the notes about their similarities and differences.

Pictures A and B *similarities*	Pictures C and D *similarities*
1 .... 2 .... 3	1 .... 2 .... 3 ....
differences 1 .... 2 .... 3	*differences* 1 .... 2 .... 3 ....

❷ When you talk about similarities, you compare things. When you talk about differences, you contrast them. Look at the words and phrases below and decide which box they should go in:

- *...and...*
- *Both of them...*
- *...but...*
- *...different from/to...*
- *Each photo shows...*
- *However,...*

- *Neither of them...*
- *...on the other hand...*
- *One similarity is that...*
- *What they have in common is that...*
- *...whereas...*

language for comparing	language for contrasting

❸ Now decide with another student which two pictures you each want to talk about. Use the language above to compare and contrast them. Take it in turns. Ask your partner to time you while you talk for a minute about your pictures.

Vocabulary

Suffixes

1 Look at your answers to question 2 on page 21. What suffixes are used to make nouns?

For example : -ar in burglar

2 In English, we often make a noun by adding a suffix to the verb: *rob* (verb) *robbery* (noun); a verb by adding a suffix to the adjective: *modern* (adjective) *modernize* (verb); an adjective by adding a suffix to the verb or noun: *use* (verb/noun) *useful* (adjective). What happens in your language?

3 Look at these common suffixes. Are they used to form nouns, verbs or adjectives? Complete the noun, adjective and verb columns.

-er/ar -able -al -ance -ate(x2) -en -ery ~~-ful~~ -hood
-ify -ion -ish -ity ~~-ise~~ -ment -ness -ous -ship

noun	example	adjective	example	verb	example
-er/ar	robber	-ful	useful	-ise	modernise

4 Now look at the words in the box. They all contain a suffix from question 3. Write them in the correct column in the chart.

ambitious calculate childhood childish comfortable
fortunate ~~modernise~~ national performance probation
punishment ~~robber~~ robbery selfishness sensitivity
simplify ~~useful~~ widen friendship

5 Can you think of any more suffixes to make nouns or adjectives?

nouns: ....
adjectives: ....

6 Complete the sentences with the correct form of the word in brackets.

1 That man is very .... He goes jogging every day. (*health*)

2 This is a very quiet .... (*neighbour*)

3 Police officers often wear .... vests so that they are not hurt in a gun fight. (*bullet*)

4 Not everyone agreed with the .... of the death penalty in Britain. (*abolish*)

5 He was always a very high .... at school and passed all his exams. (*achieve*)

6 He goes to the gym to build up his physical .... (*strong*)

7 She was .... and her parents got angry with her. (*think*)

8 You are .... if you think you'll get all that work done. (*optimist*)

9 She is one of the most famous .... in the world. (*piano*)

Phrasal verbs/expressions with *come*

1 Underline the expressions with *come* in the sentences below. Then replace them with the definitions in the box.

> to be published
> to change your opinion
> to experience something negative
> to find by chance
> to inherit to occur to reach
> to return to think of
> to visit someone

1 Why don't you come round for dinner this evening?

2 She came into a lot of money when her grandmother died.

3 The judge came in for a lot of criticism when he gave the burglar a suspended sentence.

4 I came across my school photos when I was clearing out the attic.

5 It took the jury two days to come to a decision about the case.

6 I think we should come back to this discussion after lunch.

7 I hope his next novel comes out soon. The one I've just finished reading was great!

8 The men came up with a plan of how to escape from prison.

9 I can't believe another problem has come up.

10 He eventually came round to the idea after a lot of persuasion.

2 Fill in the gaps with the correct form of the appropriate expression.

1 Have you .... an excuse yet for being so late?

2 It will be difficult for him to .... the idea of moving out of London.

3 I hope we don't .... a lot of criticism when we tell them the bad news.

4 I'm sorry. The stain still hasn't .... your favourite shirt.

5 The question of a salary increase .... at the meeting but no decision was made.

UNIT 3
The Unknown

Speaking

1 Crop circles first started to appear in the English countryside in the 1970s. Since then they have become more numerous and complex. Look at the photographs below and read the explanations.

Wind: in 1989, meteorologist George Terence Meaden put forward a theory of natural wind forces.

> Well, the weather can do strange things, but I don't believe it's the answer here.

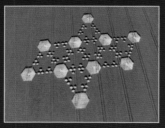

Aliens: there have been reports of UFOs near crop circles. Some believe they are messages from another world.

> If you think we're alone in the universe, you must be very arrogant. These may be messages from extra-terrestrials.

Magnetic fields: a scientist, Colin Andrews, has claimed that some crop circles are caused by changes in the earth's magnetic field. He believes crops can be 'electrocuted' by the effect.

> Strange things can happen, but complicated crop circles can't be made by natural forces. There must be some kind of planning or design, either human or alien.

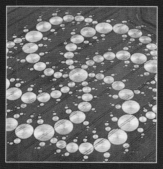

Man made: in 1992 two artists, Doug Bower and Dave Chorley claimed responsibility for all the simple circles in English fields since the mid-70s. They showed how they did it, with garden tools.

> This one's over 450 metres across. I can't believe it was made by two guys with a lawnmower.

2 How do you think crop circles are made? Compare ideas in a group.

3 Do you have crop circles or other strange things in your country? Tell another student.

Reading

1 The newspaper article on the next page is about Matthew Williams, who went out and made a crop circle last summer. Unfortunately, he didn't get permission from the farmer. The police arrested him and he was taken to court. The words below have different meanings. Which meaning do you think they will have in the article?

1 admission
1 *n* [C] when you admit that you have done something wrong.
2 *n* [U] the price charged when you go to a film, sports event, concert etc.

2 alert
1 *v* [T] to warn someone of a problem or of possible danger.
2 *adj* able to think quickly and clearly.

3 charge
1 *n* [C,U] the amount of money paid for a service.
2 *n* [C] an official police statement saying that someone might be guilty of a crime.

4 devote
1 *v* [T] to deal with one main subject or activity.
2 *adj* very loyal or loving.

5 dismiss
1 *v* [T] to refuse to consider someone's ideas, opinions etc.
2 *v* [T] *formal* to make someone leave their job.

FCE Paper 1, Part 2

2 Now, read the article. For questions 1-6, choose the answer (A, B, C or D) which you think fits best according to the text.

Fined – For Running Rings Round Crop Circles

An unemployed computer programmer yesterday became the first person to be fined for creating a crop circle. He said he did it to prove that wild theories about their origins were wrong. Matthew Williams made a seven-pointed star in a field in August. It took him three nights.

Williams, 29, from Wiltshire, decided to act after Michael Glickman, a professor of architecture, who has studied crop circles for many years, appeared on a radio show. He said that it was impossible for a human to create a seven-pointed star in a crop field – it could only have been created by aliens.

After the show, Williams contacted the show's presenter to dismiss Prof Glickman's claims. When the presenter challenged him to prove the professor wrong, Williams went to the field at Manor Farm, near Marlborough, to create the design. He then e-mailed a picture of the crop circle to the presenter. It was passed on to the professor who alerted the police and then they charged him with causing criminal damage.

Yesterday, he admitted the charge and was fined £100. Stephen Clifford, Williams' lawyer said: 'My client believes that the public were being misled. He did not make any profit from his actions. Crop circles are known to boost tourism. He was trying to prove that a seven-pointed star can be man-made.'

The magistrate told Williams: 'I suggest in future that before you make artificial crop circles you get permission from the owner of the field, otherwise you will be prosecuted for criminal damage.'

Outside court, Williams, who has set up his own magazine and Web site devoted to crop circles, said: 'There are researchers who are determined to say that all crop circles are the result of aliens – when they know this is not the case.'

Crop circle students refused to allow the courtroom admissions to detract from their beliefs. Francine Blake, coordinator of the 400-member Wiltshire Crop Circle Study Group, said she believed vandals were trying to take advantage of the interest in crop circles to get into the news. Speaking from California she added: 'There is a phenomenon here and they are trying to take advantage of the situation for self publicity.'

1 Matthew Williams wanted to show that
   A aliens couldn't make a seven-pointed star.
   B all crop circles are created by humans.
   C humans can create elaborate patterns.
   D aliens make the best crop circles.

2 Matthew Williams
   A made a crop circle then sent two e-mails.
   B sent an e-mail, made the crop circle then sent another e-mail.
   C sent two e-mails then made the crop circle.
   D appeared on a US radio show.

3 How was Matthew Williams caught?
   A He admitted creating the circles.
   B He admitted causing criminal damage.
   C Information was given to the police.
   D He gave an interview to the police.

4 The magistrate said that Williams
   A should not make any more crop circles.
   B should ask the farmer first.
   C should pay compensation to the farmer.
   D was devoted to crop circles.

5 Matthew Williams said that academic researchers
   A believe all crop circles are made by humans.
   B believe all crop circles are made by aliens.
   C want people to believe that crop circles are made by humans.
   D want people to believe that crop circles are made by aliens.

6 What does Francine Blake say in the last paragraph?
   A She welcomes his prosecution.
   B She welcomes his actions.
   C She welcomes the publicity.
   D She thought it was phenomenal.

UNIT 3
Grammar

Modals

1 Put *can*, *may*, *mustn't* or *needn't* into each space in the conversations below. You can use a word more than once and sometimes two words are possible.

1 **Prof Glickman:** It's impossible for a human to create a crop circle.
Matthew: No it isn't — I .... do it.

2 **Magistrate:** You .... stop making crop circles, but you .... do it without the farmer's permission.

3 **Reporter:** Don't you think that a lot of crop circles .... be the work of humans?
Francine Blake: Well, perhaps a few are made by vandals trying to get into the news.

4 **Matthew:** .... I make a crop circle in that field?
Farmer: Why not? It might bring in some tourists.

2 Match the first half of each sentence with either a or b and discuss the difference in meaning with another student.

1 **Matthew:** I **must** make this crop circle ☐
    I **have to** make this crop circle ☐
    a *the TV company wants to film me.*
    b *I love making crop circles.*

2 **Matthew:** I **must** finish this crop circle ☐
    I **have to** finish this crop circle ☐
    a *I'm really tired.*
    b *a journalist is waiting to interview me.*

3 Which three words can you use to replace *needn't*? Talk about it with another student.

I know this is an old car but you **needn't** drive so slowly.

4 Choose meanings from the box for each modal. Use two meanings more than once.

ability	external obligation	no obligation
general/internal obligation		permission
possibility	prohibition	

can	....	....
may	....	....
must	....	
mustn't	....	
have to	....	
don't have to	....	
needn't	....	

5 Read what people said about crop circles and then discuss the questions with another student.

If you think we're alone in the universe, you must be very arrogant. These may be messages from extra-terrestrials.

This one's over 450 metres across. It can't be made by two guys with a lawnmower.

Strange things can happen, but complicated crop circles can't be made by natural forces. There must be some kind of intelligence at work here, either human or alien.

1 *Must* can have the meaning of internal obligation. What does it mean here?

2 *Can't* can be used for ability, permission or possibility. Does it always mean these things or can it mean something else?

Theory Box

Modals

In these sentences, **must** means a *logical deduction*.

*If you think we're alone in the universe, you **must be** very arrogant.*

*There **must be** some kind of intelligence at work here, either human or alien.*

The negative form of **must** for logical deduction, is **can't**.

*I **can't** believe it was made by two guys with a lawnmower.*

6 Read about the Haunted House Hotel and complete the sentences with either *must*, *mustn't*, *can*, *can't*, *don't have to* (or *needn't*, which means the same thing) in each space.

Haunted House Hotel

The Haunted House Hotel gives a warm welcome to witches, werewolves and vampires as well as human beings. For a peaceful and restful stay, the following rules must be observed.

- It is not necessary for guests to dress formally for dinner. However, smart appearance is expected.
- Broomsticks must not be brought into the dining room.
- Witches must not fly from balconies. The hotel roof is specially adapted for take off and landing.
- Werewolves are considered to be human for registration purposes. All other animals, especially witches' cats, must be kept in the kennels.
- The chef will be pleased to consider special requests for snakes, lizards and whole frogs etc. as long as they are submitted a day in advance.
- Please note that the cocktail bar does not serve blood.
- Vampires should note that coffins must only be moved from floor to floor using the service lift. The guest lifts are not suitable for this purpose.
- Guests are expected to maintain silence in the corridors, especially after dark. Screaming is forbidden.

1 You .... fly from balconies.

2 You .... dress formally for dinner.

3 You .... drink blood in the cocktail bar.

4 You .... keep animals in the hotel rooms.

5 You .... use the service lifts to move coffins.

6 You .... keep quiet in the corridors after dark.

7 You .... bring broomsticks into the dining room.

8 If you are a werewolf, you .... stay in the kennels.

9 You .... eat whole frogs if you order them a day in advance.

7 Now write the correct form of *can, may, must, have to* or *need* in each of the spaces.

Theory Box

ability	permission	possibility
I .... make a crop circle.	You .... leave now.	We .... go swimming tomorrow.

positive internal obligation	negative obligation
I .... get some new clothes.	You .... smoke in here.
positive external obligation	**no obligation**
I .... start work at 8.30.	I .... work at weekends. or
	I .... work at weekends.

positive deduction	negative deduction
He .... be the oddest person I know.	The bill .... possibly be as big as this.

Listening

1 What do you believe in? Write each of the names in one of the boxes.

ghosts

poltergeists

fairies

telepathy

life on other planets

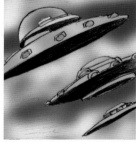
UFOs

abduction by aliens

the Loch Ness Monster

the yeti

wizards and witches

I believe

...these must exist	...these may exist	...these can't exist

2 Work with another student who believes in different phenomena to you. Explain why you believe in them. What happened to you that made you believe in these phenomena?

FCE Paper 4, Part 3

3 You will hear five people talking about strange experiences. For questions 1-5, choose which of the statements A-F refers to each speaker. Use the letters only once. There is one extra letter which you do not need to use.

A The speaker thought the object was something else.

B The speaker doesn't believe the story.

C A person in the story was insane.

D It happened to a friend of the speaker.

E It happened more than once.

F They were on holiday at the time.

Speaker 1 ☐ **1**

Speaker 2 ☐ **2**

Speaker 3 ☐ **3**

Speaker 4 ☐ **4**

Speaker 5 ☐ **5**

Speaking

FCE Paper 5, Part 3

1 You are in a film hire shop and you want to choose a DVD to watch at your friend's house. Work with another student and decide on a film you think you and your friends would all like to watch.

Grammar

Theory Box

Zero and first conditionals

If you believe in fairies, you must be mad.

This is an example of a conditional sentence.

It is made with an **if**-clause   *If you believe in fairies,*
and a **result** clause   *you must be mad.*

Usually the **if**-clause comes first, but it doesn't have to:

You must be mad if you believe in fairies.

When we start with **if** we separate the two clauses with a comma. This makes the sentence easier to read. When we start with the result clause, we do not need to use a comma.

If you believe in fairies, you must be mad.
You must be mad if you believe in fairies.

This type of conditional uses present tenses and present modals. It is used for **probable** or **likely** events in **present** or **future time**. Because it is the simplest type of conditional, we call it a **first** or **type 1** conditional.

The most common tense in **first** conditionals is the Present Simple. However, other **present tenses** are possible:

*If **he's making** crop circles, he'll be out all night.*

The most common modal is **will**, but other present modals are also possible. We used **must** above. We can also use these:

	shall	
If he's in trouble, I	*can*	*help him.*
	may	
	must	
	'm going to	

To say something is always true, we use no modal verb at all. This is called a **zero** conditional because there is no probability or possibility — it is a fact, or truth.

He's my friend. If he's in trouble I help him.

❶ For each question, match a clause from A with a clause from B to make a first conditional sentence.

A
1 If he turns up
2 He'll get into trouble
3 If he's messed up the computer
4 She must be insane
5 If you feel like a drink
6 I can have another coffee
7 She's going to finish with her boyfriend
8 If I've told you once

B
A if you can lend me some money.
B there's some beer in the fridge.
C if she can work out what to say.
D he can get somebody to fix it.
E I've told you a hundred times.
F if she's going out with him.
G if he's taken his Dad's car.
H I leave. So don't invite him.

❷ Look at your answers. One of them isn't a conditional sentence. Which one is it?

Vocabulary

Compound adjectives

❶ Match the words in the two columns to make compound adjectives to fit the descriptions.

1	absent-	a	conditioned
2	built-	b	made
3	off-	c	minute
4	world-	d	price
5	well-	e	minded
6	blue-	f	up
7	home-	g	peak
8	air-	h	eyed
9	last-	i	famous
10	cut-	j	paid

1 an .... person (someone who often forgets things)
2 a .... holiday (you book a few days before you leave)
3 .... cigarettes (a lower price than usual)
4 a .... area (where there are lots of buildings)
5 an .... office (it's never too hot)
6 a .... cake (you make it yourself)
7 a .... pianist (everyone knows who she is)
8 .... travel (you do not travel at the busiest times)
9 a .... job (you earn good money)
10 a .... baby (a baby who has blue eyes)

❷ Compound adjectives are often used to describe:

a someone's physical appearance
b someone's character
c a place
d everyday objects or things

Look at the compound adjectives in question 1. Write a, b, c or d next to them.

Use of English

FCE Paper 3, Part 3

1 For questions 1-6, complete the second sentence so that it has a similar meaning to the first sentence, using the word given. Do not change the word given. You must use between two and five words, including the word given. There is an example at the beginning.

0 You needn't take your camera to Loch Ness, there's nothing there.
have
You .... your camera to Loch Ness — there's nothing there.

If you write **don't have to take** in the space, the sentence will have a similar meaning.

1 It is possible that aliens are responsible for crop circles.
be
Aliens .... for crop circles.

2 It's necessary to ask the farmer before making a crop circle.
to
You .... before making a crop circle.

3 It's not allowed to take photos of the yeti.
use
You ...., it frightens the yeti.

4 The yeti must be shy, only a few people have seen him.
friendly
The .... not many people have seen him.

5 You don't have to dress up as a ghost for the Halloween party.
wear
You .... costume for the Halloween party.

6 I want to finish this crop circle as soon as possible.
be
This crop circle .... as possible.

Vocabulary

Word transformation

1 In English, there are some word families which have confusing forms and pronunciations. Here are seven of the most common. Use a dictionary to complete the table below.

noun	person	verb	adjective
photograph			
			analytical
economy/ economics			
	advertiser		
			advisory
	practitioner		
			judgemental /judicial

2 Mark the stress on the words. Practise saying the words in pairs.

3 Interview another student.

1 Have you ever answered or placed an advertisement?
2 Do you regularly practise a sport?
3 Do you often give people advice?
4 Have you got a photographic memory?
5 Do you have an economical scooter?
6 Do you find it difficult to economise?
7 Have you ever had your photograph in the newspaper?
8 Would you like to work in advertising?

4 **If your partner answers *yes*, ask another question to get more information.**

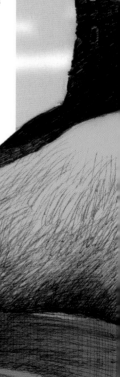

UNIT 3
Writing

1 Do you believe in UFOs? Have you, or anyone you know, ever seen a UFO? Compare your answers with another student.

2 Read this story by Andrew, who says he was abducted by aliens. What's wrong with the style of his story? What changes would you make? How would you make it better?

One day my sister Rachel and I were walking home and we decided to go to the park. Then this huge spaceship appeared in the sky and it stopped above us. Then the bottom of it opened and a big stair came down. Then we tried to run away but we couldn't. Then these aliens – they were big and shiny – walked down and took us by the hand. Then they took us up the stair into the spaceship. It was very bright inside. Then they put us in chairs and looked at us with instruments. Then we woke up on the ground outside. There was no spaceship and it was six o'clock.

3 The only word Andrew uses to introduce the next event in the story is *then*. What other words can you use instead? Look at the same story, written by Rachel. Which words does she use to introduce the events? Underline them.

One day my brother Andrew and I were walking home from school and we decided to go to the park. Suddenly a huge spaceship appeared in the sky and it stopped above us. Next, the bottom of it opened and a big stair came down. When we saw this, we tried to run away but we couldn't. Then some big, shiny aliens walked down and took us by the hand. After that they led us up the stair into the spaceship, which was very bright inside. The next thing was that they put us in chairs and looked at us with instruments. Later we woke up on the ground outside. The spaceship had disappeared and it was six o'clock.

4 Look at the cartoon in the next column. With another student, tell the story of what happened. How did the story finish? Don't forget to use a variety of words to introduce the next action.

FCE Paper 2, Part 2

5 You are going to write a short story based on the cartoon. Discuss your ideas for the story with other students. Find out if they like your ideas. Think of a good title too.

6 Now write some notes which explain the main points in your story. Think of an exciting introduction and conclusion. Decide which of the words from Rachel's story you can use to introduce each event. Now write your story in 120-180 words in an appropriate style.

Grammar

Theory Box

Order of adjectives

> Look at that lovely, big, red Italian car.

When we put a number of adjectives before a noun, we usually...

start with...	and end with...
the most personal	the most unarguable
the most subjective	the most objective
the most temporary	the most permanent

1 The car may or may not be **lovely** — that's a matter of opinion.
2 Most people would think it is **big**, but if you're used to driving big cars, it may seem normal.
3 It is definitely **red**. However, this could be changed if you paint it.
4 It is absolutely, completely and forever **Italian**.

However, this is only a general rule. You might decide to change the focus:

A **big, red, lovely** Italian car.

If you particularly like **big** red cars.

1 How could you describe this table? These adjectives might apply:

age	*old*
colour	*brown*
material	*wooden*
quality	*fine*
origin	*Italian*
shape	*round*
purpose	*dining*
size	*big*

In what order? Look at these pictures and the descriptions. Then write the names of the types of adjective in the spaces in the correct order:

quality size ....

1 a nice big hamburger
  quality size

2 a new flat screen
  age shape

3 a plastic coffee cup
  material purpose

4 a red German motorbike
  colour origin

5 a Scottish woollen scarf
  origin material

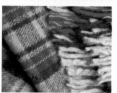

6 a small young dog
  size age

7 a round blue ashtray
  shape colour

2 Now put these words in the correct order to describe the table in question 1.

> old brown wooden fine Italian round dining big

....
.... table

3 Look at these sentences and write the adjectives for each one in the correct order.

1 garden/white/plastic/chair
  ....
2 flower/china/tall/vase
  ....
3 brown/French/pretty/wooden/chalet
  ....
4 New Zealand/white/racing/large/yacht
  ....

Progress Check 1 (Units 1-3)

1 **Choose either the Present Simple or Present Continuous for each *verb*. Use question forms where necessary.**

1 Could you help me? We .... (*do*) a survey on people's leisure interests.

2 How often .... you .... (*go*) swimming?

3 She .... (*spend*) time in cafés but she hardly ever goes to clubs.

4 He mainly grows coffee but this year he .... (*plant*) some cocoa as well.

5 Farming .... (*mean*) that you must give daily attention to the crops.

6 I always .... (*listen*) to the radio before going to bed.

7 Generally, the weather .... (*get*) warmer this week.

8 United .... (*play*) well enough to win today? What do you think?

9 Charlie still .... (*go*) on holiday with his parents every year.

10 Our company .... (*organise*) expeditions to different parts of the world.

2 **Decide if these sentences using *will* or *going to* are right or wrong. Put a tick (✔) or a cross (✘) in the box at the end of each line.**

1 I can't talk to you now — I'll meet Jim at the cinema in ten minutes. ☐

2 It's just a feeling I have — I think he'll come and see me soon. ☐

3 Look, I'm going to paint it in a minute — I've got everything ready. ☐

4 'What's the best thing to do, write or phone?' 'OK, I'll phone her.' ☐

5 ...and the Ferrari approaches the finish ahead of the rest. He'll win. ☐

6 If you're going to take a seat I'll ask Mr Martin to speak to you. ☐

7 Brian's a hopeless driver. There's no way he's going to pass the test. ☐

8 I think I'd better sit down — I feel like I'll faint. ☐

9 If I get a chance to watch this video tonight I'll return it tomorrow. ☐

10 I have to go to the doctor's, will you give me a lift? ☐

3 **Choose the most appropriate future form for each sentence.**

1 *Do you go/Are you going* out with Evan tonight?

2 What are you going to do when you *get out of/'ll get out of* here?

3 The next train from platform 7 *leaves/is going to leave* in 15 minutes.

4 When I grow up I *marry/'ll marry* a handsome prince, or at least somebody rich.

5 Do you think Trevor's *accepting/going to accept* the offer?

6 He's been in jail for five years. Who's *giving/going to give* him a job now?

4 **Choose either the Past Simple or Past Continuous for each *verb*.**

1 Mary .... (*go out with*) Fred at the time she .... (*meet*) Pete.

2 Our neighbour .... (*play*) music all the time we .... (*watch*) the film.

3 The door .... (*burst*) open and three robbers .... (*rush*) into the bank.

4 I .... (*hear*) something move and I .... (*realise*) I .... (*stand*) next to a snake.

5 Her friends .... (*arrive*) about an hour before she .... (*get*) there.

6 Petrol .... (*cost*) less in those days so many people .... (*prefer*) bigger cars.

7 They .... (*hear*) a noise and .... (*look*) round to see what .... (*happen*).

8 He .... (*turn*) and .... (*say*) goodbye to her as he .... (*leave*) the room.

9 The cat .... (*lie*) on the floor fast asleep when I .... (*get*) home.

10 Peter .... (*fix*) the explosives to the safe when the police .... (*turn up*).

5 **Decide if these sentences are right or wrong. Put a tick (✔) or a cross (✘) in the box at the end of each line. Then correct the wrong ones.**

1 I asked you to get some cheese — I didn't expect a whole one. ☐

2 Have you got a paper? I need to print a few copies of this letter. ☐

3 We need to take an action here. The situation's getting worse. ☐

4 There's far too many furnitures in this room. I can hardly move. ☐

5 Would you like a coffee? I've just made some. ☐

6 These potatoes will taste better if you add some black peppers. ☐

7 This stew will taste better if you add some chopped green peppers. ☐

8 They've taken him off to the hospital for a treatment. ☐

9 Tropical hardwoods are not popular for furniture today. ☐

10 Just put your luggages on the scales one at a time. ☐

6 **For each sentence, choose the correct modal verb.**

1 You *can/must* have some more cake if you want to.

2 You *mustn't/needn't* do electrical work with the power on.

3 It *can/must* snow here in June but it doesn't often happen.

4 I don't like identity badges but I *have to/must* wear one to get into the building.

5 We expect employees to dress smartly, but you *mustn't/needn't* wear a suit.

6 Strange things *can/must* happen when you investigate the supernatural.

7 You *can/may* well be right but I'd rather see some evidence.

8 She *can't/mustn't* be Bob's sister. She doesn't look at all like him.

7 **Complete each sentence below with the correct word from the box.**

crossing cruise excursion journey
tour travel trip voyage

1 There's an .... to the Roman ruins tomorrow.

2 The Channel .... was rough and Joe was seasick.

3 The .... to Bristol took hours because the train broke down.

4 We didn't do much at the weekend except for a short .... down the coast.

5 Is there a bus that will take us on a .... of the city?

6 After a .... of three weeks the ship arrived in India.

7 This summer we're going on a .... around the Caribbean.

8 He prefers to .... by sea because he hates flying.

8 **Choose the correct phrasal verb from the box for each space. Use the correct tense.**

go through hang around hold up
meet up with pick up set off take off
touch down

Angela and I [1].................. really early but we got stuck in the traffic and we actually [2]..................
Daniel and Chloe at the check-in. But it didn't matter because the flight was delayed and we had to [3].................. for hours. It was after dark before the plane finally [4].................. and so we didn't [5].................. till the middle of the night. After passport control we [6].................. our luggage, but we got [7].................. again because they opened all our bags and [8]..................
everything. In the end, we got to the hotel just in time for breakfast.

9 **Complete each sentence below with the correct word from the box.**

charge commit court fine barrister jury
prosecute robbery sentence solicitor

1 If you .... a crime in that country they'll put you in prison for years.

2 You can use an estate agent to sell your house but you'll need a .... as well.

3 The police have arrested him and are going to .... him with theft.

4 The .... was absolutely packed on the final day of his trial.

5 It wasn't much of a .... All they took were a couple of bracelets.

6 Five years seemed quite a light .... for armed robbery.

7 It was clear the judge thought he had done it but luckily the .... didn't agree.

8 Merv had to pay a heavy .... but he didn't go to prison.

9 Since it was his first offence the police decided not to .... him.

10 Louis's .... explained his defence to the court.

10 **Match each newspaper headline below with one of the crimes from the box.**

arson assault blackmail manslaughter
mugging slander smuggling vandalism

1 MAN ARRESTED AT AIRPORT WITH CANNABIS

2 CHEF PUNCHES CUSTOMER

3 FOUR TELEPHONE BOOTHS SMASHED

4 MP DID NOT LIE SAYS JUDGE

5 PENSIONER ATTACKED AND ROBBED

6 GUARD HIT WITH BASEBALL BAT DIES

7 SCHOOL FIRE CAUSED BY PUPIL

8 EX-WIFE THREATENED TO PUBLISH PHOTOS

11 **Put the adjectives in the right order to describe the object.**

1 man's/woollen/boring/suit

2 big/birthday/delicious/cake

3 old/Italian/beautiful/castle

4 electric/shiny/black/guitar

5 small/sandy/crowded/beach

6 wooden/sailing/graceful/yacht

UNIT 4
Languages

Vocabulary

Borrowed words

1 The words on the map have all come into English from these languages. Work with other students and answer the following questions:

1 Tick (✓) the words you know.
2 Take it in turns to explain the meaning of these words to each other.
3 Check the meaning of the remaining words in a dictionary.

DUTCH
sledge
smuggle

GERMAN
abseil
waltz

HINDI
bungalow
loot

JAPANESE
futon
tycoon

FRENCH
prestige
souvenir

SPANISH
chilli
mosquito

ITALIAN
graffiti
studio

TURKISH
horde
turquoise

PERSIAN
bazaar
tulip

CHINESE
ketchup
silk

ARABIC
hazard
lemon

2 You can find a more complete list of words from other languages in English on page 190.

Listening

1 Look at these four groups of words which have been in English longer than the words on page 190. Which languages do you think gave them to English? Discuss your ideas with another student and write the name of one of the languages in the box under each group of words. You can check your answers when you listen.

2 Work with another student and make a list of other words from your language which can be found in English.

Latin
French
Anglo-Saxon
Scandinavian

mother	giant
walk	royal
cow	beef
1	2 ....

priest	sky
bishop	skirt
candle	they
3	4 ....

FCE Paper 4, Part 2

3 You will hear a conversation about the origins of English. For questions 1-10 complete the sentences.

Alan Bertram is an expert on the [1] _____ of English.

The Anglo-Saxons arrived in England in the [2] _____

The ancestors of English and German were [3] _____

Most basic English words used today come from [4] _____

After 1066, the Normans [5] _____ England.

Words for meat are French because the Anglo-Saxon kept the animals, but the Normans [6] _____ and ate it.

Latin began to influence English [7] _____ the Normans arrived.

Anglo-Saxon and French joined together after [8] _____ years.

The Vikings invaded during the eighth and ninth [9] _____

In later years, many [10] _____ to English.

4 Work with another student and make a list of words from English or other languages which are used in your language.

5 What do you know about the origins of your language? Work with other students to prepare a talk on the history of your language for the rest of the class.

Vocabulary

Confusing words *say, tell, talk, speak*

1 Tick (✓) the correct sentences.

1 They didn't say to her that they would be late.
2 She didn't say him that they would arrive on Saturday.
3 He didn't tell to them that the TV was broken.
4 They didn't tell me to stay at home.
5 He didn't tell the whole story.
6 She didn't say the truth.
7 They didn't tell Ruth that they weren't coming.
8 She didn't say that the game was cancelled.

2 Now write *say* or *tell* on each line to complete the rules. Compare your answers with another student.

1 .... is used to give information or an instruction.
2 After .... we show who got the message with a pronoun or noun.

3 We don't always use a pronoun or noun with ....
4 If we do use a pronoun or noun, we use *to* between .... and the object.
5 In some fixed expressions — .... *the truth*, ... *the time*, etc, ... is used without a pronoun or noun.

3 Write *speak* or *talk* next to the correct definition. Compare your answers with another student.

1 To .... — two or more people having a conversation. For example, *they .... for hours and hours*.
2 To .... — one person communicating to another. For example, *I'll .... to her about the noise*.

4 Tick the best verb for each situation.

1 say
   speak   a language
2 say
   speak   hello
3 tell
   say   the time
4 speak
   talk   business
5 talk
   tell   the truth
6 talk
   tell   rubbish
7 speak
   tell   your mind
8 say
   tell   your name

5 Find someone in the class who:

1 thinks talking politics is boring.
2 can say hello in five different languages.
3 never tells a lie.
4 thinks their parents talk a lot of sense.
5 speaks three languages fluently.
6 likes telling jokes.

6 If someone answers *yes*, ask another question to get more information.

Grammar

used to/would

1 Read the sentences below. All of them contain *would* and *used to*. Some are right and some are wrong. With another student, discuss the difference of meaning between *would* and *used to*.

1　Anton **used to** work for IBM. ✓
　　Anton **would** work for IBM. ✗

2　Mark **used to** work 16 hours a day. ✓
　　Mark **would** work 16 hours a day. ✓

3　At that time Catherine often **used to** go running. ✓
　　At that time Catherine **would** often go running. ✓

4　Cheri **used to** go to school in Paris. ✓
　　Cheri **would** go to school in Paris. ✗

5　Greg **used to** own a Harley-Davidson. ✓
　　Greg **would** own a Harley-Davidson. ✗

Theory Box

used to/would

The difference between **would** and **used to** is like this:

(would　　used to)

Used to has a more general meaning, which includes the meaning of **would**.

Used to and **would** are both used for repeated actions in the past. However, **would** is used for temporary voluntary actions. It **can't** be used for who you work for — question **1**, where you go to school — question **4** or what you own — question **5**. In questions **2** and **3**, when we use **would**, we show that the person didn't just do this, but also that they **wanted** to.

*We **used to** live in Glasgow, and at the weekend I **would** go and watch Partick Thistle play.*

The sentence refers to a situation in the past. The first action with **used to** refers to a repeated action in the past which continues for a long period. The second action with **would** also refers to a repeated action in the past but this one is temporary and voluntary.

2 Think of things you did in the past which you don't do anymore. Write three sentences like the example. Use *used to* for the permanent repeated action and *would* for the temporary repeated action.

0　We **used to** live in Glasgow, and at the weekend I **would** go and watch Partick Thistle play.

1　...
　　...

2　...
　　...

3　...
　　...

Theory Box

used to or be/get used to

*Alison **used to live** in France.*
*Alison **is used to life** in France.*

The second sentence means that Alison is **accustomed to** living in France. Maybe she has lived there for a long time. Note the difference in the grammar — **used to** is followed by a **verb** and **be used to** is followed by a noun. **Be used to** can also be followed by a **gerund**:

*Alison is used to **living** in France.*

or a **pronoun**:

*Alison is used to **me**.*

We can also say:

*Alison is **getting used to living** in France.*

This means that she is **becoming accustomed** to it.

Note that **be/get used to** works with various tenses and modals:

*I **was used to** it.*　　　　*I **got used to** it.*
*I've **been used to** it.*　　*I've **got used to** it.*
*I'll **be used to** it.*　　　*I'll **get used to** it.*

3 All of these sentences are wrong. Work with another student and correct them by changing the word in bold.

1　She's **used to** smoke quite a lot. ✗
2　I'll never get used to **eat** chips. ✗
3　He used to **working** in Brazil. ✗
4　I'll never **getting** used to the cold. ✗
5　I **used to** the British weather now. ✗
6　She used to **being** quite poor. ✗
7　He's used to **drink** a lot of coffee. ✗
8　She hasn't got used to **be** rich yet. ✗

4 Now write something that you *used to* do but you don't now.

5 Write something new in your life that you *are not used to*.

6 Write something new in your life that you *are getting used to*.

Reading

1 Apart from your own language and English, how many languages do you speak?

2 If you could learn to speak one more language, which one would you choose?

3 Now compare your answers with another student.

FCE Paper 1, Part 4

4 You are going to read about the languages six British people speak. For questions 1-6, choose from the people (A-F), and for questions 7-10, choose which person's family member is referred to. The people may be chosen more than once. When more than one answer is required, these may be given in any order. There is an example at the beginning (0).

Who

■ speaks four languages? **0** **D**

■ speaks a foreign language at home? **1** ☐

■ speak a foreign language on holiday? **2** ☐
3 ☐

■ were laughed at because of their accent? **4** ☐
5 ☐

■ regrets not speaking his parents' language? **6** ☐

Whose

■ father forgot some of his native language? **7** ☐

■ parents met in another country? **8** ☐

■ parents didn't want to speak their first language? **9** ☐

■ father moved to his mother's hometown? **10** ☐

A **Nick**

I learned some French at school, but I suppose I never really saw the point. I remember that if anybody tried to use a correct accent, the others in the class would laugh at them. When I was at university, I went to France for a holiday and that's where I met Corinne and her friends, who thought my English accent was so funny. I thought, 'Right, I'll learn to speak your language properly.' Which I did, and still do with Corinne. We've been married for eight years now.

B **Catriona**

I was born on Barra, one of the islands off the west coast of Scotland, and I grew up speaking Gaelic. I didn't know a word of English till I went to school. When I was six we moved to Glasgow, and there I was in a Glasgow primary school with my basic English and my strange accent. The other kids just laughed at me, so I learned fast. Although my parents spoke Gaelic to each other, they started to speak to me in English, so I lost my Gaelic. I'm really sorry about that now.

C **Tanya**

My great-grandfather came to Britain from Italy just after the end of the First World War. The first couple of generations of my family worked in cafés and restaurants, but my father became an actor, of all things. My mum also comes from Italy and I grew up in London. My mum and dad have always spoken English to each other. They don't seem to want to use Italian, although they both know the language well enough. So I had to learn it for myself. I've become quite fluent and I spend most of my holidays in Tuscany.

D **Mahmud**

I was born and grew up in Dudley, which is to the west of Birmingham. My mother and father were born in England too, but their parents came from Pakistan. We spoke mainly Urdu in the house, but I learned Gujerati and Hindi too, as well as English. So when I want to speak to a customer in the restaurant, I can do it in one of four languages. If they don't understand any of them, they can point at the menu.

E **George**

My dad's English and my mother is Greek. They met when he was a young man and he was working in Greece. Her English is very good because when she was a teenager her family moved to New York for three years. The first languages I learned were American English and Greek. But mainly we speak English in the house because my dad's Greek is awful. We go there in the summer and I know enough to get by, but I'm not fluent.

F **Peter**

My father came to Britain from Poland. He met my mother in London, but they settled in the small town that she came from. He was the only Pole in the town, so he never spoke Polish and I remember him saying towards the end of his life that he had forgotten quite a lot of it. However, he never really learned to speak English properly. He could make himself understood, but he made a lot of mistakes. So he ended up without any language that he was fluent in.

Grammar

Present Perfect

❶ Read these sentences about the people on page 41. For each one, decide if the verb should be in the Present Perfect or the Past Simple. Look back at the text if you aren't sure. Compare your answers with another student.

1 Nick .... (speak) good French for some years now.

2 Catriona .... (spend) the first six years of her life on a small island.

3 She .... (be) back there only once since she moved to Glasgow.

4 She .... (not speak) Gaelic since she was a child.

5 Tanya's great-grandfather .... (come) to Britain from Italy in 1919.

6 Before she was born, her father .... (decide) to become an actor.

7 She .... (visit) Italy a number of times.

8 Mahmud .... (open) three Indian restaurants so far.

9 George .... (just come back) from a summer holiday in Greece.

10 Peter's father first .... (meet) his mother in London.

Theory Box

Present Perfect

We use the **Present Perfect** in one of these ways:

Now

1 for an event which started in the past and is still happening.

I've known about this for weeks.

2 for events in the past where the time isn't important.

I've been to university.

He's done that many times.

3 for a recent past event which is still relevant to the present.

Someone's stolen my car!

❷ Look back at the Present Perfect sentences in question 1. With another student discuss which use of the Present Perfect (1, 2 or 3) each one illustrates.

❸ What do the three uses of the Present Perfect have in common?

Theory Box

Present Perfect vs. Past Simple

1 *I've worked on this all morning.*

It's still morning. I'm either still working or I've just finished.

I worked on this all morning.

The morning is over — it's now later in the day.

2 *I've been to Tunisia.*

We are talking about Tunisia, it could be the answer to a question about Tunisia at the moment.

I went to Tunisia.

Perhaps you want to know where I went for my holidays last year.

3 *Fred's just left.*

Perhaps only a few minutes ago — you might catch him if you hurry.

Fred left.

We're talking about an event in the past. Perhaps you want to know what Fred did next.

When we use the **Past Simple** for an event in the past, the **time of the event is important**. We either say when it happened, or both the speaker and listener know when it happened.

❹ Complete each of these extracts taken from the listening on page 39 with either the Present Perfect or the Past Simple. Then compare your answers with another student.

Alan: I'm very interested in the way English [1]............. (develop) over the centuries — the many different languages that [2]............. (give) words to it.

Interviewer: So how [3]............. it all .... (start)?

Alan: Well, if you think of Old English you're talking about the language spoken by the invaders who [4]............. (come) over from North Germany in the fifth century — the Anglo-Saxons.

Interviewer: OK, so how much of the original Old English [5]............. (survive) in English today?

Alan: ...the Normans [6]............. (invade) England in 1066...

Interviewer: The most famous date in English history.

Alan: That's right. The Normans [7]............. (take over) the whole country, and the words they [8]............. (give) to English [9]............. (show) this — words like castle, or royal. I mean, various people [10]............. (note) that while the words for farm animals — cow, calf, sheep, come from Old English, the words we use to describe the meat — beef, veal, mutton — are French.

Interviewer: That's because the Anglo-Saxon peasants [11]............. (keep) the animals and the Normans [12]............. (eat) the meat?

Vocabulary

Compound nouns

❶ In English, you can use two nouns to make a new noun. For example:

mother + tongue = mother tongue

Can you do this in your language? With another student think of the compound noun for each object (1-6).

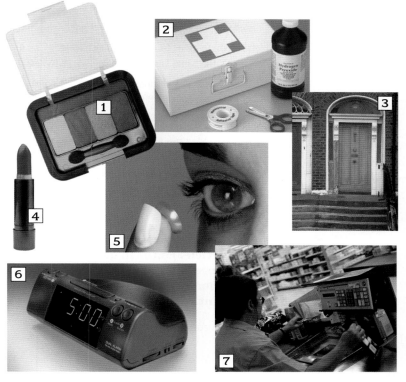

❷ Which ones are formed by:

1   noun + noun? ....

2   adjective + noun? ....

3   verb + preposition? ....

❸ Match a word from box A with a word from box B to make a compound noun for each definition (1-8).

A	junk	hitch	B	fiction	resources
	soap	current		food	sense
	generation	natural		hiker	affairs
	science	common		opera	gap

1   the difference in ideas and opinions between older and younger people

2   unhealthy food which contains a lot of chemicals and sugar

3   stories about the future

4   someone who travels by getting rides in other people's cars

5   a television programme that is broadcast at least once a week and is about the same people's daily lives and problems

6   practical knowledge that comes from experience

7   things such as trees and water which are used to make things

8   important things that are happening in the world at the moment

❹ The compound nouns in the box are all formed with a verb and preposition. Choose the best one to complete each sentence.

breakdown	breakthrough
cutback	drawback
feedback	outlook
outskirts	washing up

1   The .... for the weekend looks good with sunshine and high temperatures.

2   The company has been forced to make a lot of .... because of a fall in profits.

3   There has been a .... in communication between the management and workers.

4   The teacher was very happy because the .... from her students was very positive.

5   There has been a .... in research into AIDS.

6   I hate doing the .... after meals. Why can't we buy a machine to do it?

7   We live on the .... of the town but I'd prefer to move to the centre.

8   One .... of having a big car is that it uses a lot of petrol.

❺ Now write the compound noun next to the correct definition.

1   cleaning the dishes ....

2   a disadvantage ....

3   forecast ....

4   a reduction/decrease ....

5   a sudden failure ....

6   an important discovery/ advance ....

7   comments on someone's performance ....

8   the outer area of a town ....

UNIT 4

Grammar

ago, already, for, since and *yet*

❶ Work with another student and match each word from the box with its correct definition.

ago	already	for	since	yet

Theory Box

ago, already, for, since and *yet*

We use this word with the...

1 Past Simple to indicate **the start of a period of time that leads up to now.** ....

2 Present Perfect to indicate **the start of a period of time that leads up to now.** ....

3 Present Perfect to indicate **the length of a period of time that leads up to now.** ....

4 Present Perfect to indicate **that something we expect to happen hasn't happened.** ....

5 various tenses to indicate **that something has happened, or has been done before the moment of speaking.** ....

❷ Write one of the words from question 1 in each of the spaces below. Then compare your answers with another student.

1 There have been French words in English .... 1066.

2 There have been Norse words in English .... even longer.

3 George's father hasn't managed to learn Greek ....

4 Tanya's grandfather arrived from Italy many years ....

5 George's mum doesn't want to go to New York — she's .... been there.

6 Although he wants to go, Peter hasn't visited Poland ....

7 Tanya has lived in London .... most of her life.

8 Has Catriona started learning Gaelic ....?

9 The Anglo-Saxons came to England over 1500 years ....

10 Nick's French has improved a lot .... he met Corinne.

❸ Now write sentences about yourself using *ago, already, for, since* and *yet*. Then compare your sentences with another student. Ask each other a question about each sentence.

Writing

FCE Paper 2, Part 2

❶ You have seen this competition in an international magazine for students of English.

> You are learning English – that's why you read this magazine. But...
>
> - Do you like learning English? Is it difficult?
> - Which other languages are spoken where you live?
> - Is English your second language, your third, or your fourth?
> - Which language, or dialect, did you learn to speak as a child? Is this the same language as you speak today?
> - How many people in your area speak English? Is the number increasing or decreasing?
> - Why do people learn English?
>
> We want to know about **the languages which are spoken, or learnt, where you live**. The winning article will be published in the next issue and the winner will receive a prize of £1000.

❷ First look at these expressions which could be used in this article. For each question complete the second expression so that it means the same as the first. Then compare your answers with another student.

1 My first language is spoken by very few people.
My **m**............. tongue is a **m**............. language.

2 It is not the same as the national language.
It is a **d**............. .

3 It is mainly spoken by old people.
It tends to be spoken by the **e**............. .

4 More people are speaking it now.
Its use is **i**............. these **d**............. .

5 Some words are difficult to write because of the pronunciation.
The **s**............. of some words is difficult because of the pronunciation.

6 Some words are borrowed from English.
There are some **l**............. words from English.

7 People use it in all situations.
It is used for all **p**............. .

8 Many people speak two languages.
Many people are **b**............. .

9 People say words in different way.
People speak with different **a**............. .

❸ Now write your article in 120-180 words. Think of answers to the questions in the competition above. This will give you some ideas. You will have to think of a title for your article and organise your ideas into paragraphs.

Use of English

FCE Paper 3, Part 4

Languages quiz

1 Read the questions in the quiz below. Each one of them has a word which should not be there. Work with another student and find the unnecessary word in each question. Then choose your answer to the question — a, b or c.

1 Which of these English words itself is the oldest?
   a aeroplane
   b tin
   c house

2 Which language it has the least irregular verbs?
   a Esperanto
   b Turkish
   c Spanish

3 Which language is been spoken by the most people?
   a English
   b Spanish
   c Mandarin Chinese

4 Which is the that most widespread of these languages?
   a English
   b French
   c Spanish

5 In which country are the most languages being spoken?
   a India
   b Indonesia
   c Papua New Guinea

6 Which language is having the most difficult to write?
   a English
   b Chinese
   c Swedish

7 Which of these sounds is present in all languages?
   a /ɑ/
   b /e/
   c /i/

8 Which language there has the largest vocabulary?
   a Arabic
   b English
   c Italian

9 Which letter is entered the English alphabet most recently?
   a h
   b j
   c x

10 Which of these which is not related to any other language?
   a Arabic
   b Basque
   c Greek

2 Now look at these sentences. In each of them there is a word which shouldn't be there. Work with another student and take these words out. Look carefully at the functional, grammatical words — not nouns, verbs or adjectives.

1 Nick found there was being a good language school in the town.

2 There are so many these books that I don't know which one to choose.

3 I have to concentrate myself to understand what he's saying.

4 The class began at 6.30 on Tuesday evenings and have ended at 8.00.

5 Alice and Bob both speak French and he also speak Turkish.

6 Did you know that Lucy's boyfriend who is fluent in Japanese?

7 Has Maria caught up there with the others in the class yet?

8 This is the teacher who she taught me my first English words.

9 His spoken Spanish had got better after he went to live in Madrid.

10 Do you know where I could find it a good dictionary?

11 Shona started to learn German when she has got to secondary school.

12 You can fax the article him or send it by e-mail to him.

13 It's a language that spoken by fewer and fewer people.

14 The library which was open in the evenings for private study.

15 Clara met some British students who they were studying Italian.

Grammar

could, *might* and *have to*

❶ *Could*, *might* and *have to* all have more than one meaning. These are listed below. Work with a partner and write a sentence to illustrate this meaning *for the past*. There is an example — but write one for yourself as well.

1 *could*
   ability I could speak Gaelic when I was a kid but I've forgotten it now.
   ....
   permission ....
   possibility ....

2 *might*
   permission ....
   possibility ....

3 *had to*
   obligation ....
   logical ....
   necessity ....

❷ Now compare your sentences with other students. Then turn to page 170 for more information.

❸ Work with another student and write the correct form of *could*, *might* or *have to* in each space so that the sentence means the same as the one above it. For some questions, more than one modal verb is possible.

1 I had no choice but to tell him.
   I .... tell him.

2 He said it was OK for me to go.
   He said that I .... go.

3 It's impossible that the result wasn't correct.
   The result .... be correct.

4 It's possible that the result wasn't correct.
   The result .... correct.

5 It's possible that he was lying.
   He .... lying.

6 As a child, she was able to sing very well.
   As a child, she .... sing very well.

Speaking

FCE Paper 5, Part 4

❶ Work with another student and discuss which of these means of communication you use at the moment and which you might use in the future. Some of these are in widespread use today, some are in an experimental phase and some are only possibilities.

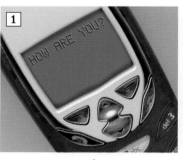

texting

the Internet

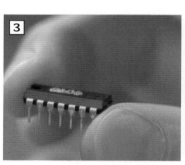

microchip implants

telepathy

virtual reality

wall screens

❷ Now write the name of one of the means of communication on each line below. Then explain your choices to another student.

1 .... this is the most useful now.

2 .... this is the least useful now.

3 .... this will be the most useful in the future.

4 .... this will be the least useful in the future.

❸ Now make a group of four with two other students. Compare your ideas. Discuss when you think the new means of communication will come into use.

Vocabulary

Ways of speaking

① Use a dictionary to find out which ways of speaking are loud (L) and which ones are soft (S)? One can be both. Compare your ideas with another student.

1 whisper ☐
2 mumble ☐
3 scream ☐
4 shout ☐
5 stutter ☐
6 shriek ☐
7 mutter ☐

② Answer each question with a way of speaking from question 1.

1 Which one is caused by a physical problem? ....

2 Which one do you do if a sign says *No talking*? ....

3 Which one do you do because you are frightened? ....

4 Which one do you do if the other person is deaf? ....

5 Which one do you do if you say something unclearly? ....

6 Which one is a short, loud, noise often in excitement? ....

7 Which one do you do quietly because you are angry?

....

③ Use an appropriate verb from question 1 to complete each sentence.

1 'I wish I could speak German,' I .... to myself in the middle of Berlin.

2 He only .... when he's nervous or upset.

3 She gave a .... of excitement when she saw she'd passed the exam.

4 She .... in my ear, but I didn't hear because the music was so loud.

5 'You're .... again. I can't hear you. Speak up.'

6 She kept on .... as the snake moved closer.

7 'There's no need .... I heard you the first time.'

④ Work with another student and match the sentence halves.

1 He keeps on boasting
2 They blamed the police
3 He always insists
4 I object
5 They always argue
6 He grumbled
7 She complained
8 She accused

A on spending the weekend with his mother.
B to people smoking in public places.
C about the parking fine but paid it anyway.
D me of eating the last chocolate.
E to the manager about the poor service.
F about his new car.
G about what they are going to watch on TV.
H for killing the man.

⑤ Complete the verb forms with the correct preposition.

1 to boast (to someone) .... (doing) something.

2 to blame someone .... (doing) something. *But* to blame something .... someone.

3 to insist .... (someone) doing something.

4 to object .... (someone) doing something.

5 to argue (with someone) .... (doing) something.

6 to grumble (to someone) .... (doing) something.

7 to complain (to someone) .... (doing) something.

8 to accuse someone .... (doing) something.

⑥ Rewrite each sentence with the correct verb and preposition from question 5. Compare your answers with another student.

1 Look. I got the best exam results in the class.
He ....

2 I know it was Stephanie who lost the necklace.
He ....

3 Really, as I said it's not a problem to drive Jane home.
He ....

4 I hate it when my neighbour plays opera really loudly.
She ....

5 My colleagues never agree about anything.
My colleagues always ....

6 We were surprised at the amount on the bill and told the manager.
We ....

7 The police say that the burglar had robbed three other houses.
The police ....

8 I don't see why I always have to tidy my bedroom.
John ....

UNIT 5
Clothes and Fashion

Speaking

FCE Paper 5, Parts 3/4

❶ Work with another student to decide which decade the different fashions in the photos belong to.

1 ☐ 1920s-1930s
2 ☐ 1940s-1950s
3 ☐ 1960s
4 ☐ 1970s
5 ☐ 1980s
6 ☐ 1990s-2000s

❷ What do you think people will be wearing in 25 or 50 years' time? Draw a sketch or write some ideas down. Discuss your ideas with another student.

Vocabulary

Adjective and noun collocations

❶ *Collocation* means words that often go together. For example, in English we can say *black coffee, white coffee, black tea* but we cannot say *white tea*. Instead we say *tea with milk*. What about in your language?

❷ Work with another student. In each group, there is one noun which does not go with the adjective. Tick [✓] the odd one out. For example :

1 strong
  rain ✗ heavy rain
  shoes ✓
  feelings ✓
  beliefs ✓

2 heavy
  punishment
  smoker
  look
  day

3 light
  clothes
  sleeper
  meal
  chance

4 dark
  room
  personality
  look
  side

5 weak
  tea
  wine
  leadership
  argument

6 strong
  possibility
  secret
  smell
  wind

❸ **Which nouns from the box go with each of the adjectives below. Compare your idea with another student. Some of the nouns can be used with more than one adjective.**

bag fine traffic fighting
sleeper heart breathing
meal argument radio signal
character storyline influence
personality economy
sea current taste impression
suspicion colour dress
housework reading wind
skin street hair

1 heavy: ....
....

2 weak: ....
....

3 strong: ....
....

4 light: ....
....

5 dark:...
....

❹ **Work with another student to complete this quiz.**

Find out...

1 Which student has a strong handshake?

2 Which city has very heavy traffic?

3 Which famous person or character has a dark side?

4 What job needs a strong heart?

5 What's a very strong wind called?

6 Which country has a strong economy?

7 Which student has the strongest personality in the class?

8 Which country has heavy rain for a short period every year?

9 Which student is a light sleeper?

10 Which student likes to wear dark colours?

Use of English

Theory Box

Word transformation

The passage below contains a number of words which you have to change into another form of the same word.

- You might have to change the part of speech:
  success (n) → *succeed* (v) or *successful* (adj)
  or *successfully* (adv)

- You might have to make it negative:
  know → *unknown*

- Give a comparative or superlative form:
  cheap → *cheaper/cheapest*

- Change it to a participle:
  notice → *noticing/noticed*

- Produce a compound form:
  post → *postcard*, *postmark*, *postscript*

- Combine two of these processes:
  agree → *disagreement* — where a verb changes to a negative noun.

FCE Paper 3, Part 5

❶ **For questions 1-10, read the text below. Use the word given in capitals at the end of the line to form a word that fits in the space in the same line. There is an example at the beginning (0).**

Hollywood Freebies

For just 90 seconds' work, Hollywood's biggest stars can receive thousand dollar treats.

Every year, as the Oscar awards come round, (0) *designers* like Calvin Klein, Giorgio Armani and John Galliano compete to dress the world's most (1)................. women.   **DESIGN**

                                                    GLAMOUR

The publicity they might gain is worth more than any (2).................. campaign.   **ADVERTISE**

Jewellers also fight hard to cover the potential winners with diamonds. Actresses have told how, from the moment they are revealed as (3)................... or presenters, they are showered with unsolicited gifts.   **NOMINATE**

The first thing that happens is that every fashion company across the world tries to catch their (4)................. , sending   **ATTEND**
over small (5)................. with photographs of their new   **FOLD**
items. The actress can choose a dozen dresses – each worth thousands of dollars, which are then (6).................. out to   **FLY**
Hollywood.

The actress will examine the (7)................. and take home   **OFFER**
the ones she likes (8)................. . She can choose to wear   **GOOD**
one of the dresses she has taken or something (9)...................   **COMPLETE**
different. Either way, she will keep them all. Money is never
(10)................. .   **DISCUSS**

UNIT 5

Reading

1 Now look at these ideas for *clever clothes*. How many of them do you think are possible in the near future? Discuss your ideas with other students.

1 clothes which clean themselves
2 clothes that can change colour to suit your mood
3 clothes which stay dry no matter how much you sweat
4 clothes which can check your health and supply necessary drugs
5 a suit you can machine wash, tumble dry and put straight back on
6 clothes containing keyboards, mobile phones and tape recorders made of soft fabric

2 You are going to read a magazine article about clothes in the future. Before you do this, work with another student and match each word from the box with its correct definition.

> garment   hollow   tight-fitting
> sweat   lapel   smart card
> to tumble dry   iron
> range   weaving

1 fitting close to the body: ....
2 a set of similar clothes from the same manufacturer: ....
3 making cloth by crossing threads over and under each other: ....
4 liquid that comes from your skin when you get hot or take exercise: ....
5 a plastic card containing information that can be read by a computer: ....
6 you put a flower in a buttonhole on this part of a coat or jacket: ....
7 it has a hot, flat metal base, you use it to make clothes smooth: ....
8 to dry clothes in hot air in a cylinder that turns round: ....
9 having an empty space inside: ....
10 a piece of clothing: ....

3 For questions 1-8 choose the correct answer (A, B, C or D).

FABRICS OF THE FUTURE

Science-fiction films often show future space explorers wearing one-piece tight-fitting suits. This may be unlikely given that the population in Western countries is growing fatter and fatter. However, one thing that is certain about the
5 future of fashion is that there are no certainties.

With fabric we are on safer ground, because fabric depends on science and science has that old-fashioned habit of taking an idea and testing it for more than a few weeks at a time. The future of fabric is already with us as science begins the
10 process of weaving intelligence into the cloth.

A British company, *Electrotextiles*, has already produced a range of intelligent clothes which includes a soft fabric keyboard
15 sewn into a pair of trousers. And, yes, the trousers can be washed and even ironed. At the moment, they are
20 planning a tie that works like a computer mouse. Potentially clothes like this could have mobile phones in
25 the lapels of jackets, or tape recorders built into the pockets. They might also keep a check on the user's
30 health and even administer any required drugs.

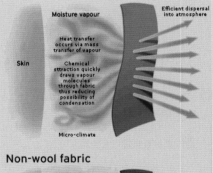

Non-wool fabric

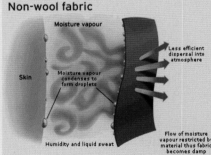

In Australia, the Woolmark Company in conjction with CSIRO, a research organisation, has developed a material
35 called *Sportwool*. Any moisture on the inside immediately spreads out over a much wider area as it passes through the fabric and evaporates quickly. This means that you can sweat and stay dry. They're looking forward to developing fibres that can change their size, becoming thinner to allow more
40 moisture through or thicker to keep out the cold.

SPORTWOOL ®

They're also working on a suit that you can machine wash, tumble dry and put straight back on, but even this development might be left behind as self-cleaning fabrics develop. A
45 research team in the US has recently worked out a way of filling hollow fibres with harmless bacteria to clean the fabric. In time, genetically engineered bacteria should be developed which can *literally* eat up dirt.
50 All very admirable, but what does it have to do with fashion? Well, a US company called International Fashion Machines is working on a fabric that contains capsules of a special ink that gets darker or lighter as it is heated or cooled.
55 This is still in its early stages, but it's easy enough to imagine the possibilities. So grey is in fashion? Let's wear grey today. The sun has come out – want to brighten up? Why not select a nice shade of red.
60 When it comes to shopping, things are moving just as fast. A 3-D measuring system will soon be available that can scan the exact size of your body and record it onto a disc. You can then look at a selection of clothes on the Internet
65 and try them on. Alternatively, you can transfer your measurements to a smart card, take it to the shop and have your garment produced on the spot.
Of course, the end result of all of this
70 development could turn out to be a disaster for the designers, the manufacturers and the stores. If you can buy one garment online, which can change its colour, its insulation and even its shape, which is self-cleaning and might never
75 wear out, well... why would you ever feel the need to buy another one?

1 What does the writer say about people in the future?
A They will wear tight-fitting suits.
B They will be fatter.
C They will wear looser clothes.
D We don't know what they will wear.

2 The writer thinks that
A fashion designers are more interesting than scientists.
B scientists are more predictable than fashion designers.
C scientists are safer than fashion designers.
D scientists are old-fashioned.

3 What kind of clothes are produced by *Electrotextiles* at the moment?
A jackets with mobile phones and tape recorders
B trousers with keyboards
C clothes which can administer drugs
D a tie which works as a computer mouse

4 What is the main purpose of *Sportwool*?
A to get rid of sweat quickly
B to keep the wearer warm
C to stop the wearer sweating
D to keep out the rain

5 In line 49, *literally* means
A effectively
B actually
C easily
D almost

6 What does the writer suggest about the machine-washable suit?
A It is made of fibres which contain bacteria.
B It may not be necessary for long.
C It may be able to clean itself.
D It isn't a practical idea.

7 What does the writer suggest about buying clothes in the future?
A The Internet will become the main method.
B Most garments will be produced in shops.
C People will still prefer to buy in shops.
D There may be a decrease in demand.

8 From the tone of the passage, what do you think the writer's job is?
A a fashion designer
B a sales executive
C a journalist
D a scientist

Grammar

Past Perfect

1 Look at each group of sentences below. For each sentence, answer the question and tick the right box: yes (Y) no (N) or maybe (MB).

	Y	N	MB

1 Did George catch the train?
   a The train left when George arrived. ☐ ☐ ☐
   b The train had left when George arrived. ☐ ☐ ☐
   c The train left when George had arrived. ☐ ☐ ☐

2 Was Louise there when the crash happened?
   a The cars crashed when Louise came round the corner. ☐ ☐ ☐
   b The cars had crashed when Louise came round the corner. ☐ ☐ ☐
   c The cars crashed when Louise had come round the corner. ☐ ☐ ☐

3 Was the shot fired before the police entered the house?
   a When the police ran into the house, the shot was fired. ☐ ☐ ☐
   b When the police ran into the house, the shot had been fired. ☐ ☐ ☐
   c When the police had run into the house, the shot was fired. ☐ ☐ ☐

Theory Box

Past Perfect

The Past Perfect has a very simple meaning. It means **before**. Look at these sentences again:

PAST   **NOW**

*When Harry **sat down**, they **ate** the soup.*

The grammar tells us the two events happened in the past. Harry sat down then they ate. Now let's add the Past Perfect to the second verb:

BEFORE   **PAST**   **NOW**

*They **had eaten** the soup when Harry **sat down**.*

The Past Perfect moves **eat** further back into the past. We can also add the Past Perfect to the first verb:

BEFORE   **PAST**   **NOW**

*When Harry **had sat down** they **ate** the soup.*

This moves **sat** further back into the past and puts more time between the two events — maybe they chatted for a while before starting on the soup.

Look at the sentences below. As you read each one, write **1**, **2** or **3** above each verb to show the order they happened in.

1 *I **answered** some e-mails and **ate** a sandwich. Then Marta **arrived**.*

We don't need the past perfect in this sentence. The order of events is quite clear. However, let's say we want to start with Marta:

2 *When Marta **arrived, I answered** some e-mails and **ate** a sandwich.*

There's nothing wrong with this sentence, except that now the order of events is different. But we could say:

3 *When Marta **arrived, I'd answered** some e-mails and **eaten** a sandwich.*

This puts the events back in the same order as sentence 1.
Remember, the Past Perfect means the same as before. In fact, you can use **before**, or **after**, instead:

*   **Before** Marta arrived, I answered some e-mails and **ate** a sandwich.

*   Marta arrived **after** I answered some e-mails and ate a sandwich.

When you use the Past Perfect, make sure that it is necessary.

2 In each sentence below indicate the order of events. Decide if you think the Past Perfect is necessary.

1 Joe had put on his new suit. Then he took the tube to work.
2 Jane sat down at her dressing table and started to do her hair.
3 The moment people had started to wear clothes, fashion began.
4 The summer sales finished when Andrea got back from holiday.
5 Olive needed a new sweater so she went to the High Street and looked for one.
6 The first nylon shirts, which had appeared in the 1960s, were awful.
7 Andrew looked at his shoes and realised that he bought a pair just like them before.
8 They already sold out of cheap shirts when Mike got to the shop.

Speaking

1 Work with other students and decide what these people should wear in the following situations.

1 A 25-year-old woman is going to meet her boyfriend's parents for the first time.

2 An 17-year-old boy is going to an interview for university entrance.

3 A 30-year-old man is going for an interview for the position of editor of a fashion magazine.

4 A 30-year-old woman is going for an interview for the position of assistant manager of a bank.

5 A 23-year-old woman is going to start work as a teacher in a secondary school.

FCE Paper 5, Part 2

2 When you speak about the photographs, you will have to compare and contrast them, and then give a personal reaction to them. Look at the expressions below to talk about preferences. Where do they go on the scale? Write one letter, A-E, on each line.

POSITIVE

A I don't like the idea of school uniforms. 1 ☐

B I'm in two minds about school uniforms. 2 ☐

C I'm all in favour of school uniforms. 3 ☐

NEUTRAL

D I prefer school uniforms to jeans. 4 ☐

E I don't mind what children wear to school. 5 ☐

F I'd rather children wear jeans to school. 6 ☐

NEGATIVE

3 Correct the mistakes in the sentences below.

1 I'm all a favour of people wearing casual clothes to work.

2 I'd rather to buy expensive clothes that last a long time.

3 I prefer buy clothes that are made of cotton.

4 I'm in two minds about buy clothes on the Internet.

5 I don't mind what young people wearing to school.

6 I don't like an idea of buying designer clothes.

4 Work with another student. Do you agree with the statements in question 3? What clothes do you like and dislike wearing?

5 Work with another student and each choose a set of photos to talk about. You should compare and contrast your photos and give your opinion about what is happening in them. Talk for about a minute.

Listening

1 You are going to hear people talking in eight different situations. Match the subjects (1-8) they will be talking about to the word or phrase (a-h) for each subject.

1	the garden	☐	**a**	psychology
2	restaurants	☐	**b**	a little bistro
3	clothes	☐	**c**	next week's friendly
4	a dog	☐	**d**	London fashion house
5	football	☐	**e**	had an injection
6	clothes design	☐	**f**	massive paws
7	the dentist	☐	**g**	rose bushes
8	a lecturer	☐	**h**	it's shrunk

2 Listen and check your answers.

FCE Paper 4, Part 1

3 Now listen to the people talking. For questions 1-8, choose the best answer, A, B or C.

1 You hear a son talking to his father. Why is he talking to him?
   A to arrange a meeting
   B to request some help
   C to postpone some work

2 You hear a student talking to a friend. What is she giving?
   A an opinion
   B some advice
   C some information

3 You overhear this conversation in a clothes shop. What is the manager going to do?
   A talk to the woman
   B change the sweater
   C return her money

4 You hear a woman talking about a dog on the phone. Why did the man buy the dog?
   A as a companion
   B to guard his property
   C for his children to play with

5 You are listening to the news on the radio. Why has David Belford lost his job as captain?
   A for being friendly
   B for being critical
   C for playing badly

6 You hear a man talking about fashion. What is he doing as he speaks?
   A announcing a competition
   B advertising clothes
   C discussing designs

7 You hear a man talking about going to the dentist. What did the dentist do?
   A filled his tooth
   B pulled his tooth out
   C checked his teeth

8 You hear a student talking about a lecture. What was it like?
   A interesting
   B boring
   C out of date

Grammar

Passive

1 In each of the texts you have just listened to, there is an example of a verb in the passive. Listen to extracts from the texts again. Complete the table below with the passive verb. The first one has been done for you. Then write the names of the tenses in the column on the right.

		example sentences	passive tense
1	son and father	were delivered	
2	lecturer and student		Present Simple
3	woman and waiter	has(n't) been cooked	
4	woman on phone		Past Continuous
5	radio news	is being replaced	
6	woman on TV		*will*
7	man talking	had been filled	
8	student talking		*should*

Theory Box

The passive

	subject	Past Simple of deliver	object	
active:	They	delivered	the rose bushes	this morning.
passive:	The rose bushes	were	delivered	this morning.
	subject	Past Simple of be	past participle of build	

We make the passive with the same tense of the verb **be** + the past participle of the main verb.

The **object** of the active sentence moves to the **subject** position of the passive sentence. If we want to keep the **active subject**, it moves to the end, after **by**, and we call it the **agent**.

	subject			agent
active:	The children	were stealing	the apples.	
passive:	The apples	were being	stolen	by the children.
	subject		object	

2 Now look at these comments about the situations in the listening activity. For each question, change the active sentence to its passive form. You must use between 2 and 5 words, including the word given. Do not change this word.

1 Joe and his father are planting the roses tomorrow.
by
The roses ....
.... Joe and his father tomorrow.

2 Metcalf is going to replace David Belford as captain.
be
David Belford ....
.... replaced as captain.

3 A lot of customers don't like the way you cook their steaks.
are
A lot of customers don't like the way ....
.... cooked.

4 A friend asked me to recommend a good, cheap restaurant.
by
I ....
to recommend a good, cheap restaurant.

5 One of our viewers has designed this outfit.
designed
This outfit ....
.... one of our viewers.

6 I think I have to take this tooth out.
be
I think this tooth ....
.... out.

7 When he bought the dog, the children had already stolen most of his apples.
been
When he bought the dog, most of the apples ....
.... stolen.

8 Psychologists were saying these things about 20 years ago.
by
These things were ....
.... about 20 years ago.

Writing

1 An international chain of clothes shops is thinking of opening a branch where you live. They have asked different young people to write a report on the shops there. You should comment on the types of shops, what kinds of clothes they sell and how a new shop could attract business. But first... let's plan what you're going to say:

An international chain of clothes shops... → You don't need to describe the chain, but you should have an idea in mind. Write the name of your favourite chain store here. ....

...is thinking of opening a branch in your town. → Let's begin with some facts about your town. Write the town's name, its population and what kind of place it is here.
....
....

They have asked you to write a report on the shops in your town centre. → Write the names of the major shops in your town centre here ....

You should comment on the types of shops and what kinds of clothes they sell. → In the report you won't have time or space to write a full description of every shop and what it sells. Either: give a brief description of 2-3 shops, or write a general description of all of them.

Write the names of the shops here and a couple of words to describe them.
1 ....
2 ....
3 ....

Write 2-3 areas you wish to cover in your description.
1 ....
2 ....
3 ....

...and how a new shop would attract business. → Think about what is needed in your town. Here are some possibilities:
- top designer labels ☐
- good, quality clothes at a reasonable price ☐
- clothes that are out of the ordinary ☐
- a shop that stays open for longer than the others ☐

Either tick one or more of these or write other possibilities here:
....
....

2 Now you must put your ideas into paragraphs. You will need an introduction, two main paragraphs and a conclusion. Make a paragraph plan which shows what you're going to say in each paragraph.

3 Finally write your report in 120-180 words in an appropriate style. The style should be formal, but not very formal. Try to use the passive if you can.

UNIT 5
Grammar

Urban legends

❶ This is the name we give to stories that people believe, but are not true. In the five questions below there are four urban legends and one true story. Work with another student and decide which one you think is true. Then check the answers on page 190.

People say that...

1 When the *Titanic* was sinking, only women and children were allowed onto the lifeboats. A man got onto one of the boats by wearing a woman's dress.
2 When Nike filmed a commercial for hiking boots in Africa, a tribesman was supposed to say, 'Just do it' in his native language. Instead, he said that he didn't want the shoes.
3 When John F. Kennedy was inaugurated as US President in 1961 he didn't wear a hat. This caused a serious decline in the sales of men's hats.
4 Donald Duck was once banned in Finland because he doesn't wear trousers.
5 The word *nylon* comes from a combination of parts of the names *New York* and *London*.

Theory Box

Impersonal passive

People say that the word nylon comes from New York and London.

Which people? Well... people in general. In fact, you might want to make this information sound more formal. You can do this by using the passive, in one of two ways.

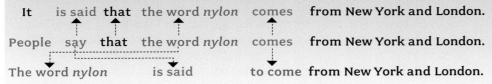

There are other verbs that we can use in sentences like these, apart from **say**: **allege, believe, calculate, claim, consider, discover, estimate, expect, fear, feel, hope, know, prove, report, say, show, think** and **understand**.

❷ Now try a transformation for yourself. This time the sentence is in the Past Simple. For the second change, use the perfect infinitive, *to have played*.

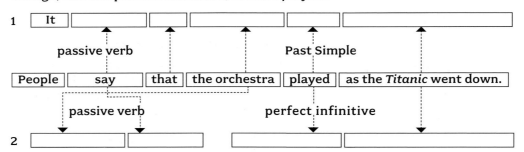

FCE Paper 3, Part 3

❸ Complete the second sentence so that it has a similar meaning to the first sentence using the word given. Do not change the word given. You must use between two and five words, including the word given.

1 A lot of people claim that aliens visit Earth regularly.
   claimed
   It is .... Earth regularly.

2 Some people believe that a monster lives in Loch Ness.
   is
   A monster .... in Loch Ness.

3 At one time people thought that the Earth was flat.
   thought
   At one time .... that the Earth was flat.

4 Some people say that they have seen large apes in the Himalayas.
   said
   Large apes are .... seen in the Himalayas.

5 We understand that the dinosaurs were killed by climate change.
   were
   It is .... killed by climate change.

Vocabulary

Clothes and accessories

1 Work with another student and list all the clothes and accessories that you can see in the pictures. Decide which person looks:

> badly dressed   casual   fashionable
> old fashioned   scruffy   smart   stylish
> trendy   well dressed

2 Match each description in the box to a piece of clothing in the photo.

> checked   flowery   flared   high heeled
> patterned   plain   short sleeved
> spotted   striped   v-necked

3 Do the materials in the box come from animals (A), plants (P), or are they man-made (M)?

> corduroy   cotton   denim   leather
> linen   nylon   plastic   silk   suede   velvet

4 Work with another student and match the questions and answers.

1 Why would you take up a skirt?
2 Why would you let down a dress?
3 Why would you let out a jacket?
4 Why would you take in a skirt?
5 Why would you try on a dress?
6 Why would you put on a jumper?
7 Why would you do up your coat?
8 Why would your jacket come apart at the seams?
9 Why would you take off your jacket?
10 Why would you change out of your school/work clothes?

A Because you were hot.
B Because you were cold.
C Because it was old.
D Because it was too long.
E Because it was the evening.
F Because it was too short.
G To see if it fits.
H Because it was raining.
I Because it was too tight.
J Because it was too loose.

Grammar

Articles — *a/an*, *the* or no article?

1 Read the information about the use of the article on page 177. Work with another student and decide whether each of the spaces below needs *a/an*, *the* or no article.

1 Could you turn down .... TV? I can't hear myself think.
2 Have you got .... pen? I need to sign this.
3 I'm looking for .... shampoo for dry hair.
4 .... fish are quite cheap at the moment.
5 Is she really .... airline pilot?
6 I needed to buy a new jersey and this is .... one I got.
7 Her daughter's at .... university. She's studying medicine.
8 You'd need .... good knowledge of German to do that job.
9 Have you ever been in .... tropics?
10 One of the biggest problems today is .... pollution.

UNIT 6
Sport, Health and Fitness

Reading

1 Are you a couch potato or a disco diva? Do the health and fitness quiz to find out. Then, check your score on page 191. Do you agree with your score?

HEALTH AND FITNESS QUIZ

1 How often do you eat fresh fruit or salad?
- a every day
- b more than once a week
- c occasionally or never

2 How often do you eat fried food?
- a every day
- b once or twice a week
- c less than once a week

3 How often do you eat sweets and/or chocolate?
- a every day
- b more than once a week
- c occasionally or never

4 Do you go for walks?
- a yes — occasionally
- b yes — regularly
- c no

6 How often do you visit a dentist?
- a every six months
- b every six months to a year
- c when you have to

5 How many hours a night do you normally sleep?
- a more than 6 hours
- b less than 6 hours
- c less than 5 hours

8 How often do you take exercise?
- a most days
- b more than once a week
- c occasionally or never

9 Which of these statements reflects how you feel about your body?
- a It's in good shape.
- b It could be in better shape.
- c I don't care what shape it's in.

7 Do you think your weight is
- a more than it should be?
- b less than it should be?
- c about right?

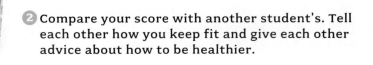

2 Compare your score with another student's. Tell each other how you keep fit and give each other advice about how to be healthier.

Vocabulary

Health and fitness

1 Look at the pictures. Who is saying what? Write each question number in the correct speech bubble.

1 I've put on a lot of weight recently.
2 I cut out chocolate last year and lost a lot of weight.
3 I know I should give up chocolate.
4 I'm in peak condition.
5 I took up jogging last year and feel much fitter.
6 I feel under the weather.
7 I'm in good shape.
8 I don't feel myself at the moment.
9 I ought to cut down on eating cakes.
10 I was feeling run down so I started taking vitamins everyday.

2 Choose a word from the box to complete each sentence. If the word is a verb, put it in its correct form.

ache	blister	dizzy	indigestion	rash
scratch	sick	sneeze	sore	weak

1 The shellfish was off and he was very .... during the night.
2 My body .... and I've got a .... throat. I think I'm coming down with flu.
3 I keep on .... I think I've picked up a cold.
4 I've got a .... all over my body and it itches. I want .... it all the time.
5 He had .... because he ate too much rich food.
6 These new shoes hurt and I've now got a .... on my toe.
7 I feel .... I think I'm going to faint.
8 She hasn't got over her operation yet and still feels very ....

3 Look at the sentences in question 2 again. Underline the five phrasal verbs. Now write the phrasal verb next to its definition.

1 to recover ....
2 to be bad ....
3 to get something unexpectedly ....
4 to become ill ....
5 to repeat the same action ....

Adjectives with prepositions

1 Choose the correct preposition to follow each adjective.

1 I'm interested **in/at** learning how to do Tai Chi.
2 They're keen **in/on** going to the gym.
3 He's very good **with/at** competitive sports.
4 Swimming once a week is good **for/with** your heart.
5 We were really shocked **by/with** his performance.
6 Snooker is very similar **to/than** pool.
7 Football is very different **from/than** rugby.
8 People never seem to get tired **of/with** watching sport on TV.
9 David Beckham is best known **for/at** playing football.
10 I'm worried **about/at** him going jogging every night.

2 Complete the questions with the correct prepositions.

1 What subjects were you good .... at school?
2 What are you interested .... doing this weekend?
3 What sport is similar .... tennis?
4 What are you shocked ....?
5 What things are good .... you?
6 What do you get tired .... doing in your job/studies?
7 What is your country best known ....?
8 What do you worry ....?
9 What are you keen .... doing for your next holiday?
10 How is London different .... your hometown?

3 Work with another student. Take turns to ask the questions: Student A asks the odd questions and Student B asks the even questions.

Reading

1 Look at the pictures of team sports below. You may not know all of them. Read the descriptions of the sports below and write the correct sport (A-F) in each box (1-6).
In Unit 1 on page 7 we saw how you can guess the meaning of unknown words. Go back and read the different strategies you can use. There are some new words here, but they won't stop you answering the questions correctly.

A **Australian Rules Football (ARF)** is popular in the south-eastern part of the country, particularly in the state of Victoria. It is played on an oval pitch with eighteen players on each team. At either end of the pitch there are four vertical goalposts. You get six points by kicking the ball between the middle posts and one point if it goes between these and the outer posts. The ball is oval, and is passed either by punching or kicking it. When running with the ball, it must be bounced on the ground every ten metres. Players can be tackled by holding them below the shoulder and above the knee.

B In the Irish game of **Gaelic Football** each team has fifteen players, including a goalkeeper. The goalposts are H-shaped, with a net across the lower part. The ball is round and slightly smaller than a football. It can be carried in the hand for a distance of four steps. After this it must be bounced on the ground or dropped onto the foot and kicked back to the hand. Players pass to each other by kicking or hitting the ball with the hand, like a serve in volleyball. To score, you must put the ball over the crossbar for one point, or under it for three points.

C **Hurling**, which is also popular in Ireland, has certain features similar to Gaelic football. The number of players is fifteen and the goalposts are the same shape. However, in this game each player carries a stick, called a hurley, and can use it to carry or bounce the ball while running. To make this easier, the stick is wider at one end and the ball has raised ridges on it. A player can score one point by hitting the ball through the upper part of the goal and three by hitting it under the crossbar.

D **Kabaddi** is popular in India and the surrounding countries. The playing area is divided into two halves. There are twelve players in each team, of whom seven are on the court at a time. The game starts when one team sends an 'invader' or 'raider' into the other team's half. His aim is to touch the players on the opposing side, while the other team try to catch him. Anybody that the raider touches has to leave the court. While the raider is in the other court he has to chant 'kabaddi-kabaddi' continuously. When he runs out of breath he has to return to his own court.

E **Rugby** is said to have begun at Rugby School in England in 1823 when a schoolboy picked up the ball in a football game and ran with it. The game divided into two types in 1895 when the northern English clubs formed a professional league. The more popular game of Rugby Union remained amateur until quite recently. The rules of the two types of rugby are slightly different but in both cases the oval ball is carried forward by running or by kicking. Players are not allowed to pass or kick the ball to a player in front of them. When there is a breakdown in play, the forwards in each team join together and push to get the ball. This is called a scrum.

F In **Shinty**, played in the Scottish Highlands, there are twelve players on each side. The goals are similar to football goals, though narrower and higher. Only the goalkeeper can handle the ball. Each player carries a stick, known as a caman. Players use these to hit the ball and use them to block an opponent's caman. Although it is possible to run while carrying or bouncing the ball on the caman, this is more difficult than in hurling because the caman is thinner at the end. Because of this, the ball is moved along the ground or passed from player to player.

FCE Paper 1, Part 4

2 For questions 1-15, choose from the sports (A-F). The sports may be chosen more than once.

Which game(s)

- uses an oval ball?   1 ☐
     2 ☐

- doesn't use a ball?   3 ☐

- uses a ball with a special surface?   4 ☐

- doesn't allow the ball to be passed forward?   5 ☐

- is played on an unusually-shaped pitch?   6 ☐

- has the greatest number of players?   7 ☐

- has the fewest playing at any one time?   8 ☐

- uses a stick designed to carry a ball?   9 ☐

- has goals with no crossbar?   10 ☐

- use H-shaped goals?   11 ☐
     12 ☐
     13 ☐

- has a goal most like the goal in football?   14 ☐

- has different versions with different rules?   15 ☐

1 Now listen to Mike, a teenager from Scotland talking about sports. For questions 1-10, complete the answers.

1 Which is your favourite sport?
....
....

2 Do you play it, or only watch it?
....
....

3 Which is your favourite team?
....
....

4 Do you watch them on TV, or go to matches?
....
....

5 Are there any sports which you dislike?
....
....

6 Which is the most popular sport in your country?
....

7 At which sport is your country most successful?
....

8 Are there any sports which originated in your country? ....

9 Where are these sports now played? ....

10 Are there any sports which are unique to your country? ....

2 Write your own answers for the questions above and talk about them with another student.

FCE Paper 3, Part 1

1 The island of Ireland is divided into two parts, the Irish Republic in the south, and Northern Ireland, which is part of the United Kingdom, in the north. Read the passage below to see how the history and politics of Ireland have their effect on sport. For questions 1-15, decide which answer (A, B, C or D) best fits each space. There is an example at the beginning (0).

In Ireland, sporting affiliation can be a complex matter. (**0**).A.. speaking, there are three choices of team games (**1**)..... offer: football, rugby and what are (**2**)..... the Gaelic sports, the most (**3**)..... being Gaelic football and the stick games of hurling for men and camogie for women. These are controlled by the Gaelic Athletic Association, which grew up in the (**4**)..... 19th century and has always had close (**5**)..... with Irish nationalism. Perhaps not (**6**)....., Protestants in Northern Ireland prefer to play football and rugby. Rugby is (**7**)..... more by the middle class. Northern Catholics (**8**)..... to play either football or the Gaelic sports. Rugby also has a middle-class (**9**)..... in Dublin and most parts of the Republic, with the (**10**)..... of Limerick, where it is played, as they say, by everyone from dockers to doctors.

Gaelic sports, as you might expect, are played all (**11**)..... Ireland, but so is rugby. However, for football the island divides (**12**)..... two separate international teams. Football, which has always had a strong (**13**)..... in the north, has in recent years grown (**14**)..... strength in the south too. This is particularly (**15**)..... of Dublin and the larger population centres. In the more conservative rural areas, Gaelic sports still retain a strong hold.

0	A Generally	B Particularly	C Approximately	D Largely
1	A under	B to	C on	D for
2	A called	B named	C being	D known
3	A prominent	B leading	C main	D chief
4	A latter	B last	C late	D end
5	A bonds	B links	C connections	D alliances
6	A amazingly	B incredibly	C remarkably	D surprisingly
7	A recommended	B selected	C favoured	D advantaged
8	A tending	B approve	C apt	D tend
9	A bias	B prejudice	C favour	D trend
10	A exemption	B exception	C exclusion	D curiosity
11	A about	B through	C on	D over
12	A into	B up	C to	D in
13	A support	B following	C follower	D passion
14	A over	B with	C in	D into
15	A correct	B real	C true	D right

Vocabulary

Phrasal verbs/expressions with *give*

1 Match a sentence from A with a sentence from B to make nine short conversations.

A
1 I need to give Monica her book back.
2 Why don't we give tennis a go this summer?
3 Oh, I give up. Why did the chicken cross the road?
4 Can you lend me a pound?
5 Look, they're giving out samples of that new perfume.
6 There's something giving off a really horrible smell in the fridge.
7 The students need to give in their books at the end of the class.
8 I wonder if the management will give in to their demand for a payrise?
9 How do you know I've stopped my diet?

B
a All that chocolate on your face gave the game away.
b Why? Have you given all your money away again?
c Yes, why not. It'll be good for us.
d I bet you have to pay for them.
e OK, I'll tell them.
f I don't see how they can — they haven't got any more money.
g It's the milk — it's off.
h Yes, you've had it for ages.
i To get to the other side!

2 Underline all the expressions with *give*. Replace them with the definitions below.

1 to give information
2 to return
3 to produce
4 to admit defeat
5 to deliver
6 to surrender
7 to distribute
8 to try something new
9 to get rid of something

Listening

FCE Paper 4, Part 4

8 ① You will hear an interview with two members of the Villa Pamphili women's rugby team, from Rome: Anna Basile, coach and Caterina, one of the current players. For questions 1-7, decide which of these statements are TRUE and which are FALSE. Write T for TRUE or F for FALSE in the boxes provided.

T F

1 Anna started to play rugby because her boyfriend encouraged her. ☐ ☐

2 Caterina's boyfriend doesn't like her playing rugby. ☐ ☐

3 Both women agree that women's rugby is a very physical game. ☐ ☐

4 Boys and girls play rugby separately from the age of fourteen. ☐ ☐

5 When girls play a lot of rugby, they are often more enthusiastic than boys. ☐ ☐

6 Caterina regrets the time she spends playing rugby. ☐ ☐

7 Anna feels that rugby players work together more than footballers. ☐ ☐

Speaking

FCE Paper 5, Parts 3/4

① Talk about the photos below with another student. What do they have in common?

② Are there sports which you think should only be played by men or women? What do you think of men or women playing sports which are traditionally played by the opposite sex? Talk about your answers with another student and then compare your ideas with another pair.

Grammar

Present Perfect Simple or Present Perfect Continuous?

❶ **In each pair of sentences below, the first sentence uses the Present Perfect Simple and the second uses the Present Perfect Continuous. With another student decide whether each sentence is possible, and what difference in meaning there might be between the two.**

1   a   He's played for United for six months.
    b   He's been playing for United for six months.
2   a   She's lived in Dublin all her life.
    b   She's been living in Dublin all her life.
3   a   He's just scored a goal.
    b   He's just been scoring a goal.
4   a   I've just tried on some new boots.
    b   I've just been trying on some new boots.
5   a   He's fallen off his horse.
    b   He's been falling off his horse.
6   a   I've spoken to him about it.
    b   I've been speaking to him about it.
7   a   You've fought.
    b   You've been fighting.

Theory Box

Present Perfect Simple or Present Perfect Continuous?

We add the continuous form to the **Present Perfect**, or any other tense, when we want to make short actions longer, *'we've been talking about going to the match,'* or longer actions shorter, *'she's been playing well all season'*.

medium length event

1   a   He's played for United for six months.
    b   He's been playing for United for six months.

six months is not too long or short. Both sentences are possible, and there is no real difference between them.

very long event

2   a   She's lived in Dublin all her life.
    b   She's been living in Dublin all her life.

All her life is a long time. We don't want to make it sound temporary. The continuous form doesn't work here.

short, single event

3   a   He's just scored a goal.
    b   He's just been scoring a goal.

Scoring a goal is a quick activity. There's no reason to make it sound longer. **b** is very unlikely.

temporary event which can take time

4   a   I've just tried on some new boots.
    b   I've just been trying on some new boots.

If you're interested in the result of the activity because now you've got some new boots, use the Present Perfect. If you want to focus on the activity because it took you all morning, use the Present Perfect Continuous to make it sound longer.

short, single event, possibly repeated

5   a   He's fallen off his horse.
    b   He's been falling off his horse.

Fall off his horse can't happen slowly, adding the continuous form makes it seem like a repeated action. **b** is possible, if he's been falling off a lot recently.

temporary event which can take time, or be repeated

6   a   I've spoken to him about it.
    b   I've been speaking to him about it.

Speaking can take a long or short time — we don't know in this situation. Adding the continuous form either makes the event longer, or suggests that it was repeated. If you want to focus on the result of the activity, use the Present Perfect Simple. If you want to focus on the activity, use the Present Perfect Continuous.

short, recent event, no context

7   a   You've fought.
    b   You've been fighting.

When you want to comment on an event without giving details, the continuous form is the best choice. It emphasises the action and makes it more significant. Turn to page 169 for information on the Past Perfect Continuous.

❷ **Read the news article below. The verbs in the Present Perfect Simple are in bold. In a group, discuss which of these could be changed to the Present Perfect Continuous.**

...and Lewis Reilly **1 has decided** to leave Manchester United. England's highest-paid footballer, who **2 has scored** seven goals in his past three games, is to leave the club **3 he's played** for for over five years, and join Arsenal. He said today, **4 'I've thought** about it a lot over the past few weeks and now the time **5 has come**.' Asked if he had discussed it with the club's manager, Norman Bradley, he said, 'Yeah, **6 I've talked** about it with the boss. I think he'll be glad to see me go. Also the shops are better.' Reilly's wife Debbie, who **7 has** just **had** the couple's second baby, said, 'I'm very happy about the decision which Lewis **8 has made**. I think we'll enjoy living in London.' The player's parents are also delighted. His father, who **9 has supported** Arsenal all his life, said, 'He's a London boy and it will be good to have him home. **10 He's been** up north for long enough.'

Vocabulary

Sports

1 Match the correct sport, equipment or venue to the information in the table below. Some of the words can be used more than once.

sport	equipment	venue
boxing golf hockey rowing skating snooker/pool	ball bat canoe club gloves paddle racket rollerblades skates trainers	court pitch field table track

sport	equipment	venue
		ring
canoeing		/
cricket		
football		
		course
	stick	
	oar	/
running		
		rink
	cue	
tennis/squash/ badminton		

2 For each question, choose the best answer (a, b, c or d).

1 I hate ...... jogging in winter because it's so cold.
   a go   **b** doing   **c** going   **d** to do

2 He ...... his hand a little when he was playing football.
   a wounded   **b** broke   **c** fractured   **d** hurt

3 He works as a ski ...... in the winter.
   a teacher   **b** coach   **c** trainer   **d** instructor

4 Arsenal ...... Chelsea six goals to two in the final.
   a beat   **b** drew   **c** won   **d** lost

5 We had to ...... a sport twice a week at school and I hated it.
   a practise **b** make   **c** take   **d** play

6 She ...... the world record when she became the first woman to run a kilometre in two minutes.
   a held   **b** won   **c** broke   **d** collected

3 Now choose one of these sporting words or expressions to fill each space in the sentences below.

draw   forty-love   foul
game, set and match   penalty   referee
serve   three-nil   umpire

1 And that's it, match point, ... It's all over. .... to Harrison.

2 With these modern rackets they .... so fast it's difficult to get to the ball.

3 Well, I think we were lucky to get a .... Last time they beat us ....

4 Oh what a cynical ....! He just tripped him up. That'll be a ...., for sure.

5 The .... must be blind. That was obviously a goal.

6 I just don't understand what the .... does in English games like tennis and cricket.

Grammar

Comparatives and superlatives

❶ Read the examples of language from this unit in groups and underline the comparative in each sentence.

1 ...the most prominent being Gaelic football and the stick games...
2 It's easier to understand what's happening when women play.
3 The ball is round and slightly smaller than a football.
4 ...the stick is wider at one end...
5 ...this is more difficult than in hurling because the caman is thinner at the end.
6 Which game or games has the greatest number of players?
7 ...the funniest thing is that when girls play rugby...
8 This is particularly true of Dublin and the larger population centres.
9 The biggest difference is that men's rugby is very physical.

Writing

❶ Do you support a football team, or a team in another sport? Write its name here:

....

❷ Why did you choose this particular team? Did these:

geographical location   age   politics   social class

or any other factors affect your choice? Write the factors here.

....

❸ Explain to another student which team you support and the reasons why.

❹ Talk with other students about the reasons why people choose to support a particular club, or play the sports in the table. Think of some other sports — ones that you are interested in or are popular in your country or region.

sport/club	factors affecting choice	comments
football		
basketball		
volleyball		
tennis		
....		
....		

❺ Now write a magazine article with the title: *Choosing a sport or football club in my country.*

length	120-180 words
purpose	to describe the appeal of different sports or clubs in your country
publication	in a student magazine in the UK
target readership	students, particularly those who may intend to travel to your country
paragraphs	1 Introduce general situation in your country 2 Factors affecting choice of sport and/or football team 3 Conclusion: summary of situation

Speaking

❶ Look at the newspaper headlines and the information in the table below and talk about the following questions with another student:

1 What are the newspaper headlines about?

2 What does the table show?

3 What's the link between the headlines and the table?

4 What might be responsible for the great improvement in women's times between 1970 and 1995?

5 Are there similar stories in your country?

6 Do you think that women might eventually catch up with men?

World record times for the 100 metres							
			seconds				
			13	12	11	10	9
	women	men					
1925-30	12.8	10.4	*		*		
1930-35	12.0	10.4		*	*		
1935-40	11.7	10.3		*	*		
1940-45	11.6	10.3		*	*		
1945-50	11.6	10.3		*	*		
1950-55	11.5	10.3			*	*	
1955-60	11.3	10.3			*	*	
1960-65	11.3	10.0			*	*	
1965-70	11.1	10.0			*	*	
1970-75	11.08	9.95			*	*	
1975-80	11.07	9.95			*	*	
1980-85	10.88	9.95			*	*	
1985-90	10.76	9.93			*	*	
1990-95	10.49	9.92				*	*
1995-00	10.49	9.85				*	*
2000-05	10.49	9.79				*	*
2000-	10.49	9.78				*	*

Mail
Done for doping

Record
Why does she run so fast

EXPRESS
Star Bunnel tests positive

1 **For each sentence, write *would* in the space if the action is temporary and voluntary. Otherwise, write *used to*.**

1 Marcus .... work for General Motors.
2 He .... get up at five a.m. and go training before he went to work.
3 Alan .... own an old car that kept breaking down.
4 Charlie .... live in a small flat in Marseilles.
5 Angie .... drink 18 cups of coffee a day.
6 I .... go skiing most weekends when I lived in the Alps.

2 **For each sentence, choose *used to* or a form of *be* or *get used to*.**

1 She can't .... being without him.
2 Dan .... drive to work but now he cycles.
3 Isabel hasn't been here long so she .... the weather yet.
4 I .... have more money before I got married.
5 I remember the way my father .... sing to me as a kid.

3 **Decide if these sentences using the Present Perfect or Past Simple are right or wrong. Put a tick (✔) or a cross (✗) in the box at the end of each line.**

1 My father has been born in the United States. ☐
2 She learned Hindi as a child in India and has spoken it ever since. ☐
3 I knew him all my life. ☐
4 The 2000 Olympics have been in Sydney. ☐
5 I wrote twelve e-mails so far this morning. ☐
6 The last time I met him was five years ago. ☐

4 **Use *for*, *since* or *ago* to write a second sentence which means the same as the first sentence. Use the word given and don't change the form of this word.**

1 Mike bought that car five years ago.
   owned ....
2 I've lived in this flat for a year.
   started ....
3 I learned to play the violin when I was a child.
   played ....
4 He's been learning Arabic for four years.
   began ....
5 The cat fell asleep over an hour ago.
   been ....
6 Eric first went out with Sandra in August.
   gone ....

5 **Use *could*, *couldn't*, *might*, *mightn't*, *had to* or *didn't have to* to complete each sentence below.**

1 We wanted to stay longer but we .... catch the last bus.
2 I knew that David .... come because he was ill.
3 I .... play this tune last year but I've forgotten most of it now.
4 You .... shout at her. She was doing her best.
5 I knew the horse .... win but I thought I'd take a chance on it.
6 She said that I .... take the films home if I wanted to.
7 Ned's mum said he .... go out till he'd tidied up his room.
8 I knew the answer .... be right because I'd checked all the maths.

6 **Choose either the Past Simple or the Past Perfect for each *verb*. Use the Past Perfect *only where necessary*.**

1 I .... (*want*) to know what he was doing so I .... (*send*) him an e-mail.
2 She .... (*be*) delighted to get the Oscar because it was the first time she .... (*win*) anything.
3 The girl .... (*run*) into the sea to save the man who .... (*fall*) in.
4 When he .... (*finish*) the essay, it .... (*be*) after one o'clock so he .... (*not watch*) TV.
5 Jake .... (*sit down*), ... (*open*) the packet and .... (*start*) to eat the sandwiches.

7 **Some of these active sentences can become passive, but others can't. Change those which can be changed.**

1 The company chose her to represent them in Paris.
2 Mervin travelled across Africa on a motorbike.
3 She was wearing a dress which her mother had designed.
4 The boss has sacked him for turning up late for work.
5 Milly tried to find a pair of shoes that were comfortable.
6 She's broken three world records this year.

8 **Complete the second sentence so that it means the same as the first sentence. Use the word given and don't change the form of the word.**

1 People say that he's been married twice before.
   said
   It is .... twice before.

2 Some people say that they have seen UFOs over London.
to
UFOs are .... over London.

3 Some people believe microscopic life exists on Mars.
thought
Microscopic life .... on Mars.

4 At one time people thought that gold could be made out of lead.
it
At one time .... gold could be made out of lead.

9 For each sentence, choose *a(n)*, *the* or no article.

1 This is .... only 6-star hotel in the world.

2 Do you have .... lipstick that will go with this ...?

3 Is John still at .... school or has he found a job?

4 Is there anything interesting on .... radio this afternoon?

5 We're driving to .... India this summer.

10 Choose either the Present Perfect Simple or Present Perfect Continuous for each *verb*.

1 Fred .... just .... (*tell*) me to get lost.

2 You can tell she .... (*cry*) — look at her eyes.

3 One of the players .... (*break*) his leg.

4 She was born in London in 1922 and .... (*live*) there ever since.

5 That phone .... (*ring*) all day.

6 'Have you .... (*see*) Alice?' 'Yes, and we're getting engaged soon.'

11 For each sentence, write the correct form of these irregular comparative or superlative adjectives and adverbs.

1 The weather's much .... (*bad*) than it was this morning.

2 That goal was the .... (*good*) I've ever seen.

3 We need .... (*much*) time to finish this job.

4 He makes the .... (*little*) money of anybody in the company.

5 Could you send me some .... (*far*) information about this?

12 Match each word from column A with its equivalent from column B.

A		B	
1	prestige	a	sauce
2	hordes	b	market
3	ketchup	c	danger
4	hazard	d	crowd
5	bazaar	e	millionaire
6	tycoon	f	status

13 Join two words from the box together to make a compound noun to complete each sentence.

> back break cut down draw
> look out skirts through

1 .... for the weekend

2 .... of this plan

3 .... in technology

4 .... in spending

5 .... of the city

6 .... in communication

14 For each question, choose the word from the box which best goes with the articles of clothing.

> corduroy linen silk suede nylon

1 .... shoes, slippers, jacket

2 .... handkerchief, shirt, suit

3 .... dress, scarf, tie

4 .... jacket, shirt, trousers

5 .... jacket, shirt, stockings

15 Complete each sentence with the correct word from the box.

> ache dizzy rash scratch sneeze sore

1 Don't hold the cat so close to your face. It might .... you.

2 I'm going to .... I've got a really bad cold.

3 After the 20 kilometre walk my legs were .... and I had an .... in my back.

4 Her son has a .... all over his face. He must be allergic to something.

5 Doctor, if I stand up suddenly I feel .... — as if the room's going round.

16 Complete each sentence with a word from the box to make a phrasal verb with *give*.

> away back in off out up

1 Are you going to keep trying or just give ....?

2 He's going to give .... a lot of his money.

3 If you heat water it gives .... steam.

4 Did you give that book .... to John?

5 When I finished filling in the form, I gave it .... to the man at the desk.

6 He was giving .... political pamphlets at the gate.

UNIT 7 *Happiness*

Reading

1 Put the two halves of each quotation together. Work with another student. Then check your answers on page 190.

1 Everywhere is walking distance
Steven Wright, comedian and actor, 1955-

2 All good things in life are either
Rajavi Kejriwal

3 Happiness is having a large, close-knit family
George Burns, actor and comedian, 1896-1996

4 The person who knows how to laugh at himself
Shirley Maclaine, film actress, 1934-

5 It isn't necessary to be rich and famous to be happy.
Alan Alda, actor, 1936-

6 Happiness is not having what you want,
Anonym

7 If everything is under control,
Mario Andretti, motor racing driver, 1940-

a in another city.
b It's only necessary to be rich.
c will never cease to be amused.
d immoral, fattening or overpriced.
e you are going too slow.
f if you have the time.
g but wanting what you have.

2 Choose the quote you agree with most. Explain to another student why you like this quote. Make some notes — no more than 10 words — to help you when you are speaking. Tell your partner how much you agree, or disagree, with their ideas.

FCE Paper 1, Part 3

3 You are going to read the Happiness Quiz. Seven answers have been removed from the quiz. Choose from the answers A-H the one which fits each gap (1-7). There is one extra paragraph which you don't need to use. There is an example at the beginning (0).

HAPPINESS QUIZ

1 **Your health routine is best described as:**

a chaotic. The best things in life are fast food, chocolate and the TV remote control.

b controlled. You're careful about what you eat and play sport regularly.

c ⬚0 ⬚G

2 **It's the end of a long day and you have nothing planned for the evening. Do you:**

a ⬚1 ⬚

b collapse on the sofa after dinner, so exhausted that you do nothing – find it difficult to sleep and feel worse in the morning.

c hurry home to finish that important project. However difficult your day has been, you have to be ready for tomorrow!

3 **Your personal space is:**

a low on your list of priorities. You're so busy that you don't have time for yourself!

b ⬚2 ⬚

c non-existent. You try to find time for yourself, but the phone never stops ringing, or you're meeting your friends.

A very important. You have your own comfortable room, where you can relax and take time out for yourself.

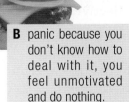

B panic because you don't know how to deal with it, you feel unmotivated and do nothing.

C at ease. You may not be a religious person, but you do have your own sense of morality and try to live your life as well as you can.

4 **How do you feel about yourself?**

a You're OK, other people just don't realise what you're worth.

b You rarely feel good about yourself – you always know you can do better.

c Great! You feel good about yourself, you solve your problems and achieve your goals.

D secure. You enjoy the feeling of setting targets and are really happy when you meet them.

E work out who can best help you with them – often you'll go straight to an expert.

F You feel uncomfortable with negative feelings and try to forget about them as soon as possible.

G varied. Your preferences and tastes guide you. As for exercise, you do what makes you feel good.

5 **When you feel bad, what's your emotional style?**

a Get angry – you love the excitement of letting off steam, even if it does cause trouble.

b [3] [ ]

c You're relaxed about your feelings. Sometimes you feel bad, but you soon feel happier. You get back on top quickly.

6 **If you're faced with a problem in life, you:**

a wait for things to get better. Everyone has problems, it's finding solutions that's important.

b [4] [ ]

c work hard to get it sorted out. You feel bad if you have any problem, no matter how small.

7 **In love, you:**

a always try to make your relationships work, but you don't feel you get it right.

b are happy overall, your relationships last, and when they finish, there's rarely any bad feeling.

c have bad luck – your relationships are stormy and end in tears.

8 **When you've got problems – in work, love or life – you:**

a [5] [ ]

b rely on those close to you – you'd be too embarrassed to get professional help.

c try to solve it alone, you don't want to worry other people with your difficulties.

9 **When you look at your life, you feel it's:**

a not as good as it could be. You often wish you'd behaved differently and you're not very confident about the future.

b good. You generally do well – you're happy! But even the bad times have taught you something, and you feel that the future is promising.

c [6] [ ]

10 **When it comes to making plans and setting goals for yourself, you're:**

a unsure. Goals? You know you should have them, but you've never really had time to make plans.

b unmotivated. You do set goals, but often you don't achieve them. Nothing you do seems to work out right.

c [7] [ ]

H confusing. Opportunities often slip away from you, or other people try to hurt you. You suspect you don't know how to make things work.

I go home and relax: watch the TV, read your favourite book or ring a friend for a chat – you deserve a break.

4 Now do the quiz and then turn to page 191 to check how happy you are. Do you agree with the explanation? Tell another student.

Nouns and adjectives to describe feelings

1 Choose an adjective from the box to describe how each person is feeling.

> angry/cross scared/frightened surprised bored sad depressed glad

2 If you say, *I feel annoyed*, are you describing a positive or negative feeling? Look at the words below and write positive (P) or negative (N) next to each one.

I feel...

1	annoyed	...N...	13	anxious	....
2	ashamed	....	14	disappointed	....
3	hurt	....	15	jealous	....
4	lonely	....	16	miserable	....
5	proud	....	17	sympathetic	....
6	astonished	....	18	guilty	....
7	terrified	....	19	nervous	....
8	furious	....	20	grateful	....
9	stressed	....	21	relieved	....
10	worried	....	22	upset	....
11	fed up	....	23	ecstatic	....
12	delighted	....	24	amazed	....

3 Mark the main stress on the adjectives. Practise saying them with another student.

4 How would you feel in these situations? Choose the most suitable adjective.

1 Your best friend has failed an important exam.
sympathetic/lonely

2 You have a lot of work to do and not much time.
relieved/stressed

3 You hear that you've won first prize in a beauty contest!
furious/astonished

4 You can't find your cat.
worried/ecstatic

5 Your sister has won the school prize for best student of the year.
disappointed/proud

6 You've got flu and can't go to a big party.
miserable/thrilled

5 Now work with another student and describe how you would feel in these situations.

1 A friend gives you a lift to the airport so that you can catch your flight.

2 You tell a lie and get a friend into trouble.

3 You find a snake in the bath.

4 You have to give a speech in front of 200 people today.

5 You didn't get the job you wanted.

6 Your parents give your brother a mini-disk player but don't give you one.

6 Use a dictionary and write the noun for each adjective in question 2. Remember to mark the main stress.

7 Underline the adjectives in the first sentences and complete the second sentences.

1 Simon is such a boring person.
I was ....

2 He was terrified when he saw the spider.
The spider was ....

3 I was amazed by the architecture in Paris.
The architecture ....

4 The end of the story is really surprising.
I was really ....

8 Discuss with another student when we use adjectives that end in *-ing* and adjectives that end in *-ed* and complete the rule.

Theory Box

We use .... adjectives to describe how you feel.

We use .... adjectives to describe the people or things that make you feel this way.

9 Choose the appropriate form of the adjective in brackets to complete the sentence.

1 The news on TV is so .... at the moment. (*depress*)

2 The athlete was .... after running 20 kilometres. (*exhaust*)

3 The twins are completely identical. It's so .... (*confuse*)

4 He gets .... when people say he's good at his job. (*embarrass*)

5 I found that book really .... when I read it. (*interest*)

Phrasal verbs/expressions with *go*

1 Choose the correct word in each sentence.

1 He's been going **round/out** with her for years. It's time they got married.

2 That milk smells awful. It's gone **off/bad**.

3 I'll set the alarm to go **off/on** at 6. I need to be at work by 7.

4 He's **had/got** a go at me for parking in front of his garage.

5 Let me **try/have** a go. I'm sure I can open it.

6 He's always going on **with/about** the noise from the neighbours.

7 That child is very ambitious. He'll go **long/far** in life and be very successful.

8 She's **in/on** the go from the moment she wakes up till she goes to bed.

9 Go **next/on**. What happened next?

10 You must go **by/through** your homework to make sure you haven't made any silly mistakes.

11 Which one are you going to go **at/for**? The blue or the red?

12 What's going **on/in** here? Why are you crying?

2 Write the appropriate phrasal verb/expression next to the correct definition.

1 to choose...

2 to continue..

3 to date someone ....

4 to complain..

5 to try..

6 to ring..

7 to check...

8 to not stop ....

9 to happen..

10 to be bad ....

11 to achieve a lot ....

12 to criticise or be rude to someone ....

Listening

1 If you could have only two of the things below, which two would you choose? Explain your choices to the other students in your group. Do you think that any one of these things are incompatible? For example, is it possible to have a lot of money and a lot of love?

| MONEY | LOVE | CONTENTMENT |
| TALENT | WISDOM | FAME |

FCE Paper 4, Part 3

2 You will hear five people talking about their lives. For questions 1-5, choose which of the opinions (A-F) each speaker expresses. Use the letters only once. There is one extra statement which you do not need to use.

A My only ambition is a material one. — Speaker 1 ☐

B I'm ready to work very hard to make money. — Speaker 2 ☐

C I believe I will become successful. — Speaker 3 ☐

D Having a lot of money isn't really important to me. — Speaker 4 ☐

E I'm looking for a new direction in my life. — Speaker 5 ☐

F I sometimes regret the choices I made.

❶ Read the article about how to be happy. Think about what type of word is needed in each space, a noun, verb, adjective or adverb, etc. The words before and after each space are important so study each sentence carefully. Compare your ideas with another student.

FCE Paper 3, Part 2

❷ For questions 1-15, think of the word which best fits each space. Use only one word in each space. There is an example at the beginning (0).

HOW TO BE HAPPY

For the first time [0] **in** history, the developed world faces the problem [1] producing too much. There are so many cars that we are running [2] of roads to drive them on. We have so [3] food to eat that we are suffering from an epidemic of obesity. There are so many things to buy, see and do that we cannot find enough time to enjoy them.

However, recent studies have shown [4] levels of reported happiness have stayed the same and [5] some cases declined over the past thirty years. The explanation may lie in the pyramid that Abraham Maslow, a behavioural psychologist, drew [6] in 1943. Maslow said that there were various

levels of need, each of [7] had to be satisfied before people could progress to [8] next level.

Clearly, money is very important. [9] it, people cannot satisfy their basic needs and [10] unlikely to progress beyond the lowest level of the pyramid.

The trouble is that people – and governments – have spent [11] their entire history in the struggle [12] subsistence. Because of this, they have [13] to believe that greater prosperity is the key [14] greater happiness. And they continue to believe this even beyond the point [15] which basic levels of comfort have been achieved. Maslow's pyramid suggests otherwise.

Self-actualisation
Pursue inner talent, creativity, fulfilment

Self-esteem
Achievement, recognition, respect

Belonging, love
Friends, family, spouse, lover

Safety
Security, stability, freedom from fear

Physiological
Food, water, shelter, warmth

Speaking

FCE Paper 5, Parts 3/4

❶ Read what the speakers say below. In a group, talk about where you would place each of these ambitions on Maslow's pyramid.

I had a difficult childhood — my parents split up when I was quite young. That's why I'm so happy now I've met Juan.

I've been homeless for over a year now. It's no fun at all. Most nights it's very cold and I often don't get enough to eat.

Well, the flat itself is lovely. We did it up last year. But it's a difficult area. There's a lot of crime and I get scared sometimes.

I've been captain of the football team this season, and I really enjoy it. The younger players look up to me, and I get to meet some interesting people.

The time when I'm most happy is when I'm playing my guitar. I get completely lost in the music I compose.

❷ Now, write your own ambitions for each line of the pyramid. At the lowest level, these can be quite simple, such as 'I'd like to have a sandwich for lunch.' As you climb the pyramid, think of more complex, long-term ambitions. Then talk about your ambitions with the others in your group.

Vocabulary

Sleep

1 Read the sentences and decide if the people are awake (A) or asleep (S).

1 [S] Dominic is fast asleep.
2 [ ] Joseph is having a nightmare.
3 [ ] Liz is tossing and turning.
4 [ ] Guy is sleep walking.
5 [ ] Adam is having a nap.
6 [ ] Paul is dozing.

7 [ ] Sally is snoring.
8 [ ] Linda is stretching.
9 [ ] Ruth feels drowsy.
10 [ ] Peter is sleepy.
11 [ ] Sally is yawning.

2 Now look at the pictures and check your answers. Write the question number next to the correct picture.

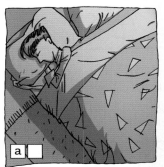
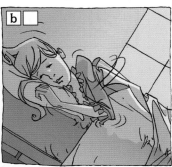

3 Complete the sentences with the correct form of the words in the box.

sleep   lie in   insomnia   oversleep   asleep

1 He always .... if he doesn't set his alarm.
2 I really like the weekends because I can have a ....
3 I suffer from .... and often have to take a sleeping pill to get to sleep.
4 She fell .... watching TV and didn't wake up until three in the morning.
5 I .... like a log last night and didn't hear the storm.

4 Work in pairs. Use the expressions to talk about your sleeping patterns. For example, *It takes me a long time to fall asleep. I toss and turn for a while.*

UNIT 7

Grammar

Second conditionals

❶ Work with another student. For each situation, decide which sentence fits best. What type of sentences are these? We looked at first conditionals in Unit 3. Do you remember how to make them and what they mean?

1a I don't have a clue. If I know, I'll tell you.

b I don't have a clue. If I knew, I'd tell you.

2a If I speak German, I may know what she's saying.

b If I spoke German, I might know what she's saying.

4a If I'm a man, I can give him some advice, but it's so difficult to understand boys.

b If I was a man, I could give him some advice, but it's so difficult to understand boys.

3a If he's alive today, he'll be 100 next week.

b If he was alive today, he'd be 100 next week.

❷ Read these sentences from the listening tapescript and complete each space with the correct word from the box.

> could   I'd be   I'd rather   if only   imagine
> it's time   might   should   suppose   wish

1 I sometimes .... my family was rich...

2 I don't want a yacht in the Mediterranean. .... I had house in the country...

3 .... I just went off on my own, what would it be like?

4 Well, I'm what you .... call a struggling artist.

5 I really think .... people started to take some notice of me.

6 .... if I was on a big Ducati or maybe a Harley.

7 .... I had a really big bike, ... the happiest guy alive!

8 Maybe I .... do something more with my life.

9 You know, with the money I've got, I .... do a lot of good.

Theory Box

Second conditionals

This is an example of a **first** or **type 1 conditional**:

If he's alive today, he'll be 100 next week.

However, this is highly unlikely. If we know that he's already dead, and we want to describe a situation that is impossible, we need to change the verb and modal to their past forms:

*If he **was** alive today, he'**d** be 100 next week.*

We call this a **second**, or **type 2, conditional**.

When we want to describe something in English that is **improbable** or **impossible**, in the present or future time, we use the second conditional and past tenses or modals.

❸ Work with another student. Match the pictures to the sentences 1-6, then think of different ways of finishing them. Remember to use the past tense.

1 Make a suggestion to Brian:
  It's time ....
  ....

2 Indicate a possibility to Hannah:
  Suppose we ....
  ....

3 Help Fred make a wish:
  I wish I ....
  ....

4 Help Marta express a preference: I don't want to visit your mother again.
  I'd rather we ....
  ....

5 Help Tracy with her talkative friend.
  If only you ....
  ....

6 Help Mike make a wish:
  If only I ....
  ....

❹ Read the conversation below with another student. In each sentence, one, two, or all three of the modals are possible. Talk about the meaning of each modal and underline the ones which are possible.

Ella: I wish I ¹ *could/might/would* play like that.

Jack: You ² *could/ought to/should* practise more. If you did, you ³ *could/might/would* get better.

Ella: I ⁴ *might/ought to/would* if I had more time, but I'm so busy these days.

Jack: Oh yeah? What about yesterday? You spent all afternoon watching football on TV.

Ella: OK, you ⁵ *could/might/would* be right. But the guitar I have is rubbish.

Jack: You know my brother said you ⁶ *could/ might/ought to* borrow his if you wanted to. You know, I think you ⁷ *might/should/would* be running out of excuses.

Theory Box

Past tenses and past modals

We use the **past tenses** and **past modals** in English for:

- **real** events in **past** time.
- **imaginary, hypothetical, improbable** or **impossible** events — **unreal** events in **present** or **future** time.

real past time	**real** present/future time	**unreal** present/future time

I was rich   I am poor   If I / If only / Suppose / I'd rather / I wish I was rich again

Vocabulary

Senses

1 Complete the mindmap with the words from the box.

> blind   deaf   feel   hear   listen   look
> press   salty   scented   sip   smell
> sniff   sound   stare   tap   taste

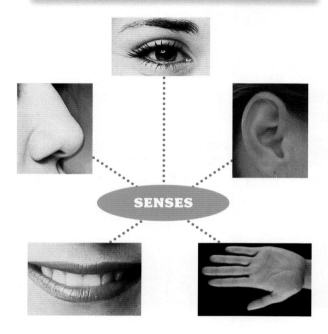

SENSES

2 Which of the words in the box can be adjectives, verbs, or nouns?

3 Make sure you understand the words in question 1 and then decide if these sentences are true or false.

1 If you can't see, you're deaf.
2 To see if you like the perfume, you sniff it.
3 To see if you like a cocktail, you might sip it first.
4 Tap someone on the shoulder if you want to get their attention.
5 You hear music on a walkman.
6 If you have a cold, you might smell a lot.
7 If you don't make a sound, you are silent.
8 It's rude to stare at people in some cultures.
9 To see if you like a kind of food smell it.
10 In a lift, tap the button to go up or down.

4 Read the sentences and answer the questions.

1 We watched the football match. *Did we follow the match?*
2 I saw the accident happen. *Did I see the accident by accident or on purpose?*
3 He glanced at the headline as he walked past the newsagent. *Did he look at the headline for a short or long time?*

4 She caught a glimpse of him in the crowd. *Did she look at him for a short or long time?*
5 The child stared at the man's red hair. *Did the child look at the man for a short or long time? Why?*
6 He peered at his watch in the dark to see what time it was. *Was it easy or difficult for him to see his watch? Why?*
7 She gazed at the view from the top of the mountain. *Did she look at the same view, or did she look at different things at the same time?*
8 The teacher looked at the students before she left the classroom. *Did the teacher look at the students on purpose or by accident?*

5 Fill in the gaps with the correct form of the verbs from question 4.

1 He .... at the menu because he had left his glasses at home.
2 They sat and .... at the beautiful painting.
3 She .... at the man on the train, hoping he would give up his seat but he didn't!
4 I like .... people in the street to see what they do.
5 We .... our son for a moment as he got on the plane.
6 He .... quickly at his watch and decided to stay in bed for five more minutes.
7 Can you .... at that notice and tell me what time the library shuts?
8 I .... a beautiful dog in the park today.

make or *do*?

1 English has two verbs, *make* and *do*, but many languages use one verb for these two. What happens in your language? Do you use the same verb with:

- *the shopping?*   do the shopping
- *a mistake?*   make a mistake

2 Add *make* or *do* to the phrases below.

1 .... a course
2 .... a decision
3 .... a difference
4 .... a mess
5 .... a phone call
6 .... a profit
7 .... business
8 .... noise
9 .... research
10 .... sense
11 .... someone a favour
12 .... the best of
13 .... the housework
14 .... your best
15 .... your homework

3 Work with another student and write at least two more expressions with *make* or *do*.

4 **Complete the following sentences with one of the expressions from question 2.**

1 He's very good at .... and his new company is ....

2 Don't worry about the exam, you can only ....

3 I know it's raining but let's .... it and go to a museum.

4 I don't understand you. You're not ....

5 I'd like to .... on Web site design in the autumn.

5 **Find out how many people in the class:**

1 always do their homework?
2 have done someone a favour recently?
3 like doing the housework?
4 made more than three phone calls last night?
5 often make a mess at home?
6 like the idea of doing research at university?
7 have bought something on the Internet?
8 don't mind making mistakes in English?

6 **If you get the answer *yes*, ask another question to get more information.**

Writing

FCE Paper 2, Part 1

1 Carla is planning her 18th birthday party. She has sent you an e-mail telling you about her ideas and asking for your opinion. You have printed out the e-mail and written some notes on it. You think her ideas are rubbish and the party she is planning will be a disaster. Read Carla's e-mail and your notes. Then using the information write a reply to Carla.

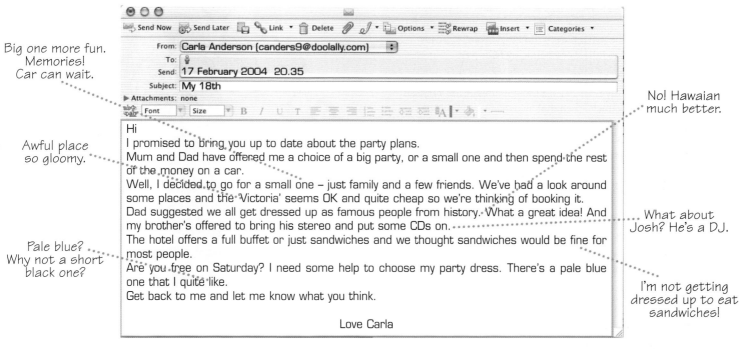

Big one more fun. Memories! Car can wait.

Awful place so gloomy.

Pale blue? Why not a short black one?

No! Hawaian much better.

What about Josh? He's a DJ.

I'm not getting dressed up to eat sandwiches!

From: Carla Anderson [canders9@doolally.com]
Send: 17 February 2004 20.35
Subject: My 18th
Attachments: none

Hi
I promised to bring you up to date about the party plans.
Mum and Dad have offered me a choice of a big party, or a small one and then spend the rest of the money on a car.
Well, I decided to go for a small one – just family and a few friends. We've had a look around some places and the 'Victoria' seems OK and quite cheap so we're thinking of booking it.
Dad suggested we all get dressed up as famous people from history. What a great idea! And my brother's offered to bring his stereo and put some CDs on.
The hotel offers a full buffet or just sandwiches and we thought sandwiches would be fine for most people.
Are you free on Saturday? I need some help to choose my party dress. There's a pale blue one that I quite like.
Get back to me and let me know what you think.

Love Carla

2 **Before you start, look at these notes that you have written:**

Big one more fun. Memories! Car can wait.

If you want to say this to Carla, you might write:

I think a big party will be more fun. It will leave you with memories that will last much longer than a car.

But this might be too direct. How can Carla make her suggestion more diplomatic? She could change the modals to their past forms:

*I think a big party **would/might/could** be more fun. It **would** leave you with memories that **would** last much longer than a car.*

When you write to Carla, use...

■ *could, should, ought to, would* and *might*

■ the **Past simple** and **Past Continuous** with *if, if only, imagine, suppose* and *wish*

3 **Write a letter of between 120 and 180 words to Carla. Be as polite and diplomatic as possible. Remember that Carla is your friend and you don't want to offend her.**

UNIT 8
Connections

Listening

10 ❶ **Read the song below. What is it about? Tell another student. Then complete each gap with one of the words from the box. Listen to the recording to check your answers.**

daughter	grandchild (x 2)	grandmother
mother	son-in-law	step-mother	uncle

I am my own grandpa

Many, many years ago when I was twenty-three
I was married to a widow who was pretty as could be
This widow had a grown-up ¹.................. who had hair of red
My father fell in love with her and soon they too were wed.

This made my dad my ².................. and changed my very life
For my daughter was my ³.................., 'cause she was my father's wife
To complicate the matter, even though it brought me joy
I soon became the father of a bouncing baby boy.

My little baby then became a brother-in-law to dad
And so became my ⁴.................., though it made me very sad
For if he was my uncle, then that also made him brother
Of the widow's grown-up daughter, who, of course,
was my ⁵.................. .
Father's wife then had a son who kept them on the run
And he became my ⁶.................., for he was my daughter's son
My wife is now my mother's mother, and it makes me blue
Because, although she is my wife, she's my ⁷.................., too.

Now, if my wife is my grandmother, then I'm her ⁸.................. .
And every time I think of it, it nearly drives me wild
For now I have become the strangest case you ever saw
As husband of my grandmother, I am my own grandpa.

❷ **Now listen to the song again and use the words in the box to complete the family tree.**

daughter	father	husband
mother	son (x2)	widow

Boxes like this [   ] are for people who are not mentioned.

Red arrows ⟷ mean married.

Blue arrows ↓ are for children.

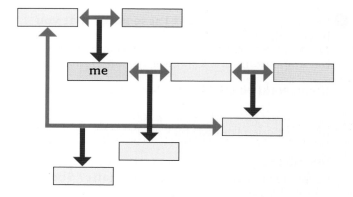

❸ **Think of your own family. Do you know what your great-grandfather and great-grandmother were called, where they lived and what they did? How far up your family tree can you go? Work with other students and tell them as much as you can about your family.**

Vocabulary

Phrasal verbs for relationships

❶ Read the story and answer the questions.

1 How were their childhoods similar?

2 How were their personal lives different?

Paul and Simon got on well as children. They grew up in the same village. Although they were completely different in character, any arguments they had were quickly made up. Paul learned to put up with Simon's teasing and Simon came round to the fact that Paul was better than him at school. Their parents brought them up strictly, teaching them that they should never let people down. Paul took after his father in character whereas Simon was much more like his mother. However, although they shared the same childhood, their adult lives were very different. Simon left school at sixteen and trained as a plumber. He met Sandra, went out with her for four years, got married, settled down, had a family and was very happy. Paul, on the other hand, went to university and got a job as a mechanical engineer. He met Rebecca and they got engaged after a year. However, after six months, she broke off the engagement. He immediately met Ruth and got married the next year. Unfortunately, the marriage broke down and they split up after two years. He never remarried.

❷ Read the story again and underline all the phrasal verbs.

❸ Replace the underlined phrasal verbs with the correct form of the definitions below. Compare your answers with another student.

1 to accept an idea
2 to separate (from someone)
3 to relax into your job and personal life
4 to date someone
5 to be unsuccessful
6 to be good friends
7 to tolerate (someone or something)
8 to resemble (someone)
9 to resolve (an argument)
10 to end (an engagement)
11 to disappoint people or make false promises
12 to spend your childhood and adolescence
13 to raise (a child)

❹ Choose the correct phrasal verb from the box for each stage in the relationship illustrated opposite.

to ask s/o out   to chat s/o up   to fall in love
to get divorced   to get engaged
to get married   to get on well together
to get to know s/o   to go off s/o
to split up   to walk out on s/o

FCE Paper 1, Part 2

1 You are going to read an article about an unusual discovery. For questions 1-8, choose the correct answer A, B, C or D.

Descendant of Stone Age skeleton found

The village of Cheddar in the south-west of England is best known for the cheese of the same name. However, nearby is Cheddar Gorge, which contains a number of interesting caves. These are believed to have been home to a
5 community of Stone Age people. In one of them the 9000-year-old skeleton of Cheddar Man was found. The conditions in the cave helped preserve it until its discovery in 1903.
Now scientists have matched Cheddar Man's DNA with that of a 42-year-old history teacher who lives less than a kilometre from the cave.
10 The skeleton, now in the Natural History Museum in London, drew the attention of TV producers preparing a documentary on archaeology in Somerset. They contacted scientists at Oxford University, who spent months analysing samples from the skeleton and succeeded in extracting mitochondrial DNA from one of its teeth. This type of DNA passes unchanged down the female line. It is easier
15 to recover from ancient bones than nuclear DNA, which carries genes from both mothers and fathers.
Then came the detective work. Scientists and a camera crew appeared one day at Kings of Wessex school in Cheddar. 'They wanted to take DNA samples from some of the students whose families had lived longest in the area,' history
20 teacher Adrian Targett said. 'I gave a sample too, just to encourage the children.'
Professor Chris Stringer, a researcher at London's Natural History Museum, said one problem with the research 'is that we don't know that Cheddar Man had any children. This is mitochondrial DNA so it would come from Cheddar Man's
25 mother or his sister.' Adrian Targett may not be a direct descendant. However, according to Bryan Sykes, one of the Oxford scientists, 'They would have shared a common ancestor about 10,000 years ago, so they are related.'
Adrian Targett's family has lived in the area since at least the mid-19th century, but it was only a coincidence that he moved to Cheddar after he began
30 teaching there 20 years ago. 'I was astonished when the scientists told me,' said Targett. 'Appropriately enough, I am a history teacher. But I teach modern history, so Cheddar Man's a bit out of my period. I have to admit I know next to nothing about him. I suppose I should try to include him in my family tree. I've been in the cave a few times, but I never realised it was home.'

1 Most people associate Cheddar with
   A Cheddar Gorge.
   B cheese.
   C Cheddar Man.
   D caves.

2 What does *it* in line 6 refer to?
   A Cheddar Gorge
   B a skeleton
   C the cave
   D the community

3 The scientists analysed Cheddar Man because
   A they were interested in Stone Age life.
   B they were interested in archaeology.
   C they were doing research for a television programme.
   D they wanted to try to take DNA from an old skeleton.

4 The scientists extracted mitochondrial DNA from the skeleton because
   A it was the most practical solution.
   B they were interested in the female line.
   C it is contained in teeth.
   D it doesn't change with time.

5 Adrian Targett gave a DNA sample because
   A he lives close to Cheddar Gorge.
   B he is interested in history.
   C his family had lived for a long time in the area.
   D he wanted to help the scientists.

6 Which statement best describes Adrian Targett's relationship with Cheddar Man?
   A Cheddar Man is a direct ancestor.
   B Targett's mother or sister is a direct descendant.
   C They are both descended from the same person.
   D They are relatives.

7 Adrian Targett's family
   A has always lived very close to Cheddar Gorge.
   B has lived in that part of England for over a century.
   C moved to the area in the mid-19th century.
   D have lived in Cheddar Gorge for 20 years.

8 What does Adrian say about the discovery?
   A He knows a lot about the Stone Age because he teaches history.
   B He wants to go and live in the cave.
   C He wants to trace his family tree back further.
   D He doesn't know much about Cheddar Man.

Listening

1 Work with another student and write a definition for each of these words associated with computers and the Internet. Then compare your definitions with another pair.

1 to log on ....
....

2 a message board...
....

3 to register ....
....

4 a search engine..
....

5 a server ....
....

6 spam...
....

7 to upgrade...
....

8 a Web site ....
....

2 In your group check your definitions in a dictionary and:

1 see which of you came closest to the correct meaning.

2 Whose definition do you prefer: yours, one of your friends, or the dictionary's?

FCE Paper 4, Part 4

3 You will hear part of an interview with one of the founders of a very popular Web site in the UK. For questions 1-8, choose the best answer A, B or C.

1 Julie Pankhurst wanted to contact old friends because
   A she knew about computer programming.
   B she couldn't go out to work.
   C she was going to have a baby.

2 Why did Julie not help with building the Web site?
   A she didn't have the skills.
   B she didn't have enough time.
   C she wanted Steve to do it.

3 Steve and Jason
   A stopped working to build the site.
   B built the site when they had time.
   C went bankrupt building the site.

4 The site first became popular
   A because of a radio programme.
   B because they worked through the night.
   C because it was featured on television.

5 How does Steve feel about marriages breaking up?
   A He is sorry that Friends Reunited caused this.
   B The only important thing is to make money.
   C People's actions are their own responsibility.

6 Friends Reunited makes money from
   A advertising.
   B fees from members.
   C e-mails.

7 The new site allows people to
   A find their relatives.
   B contact millions of people.
   C see their complete family trees.

Grammar

Theory Box

Third conditionals

In Unit 7 on page 76 we looked at the **second**, or **type 2**, conditional:

> *If he was alive today he'd be 100 next week.*

We saw that when we want to describe something in English that is **improbable** or **impossible**, in **present** or **future time**, we use **past tenses** or **modals**:

> *Suppose I just **went** off on my own for a while, what **would** that **be** like?*
>
> *Well, I'm what you **might call** a struggling artist.*
>
> *Imagine if I **was** on a big Ducati or maybe a Harley.*

If we use the **past** tenses and modals in the **present** to show that something is improbable or impossible, what do we use in the **past** to show that something is impossible?

We have to use the **Past Perfect**:

> *Imagine if I**'d been** on a big Ducati or maybe a Harley.*

Or **past modals + Present Perfect**:

> *Well, I was what you **might have called** a struggling artist.*

or both:

> *Suppose I**'d** just **gone** off on my own for a while, what **would** that **have been** like?*

We can simplify these sentences like this:

> *If I**'d owned** a big motor bike, I **would have been** happy.*
> *If I**'d been** a successful artist, I **would have been** more comfortable.*
> *If I**'d just gone off** on my own for a while, I **might have enjoyed** it.*

These sentences are called **third** or **type 3**, conditionals. We use them to talk about how things in the past could have been different. However, they refer to **impossible situations** because we can't change the past.

In Unit 5 on page 52, we saw that we can use the Past Perfect to make it clear that one event happened before another in the past:

> *When Harry arrived, they**'d eaten** the soup.*

If **when Harry arrived** is in past time, what do we call the time when they ate the soup? We can call it **earlier past** time. So, we use the **Past Perfect** and/or **past modals + Present Perfect** for:

- **real** events in **earlier past time**.
- **unreal** events in **past time**.

If we put the whole picture together it looks like this:

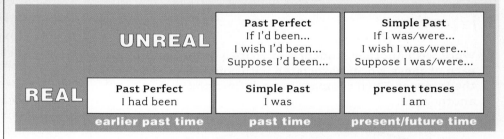

	Past Perfect	Simple Past
UNREAL	If I'd been... I wish I'd been... Suppose I'd been...	If I was/were... I wish I was/were... Suppose I was/were...

	Past Perfect	Simple Past	present tenses
REAL	I had been	I was	I am
	earlier past time	*past time*	*present/future time*

Now turn to page 174 of the Grammar File for more information.

Use of English

FCE Paper 3, Part 3

1 For questions 1-10, complete the second sentence so that it has a similar meaning to the first sentence, using the word given. Do not change the word given. You must use between two and five words, including the word given. Here is an example (0).

0   She did not buy the dress because it was too long.
    it
    She would have bought the dress ....*if it hadn't been*............ so long.

Remember that in each case, you will be moving between two of the areas in the diagram:

PAST PERFECT	UNREAL	PAST SIMPLE

PAST SIMPLE	REAL	PRESENT SIMPLE

1 I'm sorry I didn't go to see the game.
   wish
   I .... to see the game.

2 I'd prefer you not to leave all these books lying around.
   rather
   I .... leave all these books lying around.

3 Jon regrets lending her the money.
   wishes
   Jon .... her the money.

4 It's a good thing you stopped him driving home or he might have crashed.
   you
   He might have crashed .... him driving home.

5 I was supposed to answer those e-mails yesterday.
   ought
   I .... those e-mails yesterday.

6 Vicki only went to see the film because Darren suggested it.
   gone
   If Darren hadn't suggested it, Vicki .... to see the film.

7 She was in the room so I'm sure she saw what happened.
   must
   She was in the room so .... what happened.

8 I advise you not to get involved with this company.
   shouldn't
   You .... with this company.

9 She didn't buy the CD because she didn't have enough money.
   bought
   If she'd had enough money, ... the CD.

10 I'd rather he didn't wear so much aftershave.
   prefer
   I'd .... wear so much aftershave.

Vocabulary

Adjective and preposition collocations

① Choose the correct preposition for each adjective. Compare your answers with another student.

1 He was afraid .... the dark when he was a child.
   a with   **b** for   **c** of

2 They were very proud .... their son when he won the competition.
   a of   **b** with   **c** to

3 She says she's related .... the British royal family!
   a by   **b** to   **c** with

4 He's very good .... his son and never loses his temper.
   a at   **b** for   **c** with

5 I'm very fond .... my aunt. She's so sweet.
   a of   **b** with   **c** for

6 I'm really annoyed .... her behaviour.
   a of   **b** for   **c** about

7 The restaurant is famous .... French cuisine.
   a for   **b** by   **c** with

8 He's capable .... being really extrovert if he wants to be.
   a at   **b** of   **c** in

9 She's responsible .... organising all the office meetings.
   a for   **b** with   **c** at

10 I was shocked .... the parents' attitude.
   a with   **b** by   **c** for

11 I'm always suspicious .... people who are over-confident.
   a with   **b** at   **c** of

12 He was allergic .... the prawns and was sick.
   a to   **b** with   **c** at

② Complete each sentence with the correct preposition. Compare your answers with another student.

1 Most teenagers are good .... sending text messages.

2 The restaurant is famous .... its fish dishes.

3 I was very shocked .... their rude behaviour.

4 My brother is allergic .... aspirin.

5 My children are very fond .... sweets.

6 I'm very suspicious .... his behaviour — he's usually so rude.

7 The neighbours were annoyed .... the loud music and rang the police.

8 My sister is capable .... being very nice if she wants something from me.

9 My father is responsible .... the whole of his department at work.

10 He's always been afraid .... spiders and snakes.

11 The young man was very proud .... his new car.

12 Maria is related .... Freddie through his grandfather.

Vocabulary

Describing appearance

1 Do you know all these features? Which features can you see in the pictures? Work with another student.

Complexion: pale, suntanned, dark, fair, black.

Eyes: blue, grey, brown, green, long eyelashes.

Hair colour: red, blonde, fair, dark, grey.

Hairstyle: long, short, shoulder length, straight, wavy, curly, bald, receding.

Facial shape: thin, long, round, oval, heart-shaped.

Facial features: high cheekbones, high forehead, thin lips, full lips, straight nose, turned up nose, a pointed chin.

Other features: beard, moustache, clean shaven, scar, mole, freckles, dimple, wrinkles.

2 For each question, place the adjectives in the box in order on the scale.

| elderly   in her teens |
| in her mid twenties   middle aged |
| old   young |

1 ....>.................>.................>
.................>.................>.................

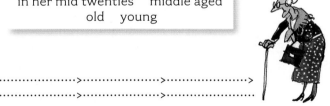

| skinny   fat   obese   overweight |
| plump   slim   thin   well built |

2 ....>.................>.................>
.................>.................>.................

| of medium height   short   tall |

3 ....>.................>
....

3 Complete this description of one of the people in question 1. Which picture is it?

He's got .... eyes and ....
eyelashes. He's got ....,
............., ... hair and a
.... He's quite .... and
he's got a .... face. He's got
.... lips and a .... chin
with a .... He's also got
.... on his nose. He looks as if
he's ...., is ....
and quite ....

4 Work with another student. Student A describes a picture in question 1. Student B guesses which one it is. Then do the same with people in the class.

Writing

1 For each question, put a word from the box into the correct place. It may come at the beginning, or in the middle. Add the correct punctuation. Each question may be one sentence or two.

| but   however |

1a appropriately Adrian Targett is a history teacher he teaches modern history

b appropriately Adrian Targett is a history teacher he teaches modern history

| so   therefore |

2a the scientists wanted to see if Cheddar Man's DNA had survived they took samples from local children

b the scientists wanted to see if Cheddar Man's DNA had survived they took samples from local children

| as well as   not only |

3a being famous for cheese Cheddar is also known for Cheddar Gorge

b is Cheddar famous for cheese it is also known for Cheddar Gorge

although   despite/in spite of

4a their DNA is almost identical Adrian Targett may not be a direct descendant of Cheddar Man

b their DNA being almost identical Adrian Targett may not be a direct descendant of Cheddar Man

and   in addition to

5a taking samples from the local children they took one from history teacher Adrian Targett

b they took samples from the local children from history teacher Adrian Targett

furthermore   moreover

6a scientists have matched Cheddar Man's DNA with that of a 42-year-old history teacher he lives less than a kilometre from the cave

b scientists have matched Cheddar Man's DNA with that of a 42-year-old history teacher he lives less than a kilometre from the cave

❷ Now look at the words or phrases in the box and write them in the correct section below.

> although   and   as well as
> but   despite/in spite of
> furthermore   however
> in addition to   moreover
> not only   so   therefore

1 Six of them are used to introduce an additional fact.

....
....
....
....
....
....

2 Four of them are used to introduce a contrasting fact.

....
....
....
....

3 Two of them are used to introduce a consequence.

....
....

❸ Work with another student and write the correct word from the box on the correct line of the table.

> although   as well as   despite/in spite of   furthermore
> however   in addition to   moreover

		position		followed by	
		beginning of sentence	middle of sentence	pronoun + verb	pronoun, noun or gerund
1	....	✓	✓	✓	✗
2	....	✓	✓	✓	✗
3	....	✓	✓	✓	✗
4	....	✓	✓	✗	✓
5	....	✓	✓	✗	✓
6	....	✓	✓	✗	✓
7	....	✓	✗	✓	✓
8	....	✓	✗	✓	✗

❹ Read these contrasting ideas about families:

God gives us our relatives. Thank God we can choose our friends.
Ethel Watts Mumford (1878-1940)
Blood's thicker than water.
Proverb

❺ Work with other students and discuss what you think these sayings mean. Then think of arguments in support of each one. Write an argument in each of the white boxes below.

Friends are more important than family because:

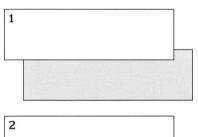

Family is more important than friends because:

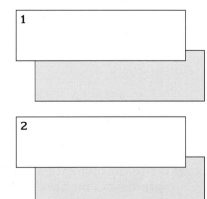

❻ Now in each of the blue boxes, write an event from your own life to support your argument.

FCE Paper 2, Part 2

❼ Compare your ideas with other students. To write a balanced composition think of arguments in favour of both statements before you reach a conclusion. Now write a composition of 120-180 words about one of these statements:

Friends are	more important	than family
Family is		than friends

UNIT 8
Vocabulary

Describing character

1 Work with other students and write down as many adjectives as you can to describe people.

2 Complete the definitions below with a suitable adjective from box A. Then write definitions for the adjectives in box B. Compare your answers.

> **A**
> cheerful   gentle   mean   reliable
> selfish   sensible   sensitive   shy
> strict   sympathetic

1   Someone who only thinks of themselves is ....

2   Someone who does what they say they are going to do is ....

3   Someone who does not like spending money is ....

4   Someone who has feelings which are easily hurt is ....

5   Someone who is reasonable and does not do stupid things is ....

6   Parents who make you obey a lot of rules are ....

7   Someone who doesn't hurt people or shout at them is ....

8   Someone who is in a good mood is ....

9   Someone who listens to people's problems and understands them is ....

10   Someone who finds it difficult to talk to people is ....

> **B**
> amusing   bossy   clever   cold
> entertaining   foolish   helpful   lively
> patient   responsible

3 Write the opposite adjective next to each definition. Compare your ideas with another student.

1   bad-tempered ....
2   unsympathetic ....
3   tough ....
4   silly ....
5   easy-going ....
6   unreliable ....
7   outgoing ....
8   generous ....
9   unselfish ....
10   insensitive ....

4 Work with another student. Use the definitions to test each other. For example :

Student A: someone who only thinks of themselves is ....?

Student B: selfish

Student A: what's the opposite?

Student B: unselfish

5 Use a dictionary to check the meaning of the adjectives below which you don't know. Then complete the chart.

adjective	opposite adjective	noun
ambitious	*unambitious*	
considerate		
obedient		
tolerant		
honest		
faithful		
intelligent		
organised		
careful		

6 Work with other students and make a list of three adjectives which you think are the most important for the ideal teacher. Then compare your ideas as a class. Find out what three adjectives your teacher has to describe an ideal student!

7 Now decide which three adjectives in question 2 and 5 are the most important for:

1   an ideal husband/wife
2   an ideal son/daughter
3   an ideal mother/father
4   an ideal best friend

8 Match each question to its correct answer.

1   What does your mother look like?   a   She's very patient and loving.

2   What is she like?   b   She likes going to the cinema.

3   What does she like?   c   She's quite tall with blond hair.

9 What are the answers to these questions?

1   What does your teacher look like?
2   What is he or she like?
3   What does he or she like?

Speaking

FCE Paper 5, Part 1

1 Which features do you notice when you first meet someone? Work with another student and discuss the three most important features and the three least important ones. Compare your ideas with other pairs.

accessories (e.g. jewellery) build clothes

4 How high is she?

5 What colour of eyes has she got?

6 What kinds of cloths does she like?

7 What's voice like?

8 What kind of figure has she?

9 Does she wear lots of jewellery and makes up?

10 What kinds of things does she like do in her free time?

11 Why you like her?

4 Ask your partner the questions in question 3 to find out about your mystery person.

Vocabulary

Homographs

1 In English, there are some words which have the same spelling but a different meaning and pronunciation. These are called *homographs*. Look at the use of desert in these two sentences. Which one means:

1 a place where there is no water ☐

2 to leave someone or somewhere ☐

a I'll never desert you whatever happens.

b We saw a few camels as we drove through the desert.

2 Now mark the stress on desert in each sentence. How does the second vowel sound differ?

---

3 Do you know any other homographs in English? Underline the homographs in each pair of sentences. What do they mean in each sentence? Compare your answers with another student.

1a They had a huge row and didn't talk to each other for a week.

b It was very hard work to row across the lake in a small boat.

...he diamond in the ring was so ...inute that we could hardly see it.

...here are sixty minutes in a hour.

...so hard that the tree

...ind the bandage ...inger tightly to stop

...nt at the meeting but ...ne immediately after

...presented him with a special ...his hard work.

...ed after a year in prison for good

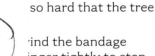

b They are going to conduct an inquiry into the situation.

6a The little girl had a pink bow in her hair.

b Japanese people often bow instead of shaking hands when they meet people.

7a Where do you live?

b They broadcast the concert live.

8a They are a very close family and see each other every weekend.

b Could you close the door? It's freezing in here.

9a The child was crying and had tears running down his cheeks.

b Be careful! You're going to tear your shirt on the nail.

4 Listen to how the homographs are pronounced. Practise saying the sentences.

UNIT 9
A Place to Live

Speaking

Town and country

❶ Work with another student. Match the houses in the photos with the places in the box.

a on the Spanish coast
b in Venice
c in Texas
d in London
e in France
f in the Alps
g in Tahiti
h in the Scottish Highlands

1 ☐ a palace

2 ☐ a farmhouse

3 ☐ a hut

4 ☐ a chalet

5 ☐ a holiday home

6 ☐ a cottage

7 ☐ a ranch-house

8 ☐ a flat

❷ Now think of the three places where you would most like to live. Write them on the lines below.

1 ....

2 ....

3 ....

❸ Tell your partner about the places you have chosen.

❹ The photos on the next page show more unusual places to live. Work with other students to match each of them with one of the names in the box. Write the correct name of the house under each photo.

1 cave appartment
2 loft
3 historic flat
4 windmill
5 castle
6 multi-storey flat
7 underground house
8 narrow boat

A ....

B ....

C ....

D ....

E ....

F ....

G ....

H ....

5 Which of these homes would you most like to live in? Explain your choice to another student.

Listening

1 You will hear people talking about eight different types of accommodation. The first time you listen, decide which person (1-8) each of these statements refer to:

Who

1 had a difficult childhood.
2 talks about a very safe form of housing.
3 finds shopping locally difficult.
4 found an unusual location for their business.
5 talks about a temporary building.
6 designed her own house.
7 makes less money than he used to.
8 doesn't worry about the cold.

FCE Paper 4, Part 1

2 Listen again and for questions 1-8, choose the best answer, A, B or C. You will hear each recording twice.

1 You overhear a woman talking in a restaurant. How does she make most of her money?
   A from overnight guests
   B from restaurant customers
   C from tourists

2 You hear someone talking on the radio. What does he want to do?
   A move to a new area
   B improve the area he lives in
   C continue living in the same area

3 You overhear a woman talking about her flat. Why did she buy it?
   A She likes living in an old building.
   B She wanted to design her own accommodation.
   C She wanted a lot of space.

4 You overhear someone talking about the owner of a castle. Who is the speaker?
   A a visitor
   B a tourist guide
   C a historian

5 You hear a man talking on the radio. What is his attitude to his way of life?
   A realistic
   B unrealistic
   C negative

6 You overhear a man talking about the houses he's lived in. How does he feel?
   A He likes where he lives.
   B He would prefer to live somewhere else.
   C He would rather live where he used to live.

7 You hear a man talking on the radio. What type of housing is he describing?
   A underwater
   B above ground
   C underground

8 You overhear someone talking about a hotel. Who is the person?
   A a travel agent
   B a worker at the hotel
   C a guest in the hotel

Grammar

1 Look at these sentences from the listening activity. On the left they appear as you heard them, in direct speech. Their reported speech forms are on the right. Look at both forms and write the names of the tenses in the table.

Direct speech | Reported speech

1 'They only have one fire in the winter.' > She said that they only had one fire in the winter.
2 'You're living in a different place now.' > She said that he was living in a different place now.
3 'He's done a huge amount of work.' > She said that he'd done a huge amount of work.
4 'I grew up in an old house in the city centre.' > He said that he had grown up in an old house in the city centre.
5 'We were looking for a location for a new restaurant.' > She said that they'd been looking for a location for a new restaurant.
6 'Tornados and hurricanes won't affect it.' > He said that tornados and hurricanes wouldn't affect it.
7 'It can be noisy.' > He said it could be noisy.
8 'Do you regret your decision?' > She asked if he regretted his decision.
9 'What made you decide to buy a windmill?' > She asked what made them decide to buy a windmill.
10 'Try it yourself!' > He told her to try it herself.
11 'Don't tell me about tourists.' > He told her not to tell him about tourists.

Theory Box

Reported Speech (1)

direct speech	...changes to...	reported speech
Present Simple	⟶	....
Present Continuous	⟶	....
Present Perfect	⟶	....
Past Simple	⟶	....
Past Continuous	⟶	....
will	⟶	....
can	⟶	....
yes/no questions	⟶	use .... and ....
What/where/when/how etc. questions	⟶	use .... and ....
imperatives	⟶	....
negative imperatives	⟶	....

2 Look at the conversations in the cartoon on the next page. The people are using a mixture of direct and reported speech. Complete the sentences below. Then compare your answers with another student's.

1 They said, '.. .'
2 She asked, '..?'
3 He said, '.. .'
4 He said, '.. .'
5 He said, '.. .'
6 He asked, ...
7 Peter said, 'We ....'
8 He said, '.. .'
9 She ....
10 He ....

Association of Estate Agents Annual Ball

1 Imagine yourself in ten years' time. What kind of house would you like to live in? Is there anywhere else you'd prefer to live in, like a castle or a boat? Who do you think you will be living with in ten years' time? Discuss your ideas with other students.

2 Read the title of the article: *An Englishman's Castle*. What do you think it means? Read the extracts from a Web site.

Phrase Finder

An Englishman's home is his castle

Posted by Alice on May 11, 2004 at 10:32:19

Can anyone out there tell me where the saying 'An Englishman's home is his castle' comes from? I need to find out urgently. Thanks.

Re: An Englishman's home is his castle

Posted by JPR on May 12, 2004 at 11:55:42

In Reply to: *An Englishman's home is his castle posted by Alice*. This is a very old idea. It means that you are the boss in your own house and nobody can tell you what to do there. No one can enter your home without your permission. In the United States the word 'man' usually replaces 'Englishman'.

FCE Paper 1, Part 1

3 You are going to read an article about buying houses. Choose the most suitable heading from the list A-I for each part (1-7) of the article. There is one extra heading which you do not need to use. There is an example at the beginning (0).

A A compact solution

B Smaller houses or longer payments?

C Mortgaged for life

D Can prices get any higher?

E A nation of homeowners

F Keeping payments down

G Risking your money

H Need for more houses

I A good investment

An Englishman's Castle

0 | E |

'An Englishman's home is his castle', goes the saying and the British seem more obsessed with property than some other nations. 68% of households in the UK are owner-occupied. Even though this is not the highest in Europe – in Ireland 78% of houses are occupied by their owner and in Spain the figure is 82% – the UK stands out because of the high level of mortgage debt, with a figure of 58.8%, compared to Ireland's 29.9% and Spain's 27.4%.

1 | |

The cause of high levels of borrowing are high prices. House prices have been going up in every region of Britain – with last month's increase being a record. The average house price in Britain is now more than £100,000 and is going up by £28 a day. This means that it is rising at a rate of roughly 15% to 18% a year.

2 | |

The race to buy your first house is made more difficult by the shortage of housing. The government says that in the next 20 years in England nearly 4 million new households will require homes. The shortfall between supply and demand drives up prices, and make people more desperate.

3 | |

Now, in some cities, desperation to own a home has sparked the invention of the 'microflat'. These small microflats have 30 sq/m of living space. The flats are factory-built and assembled one on top of the other. Richard Connor and Stuart Piercy designed the microflat because although they earn £30,000-35,000 a year, this is not enough to buy a house in London. Stuart said, 'We're trying to keep the price below £100,000 per flat, compared with average London prices of about £180,000-£190,000.'

4 | |

Earlier this month, there was speculation that mortgages in the UK would double in length to 50 years, so that ordinary homebuyers could afford to pay the monthly repayments. 30-year mortgages are already available from most lenders, but if house-price inflation remains ahead of salary inflation the only way mortgages will remain affordable is by increasing the term to 30, 40 or even 50 years.

5 | |

If it sounds like the property situation in this country is getting out of control, spare a thought for the Japanese. Owning a property in Japan is even more expensive. Despite near-zero interest rates, some mortgages come with terms as long as 100 years. Borrowers never in fact pay off the loan, leaving the property in the hands of bank and the mortgage in the hands of the children.

6 | |

And although microflats and permanent mortgages may not please every one, this is the price that some British people may have to pay if the property market doesn't change. For young people especially, the dream of having their own 'castle' seems more distant now than it used to be.

7 | |

However, things may change. House prices in London have dropped slightly in the past few weeks. It is too early to say if this is just a temporary event or the beginning of a long-term decline. Some people believe that the latter may be the case. Prices may go on dropping for a number of years.

4 Read the tables below. The one on the left shows mortgage debt, the amount of money that people have borrowed to buy houses. The one on the right shows what percentage of the population own their own houses.

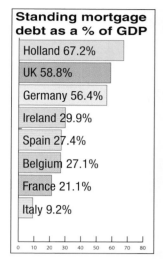

5 Work with other students and answer the questions below.

1 In which countries is the mortgage debt lower than the percentage of owner occupied households?
2 In which countries is it higher?
3 Of these countries, which has the highest percentage of owner occupied households?
4 If people own houses, and are not paying a mortgage, how do you think they got the houses?
5 Do people traditionally buy or rent a house in your country?

Vocabulary

Phrasal verbs/expressions with *have*

1 Match a clause from A with a clause from B to make complete sentences.

A

1 Flying always has a bad effect on me,
2 This computer has had it,
3 I've done with this job,
4 Her boss has really got it in for her,
5 What have you got against him?
6 She had a black dress on when I saw her,
7 I need to have this tooth out,
8 What have you got on today,
9 I'm sorry he lost his job but he had it coming,
10 I've got a lot on at the moment,

B

☐ A he was so lazy.
☐ B it's completely rotten.
☐ C I'm going to throw it out.
☐ D it makes me really nervous.
☐ E He's always charming to me.
☐ F another meeting with the boss?
☐ G I'm going to find another one.
☐ H it really suited her.
☐ I he's always criticising her work.
☐ J I'm not sure I'll get everything done

2 Write the phrasal verb or the expression with *have* next to the definitions.

1 to deserve something, usually bad
2 to be useless or ruined
3 to influence you
4 to be unkind to someone
5 to be planned
6 to dislike someone for a particular quality
7 to wear something
8 to remove
9 to be finished with something
10 to be very busy

3 Work with two other students. Choose three of the statements below. Interview as many students in the class as possible. If a student answers *yes* to one of your questions, ask another question to find out more information.

Find out who in the class:
1 has got make-up on.
2 thinks hot weather has a bad effect on them.
3 has had a tooth out.
4 has got a party on at the weekend.
5 has had it with their scooter.
6 has a lot on at the moment.
7 has something against tourists.
8 has done with studying English!
9 has got it in for someone.

UNIT 9

Use of English

1 In each of the sentences below there is a word missing. Choose one of the words from the box to complete each sentence.

> been   for   hardly   some   the
> too   used   which

1   It's a small house. There should be lots of room for all of them.
2   The place has standing empty now for about twenty years.
3   Jenny's gone to school to have a chat with her son's teacher.
4   The transport system's absolutely awful but I'm getting to it.
5   There are just many people trying to park their cars around here.
6   The house, he bought five years ago, has almost doubled in value.
7   He's been thinking of moving out of the city centre a long time.
8   That's mortgage they've got. They're paying over a £1,000 a month.

2 What about taking words which are in the wrong place out of sentences? In each of the sentences below, one of the pair of *words* is not necessary. With another student, decide which one you should take out.

1   They've *been* owned the house for five years and they've mostly *been* happy there.
2   Are there any disadvantages to *the* living in *the* old centre of the city?
3   I learned *too* various things about the property market and a lot about people *too*.
4   It's raining *hardly*, but I *hardly* think that's an excuse to stay inside.
5   He might *for* buy a house if he can find the kind that he's looking *for*.
6   There are *some* twenty houses around here, *some* which are worth over a million pounds.
7   The house *which* they used to live in *which* was a bungalow.
8   It's his dream *used* to live on a boat and she has to get *used* to it.

FOR SALE

FCE Paper 3, Part 4

3 Read the text below and look carefully at each line. Some of the lines are correct and some have a word which should not be there. Each of the words is a preposition or an adverb. If a line is correct, put a tick (✓) at the end of the line. If it is wrong, circle the word.

An Englishman's home is a Scottish castle

O The Dobson family home has nine ⟨of⟩ bathrooms but no hot water.
OO They can choose from thirty toilets but until last week none of them ✓
1 was working. They are already worried about winter coming by because
2 they have no heating. However, this is at their dream house and they wouldn't
3 swap it for anything. Duncraig Castle, in to the Scottish Highlands, had not
4 been occupied for nearly twelve years and was up on sale for £500,000. So
5 three generations of the Dobsons – seventeen men, women and children in all
6 – sold their houses in England to raise money and moved off 500 miles north.
7 Mr Dobson said, 'We decided to put our money together to get away somewhere
8 we could all live in. The castle is fantastic, for although it does need a lot of work.'

4 Read the rest of the story. Some lines are correct and some lines have an extra word. This time it could be any kind of word. The first two have been done for you.

O His mother added, 'I thought he was joking, but then we came to see it ✓
OO and fell ⟨very⟩ in love with the place – everything is absolutely ideal.' The
1 Dobsons have not just now bought a new house, but a new way of life.
2 The nearest supermarket may be nearly 200 miles far away, but the view
3 from the back of the castle is of Loch Carron and the mountains. Because
4 the location is just one of the many attractions, said Mrs Dobson. 'People
5 here can only leave their doors open and their keys in their cars,' she
6 continued. 'Bikes are left on the street and they are hardly still there the next
7 day. Everyone has been very much welcoming and everyone has time to talk.'

Vocabulary

Phrasal verbs/expressions for housing

1 Read the newspaper report and answer the questions.

1 What does the council want to do?

2 Why is the Residents' Association against the plan?

3 Has the Residents' Association stopped the council's plan?

> A spokesperson for the local Residents' Association said that although their petition to save the houses in Duke Street had been **1** *rejected* by the council, they would **2** *continue* the fight. The council proposes to **3** *demolish* the old houses and **4** *erect* a new office block on the site. Thirty families will be **5** *evicted* in an area where there is already a housing shortage. The residents want the council to **6** *renovate* the properties, including **7** *installing* central heating, and give guarantees that more houses will be built.

2 Underline the phrasal verbs in the conversation below. Match them with the verbs (1-7) in the report above.

Tom : Have you heard? The council's putting up that new office block in Duke Street.

Bob : They can't do that. What about the petition?

Tom : Oh, they just turned it down. They're going to pull the houses down.

Bob : But they're not in a bad condition. They just need to put in central heating and do them up.

Tom : They say it's too expensive — it's more economical to knock them down.

Bob : But what about the people who live there? They can't just turn them out without anywhere to live.

Tom : We told them it's more houses we need, not office blocks, but they wouldn't listen.

Bob : But we can't stop now.

Tom : No, we're going to carry on, even if it means another petition.

3 Complete the sentences using the correct phrasal verb from question 2.

1 I think they should .... that building — it looks dangerous to me.

2 The council .... our application to cut down the tree.

3 I'd like to .... a new speaker system.

4 He buys old houses, ... them .... and then sells them for a profit.

5 They're .... a new shopping centre.

6 We need to .... this discussion after lunch.

7 They can't .... the old man .... from his home — he's lived there all his life.

Grammar

1 Work with another student, what's the difference between these two sentences?

1 Do you want something to eat?

2 Do you want anything to eat?

2 Write one word in each space.

1 Nobody is coming, ... they?

2 Everybody likes her, ... they?

Theory Box

1 When we use **some** we're thinking of something **specific**. When we use **any**, we're thinking of a **number of possible things**.

*I'm looking for **somebody** who understands computers.*

*I'm looking for **anybody** who might be able to help me.*

*I know he's **somewhere** in this house.*

*He could be **anywhere** in the world.*

When we **give an invitation**, we use **something** when we expect a **positive answer**. We have something definite in mind. We use **anything** when we are not sure what the answer is going to be.

2 Although **nobody** and **everybody** are singular, we use **they** in tag questions to avoid the awkward **he** or **she**. So we say:

*Nobody is coming, **are** they?*

*Everybody likes her, **don't** they?*

3 Now put one of the words in the box into each space. Some words can be used twice.

some/any/no/every	+	thing body/one where

1 After the main course I was too full to eat .... else.

2 There's .... here at all.

3 Look, there's .... in the bushes, a small animal moved.

4 If .... wants more food they'll have to go to the chip shop.

5 You look thirsty. Would you like .... to drink?

6 He'll be difficult to find — he could be .... by now.

7 There's .... interesting about this film at all.

8 Tell .... at home that I'm OK.

9 She looks so happy. I think she's found .... special.

UNIT 9
Speaking

1 Conversations often have similar structures. Sally and Charles are university students who are going to share a flat. They are discussing what they need to buy for the flat. Read the conversation in pairs and underline the expressions used for each function:

Charles

1 Starting the discussion Why don't we start by looking at what we really need.

3 Making a positive suggestion It might be a good idea to think about the kitchen first. What about a dishwasher?

5 Agreeing with a suggestion Yes, that's a good idea.

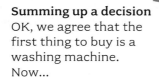

Making a positive suggestion We could think about getting an iron at the same time.

7 Summing up a decision OK, we agree that the first thing to buy is a washing machine. Now...

Sally

2 Asking for the other person's suggestion What do you think we should buy first?

4 Disagreeing with a suggestion I don't think we need a dishwasher. They're a waste of money.

Making a positive suggestion I think we should get a washing machine first.

6 Making a negative suggestion There's no point in buying an iron. I'm not going to iron my jeans and T shirts!

2 Charles and Sally continue their discussion. Put the conversation in the correct order.

- ☐☐ Yes, I think we should definitely do that. I can't cope in the morning without a cup of coffee.
- ☐☐ Why don't we get a microwave? They're really useful.
- ☐☐ So that's the second thing that we've decided to buy.
- ☐☐ I'm not sure we need it. We've already got an oven. It would be better to buy a kettle.
- 1☐ What do you suggest we buy next?

3 Write the correct function (1-7) in each box and then practise the conversation with another student.

4 Write the function next to each expression.

expression	function
1 Shall we look at what we need first?	1
2 Do you think we should buy a breadmaker?	☐
3 It's a waste of money buying a breadmaker.	☐
4 Let's get an ice-making machine instead.	☐
5 It's not worth buying an ice-making machine.	☐
6 How about buying a toaster?	☐
7 It would be best to see how much it costs, first.	☐
8 It's no good having a kitchen without a toaster!	☐
9 OK, we can go and look at the prices tomorrow.	☐
10 Let's think about the bathroom now...	☐

FCE Paper 5, Part 3

5 Work with another student. You are going to share a flat. Look at the flat and label the furniture already in it. Then look at the list of things that you could buy. You each have £250. First, make your own list of what you think are the most important things. Then decide what you are going to buy together. Use the expressions you have studied.

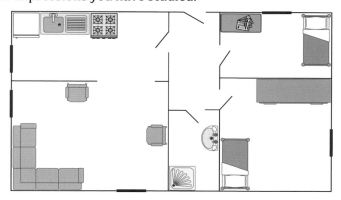

THINGS TO BUY

washing machine	£100
dining table and chairs	£70
stereo system	£60
TV	£50
DVD player	£40
microwave oven	£30
crockery	£30
cutlery	£30
hoover	£30
iron	£20
saucepans	£20
bookshelf	£15 each
electric kettle	£10
toaster	£10

Writing

1 Read the tourist information about Cardiff. What aspects of the city does the writer mention? Does the writer use a lot of details? How would you describe the style the writer uses?

VISIT CARDIFF
Capital of Wales

Cardiff's name in Welsh means the 'fort on the Taff', because the Romans built a fort here on the River Taff in AD75. You can see the remains at Cardiff Castle.

In the 19th century, Cardiff became the centre for exporting coal from the Welsh valleys. Following the decline in heavy industry, Cardiff Bay has now been redeveloped. It is also the location of Techniquest, the UK's leading science discovery centre.

In spite of its long history, Cardiff is Europe's youngest capital city. It was recognised as the official capital of Wales in 1955. Then, in 1999 the Welsh Assembly brought a level of self-government to the country.

In the same year, Cardiff hosted the Rugby World Cup at the Millennium Stadium. The Music in the Bay Festival organises regular concerts featuring stars from around the world.

During the month-long summer street festival, the streets are alive with entertainers of all kinds.

Cardiff is also one of the finest shopping centres in Great Britain. There is an impressive covered Victorian market as well as modern shopping centres.

Cardiff is a great starting point for touring Wales. You can see ancient castles, beautiful mountains and valleys, and a breathtaking coastline.

2 With other students, make a list of the places to see and things to do where you live. Write one or two sentences about each attraction. You should also say something about the history of where you live.

FCE Paper 2, Part 2

3 A class of students from Cardiff is going to come and study in your town. They would like to know some things about the places they can visit and things to do. Write a similar report of the place where you live for their school magazine. Write between 120-180 words.

Progress Check 3 (Units 7-9)

1 Use one of these words or phrases to fill the gap in each sentence.

I'd rather	if only	imagine	it's time
	suppose	wish	

1 I don't want to go out tonight. .... we just stayed in and watched TV.

2 .... I had a bit more money, I'd be able to buy that DVD.

3 It's getting pretty late. I think .... we went home.

4 I .... he was here now. Things would be much more fun.

5 .... if you were a millionaire — what would you do with the money?

6 .... I hadn't told her about John, she'd still be speaking to me.

7 He wants me to help him but .... he finished the job himself.

8 I know he's only 16 but .... he grew up a bit.

9 I don't think London's a good idea. .... it rained all the time?

10 I .... I could see better and didn't have to wear glasses.

2 Choose the most likely modal for each of the sentences below.

1 Bert wishes he **could/might** get out more but he's so busy studying.

2 **Might/Would** I make a suggestion? Why don't you just calm down a bit?

3 I don't think travel to other galaxies **could/would** happen in our lifetime.

4 If the doctor thinks you **might/should** lose weight, you'd better go on a diet.

5 If you join these two wires together, anything **might/would** happen.

6 I know I **could/should** phone her more often but I just don't have the time.

7 Why **ought to/should** I have to do all the work around here?

8 You're going out with Trev? You **could/ought to** have your head examined!

9 Alice **could/should** still be at work but I don't think so. It's a bit late.

10 I know what she **might/would** say but I'm going to ask her anyway.

3 Some of these sentences are correct and others are wrong. Make changes where necessary.

1 If she arrives before 6.00 she can come out with us.

2 If I know what to do here, I'd be a lot happier.

3 Greg would help you if he's here. It's a pity he's off work today.

4 If it wasn't for his brother, he'd be living on the street.

5 If Mozart is alive today he'd be writing club dance music.

6 If you didn't make so much noise you'd be easier to live with.

7 If I was rich I'll travel round the world.

8 I'd be able to help him if I understand French.

9 If I don't like this house so much I'd probably move out of town.

10 If you don't sell that car you're going to have no money at all.

4 Change the verbs in brackets either to the Past Perfect (with *had* or *'d*) or *would/'d* + Present Perfect to make 3rd conditional sentences — referring to unreal situations in past time. The first one has been done for you.

0 If you ....had studied.... (*study*) something more useful you ...would have got.. (*get*) a better job.

1 If I .... (*buy*) this in the sales it .... (*cost*) a lot less.

2 We .... (*win*) if he .... (*not miss*) that penalty.

3 It .... (*be*) better if you .... (*not shout*) at him.

4 If you .... (*not leave*) the money on the table, they .... (*not steal*) it.

5 If I .... (*live*) in the Middle Ages I .... (*want*) to be rich.

6 If his father .... (*not be*) president they .... (*not elect*) him.

7 If you .... (*eat*) a bit less you .... (*not feel*) so ill.

8 You .... (*not get*) into trouble if you .... (*stay*) away from him.

9 If Maria .... (*not be*) there I .... (*not go*) myself.

5 Write sentences that are similar to those below using the word given.

1 I'm sorry you failed your driving test.
wish ....

2 It's possible he went home.
might ....

3 It's a pity you spoke to her.
shouldn't ....

4 It isn't possible that he didn't get the message.
must ....

5 Why didn't you listen to what she said?
ought to ....

6 If we assume that I was here — what would have happened?
suppose ....

7 He didn't tell you because he didn't want to.
if ....

8 I regret meeting her in the first place.
wish ....

9 I'd prefer it if you hadn't said anything to Mike.
rather ....

10 I only went out with him because I thought he was lonely.
gone ....

6 Change these sentences from direct speech into reported speech or the other way round.

1 'I don't like your hat,' she said.
....

2 'I can swim quite well,' Bob said.
....

3 He asked me if I knew Kevin.
....

4 'What's your mother's maiden name?' he asked.
....

5 'Put it back in the box,' he said.
....

6 Jack said that nobody was coming.
....

7 He said that he'd lived in the house all his life.
....

8 Mum told me not to speak to him again.
....

9 'I'll see you later,' he said.
....

10 'I've met her a few times before,' Harold said.
....

11 'I was working in France at the time,' she said.
....

12 Joe said that he wanted to quit his job.
....

13 He said that he'd lend me the money if he could.
....

14 Hannah told me to phone back later.
....

15 'Do you like strawberries?' she asked.
....

16 The boss asked me when I was leaving.
....

17 'Don't even think of cheating,' Al said.
....

18 'I bought them on the way home,' Sheila said.
....

7 Make the second sentences mean the same as the first sentence by writing one of these words in each space.

something	somebody	somewhere
anything	anybody	anywhere
nothing	nobody	nowhere
everything	everybody	everywhere

1 They stole all my things.
They stole ....

2 I don't know a single person here.
I know .... here.

3 I've no idea where he is.
He could be ....

4 I have some news for you.
There's .... I want to tell you.

5 It must be in this room.
It must be .... here.

6 He isn't in this town at all.
He's .... in this town.

7 I don't want to say even one word.
I don't want to say ....

8 All the people we know are coming.
.... is coming.

9 Don't tell this to a single person.
Don't tell this to ....

10 There must be a person who likes you.
.... must like you.

11 There isn't a thing we can do.
There's .... we can do.

12 There are cameras all over the place.
There are cameras ....

UNIT 10
Discoveries and Inventions

Speaking

1 Work with other students. Which of these everyday objects have you used, or eaten, in the last 24 hours?

windscreen wiper

tin opener

photocopier

sandwich

mobile phone

basketball

2 In your group, match each of the inventions with its inventor and the date it was invented.

a   John Montagu, 1762
b   Ezra J Warner, 1858
c   James Naismith, 1891
d   Mary Anderson, 1903
e   Chester Carlson, 1938
f   Dr Martin Cooper, 1973

3 Now put the inventions in order, with the most useful at the top of the table. Then compare your ideas with the others in your group. Discuss why you think the inventions are more, or less, useful.

	most useful
1	
2	
3	
4	
5	
6	
	least useful

Listening

1 Before you listen, look at these extracts from the interview. One word, a noun, has been removed from each one. Work with another student to decide which word from the box to write in each space.

> business   Centre   departments   event   Fair   money
> music   Organiser   prize   products   success   videos   Year

1   National Inventions ....
2   develop new ....
3   invest ....
4   show ...., play ....
5   National Exhibition ....
6   one-day ....
7   university ....
8   16 million pounds' worth of ....
9   Inventor of the ....
10 a sponsor for this ....
11 Inventions Fair ....
12 a huge ....

2 Now listen to the interview to check your answers.

3 You will hear someone being interviewed about the International Inventions Fair. For questions 1-10, complete the sentences. But before you begin, work with another student to predict the information you need to answer each question.

Do you have an invention?

Would you like to put it on display?

Would you like to develop new 1 ☐ ?

Then take a 2 ☐ at the

INTERNATIONAL INVENTIONS FAIR

The National Exhibition Centre Birmingham

Date: 3 ☐

More than 4 ☐ visitors attended last year's event!

Over 150 inventions from individual inventors, 5 ☐ and universities.

Over 6 ☐ of business created!

Many awards – the main prize is

£ 7 ☐ for the Inventor

of the Year

sponsored by the 8 ☐

For further details contact Cath 9 ☐

Inventions Fair 10 ☐
Tel: 08696 547812

Discoveries and Inventions
Vocabulary

Phrasal verbs/expressions with *turn*

1 Choose the correct word (a, b or c) to complete each sentence. Then compare your answers with another student.

1 We decided to turn .... for home because the weather was so bad.
   a up   **b** in   **c** back

2 This sofa turns .... a bed.
   a for   **b** into   **c** back

3 They eventually turned .... at the party but they were really late.
   a up   **b** in   **c** round

4 He was very disappointed when they turned him .... for the job.
   a up   **b** to   **c** down

5 Although she said it would be easy, it turned .... to be a really difficult interview.
   a in   **b** out   **c** off

6 You need to turn .... the motorway at the next exit and follow the signs for Oxford.
   a into   **b** down   **c** off

7 The car turned .... in the accident and ended up on its roof.
   a up   **b** over   **c** round

8 Could you turn .... the music? I'm trying to sleep.
   a down   **b** up   **c** in

2 Write each phrasal verb next to its correct definition.

1 to roll upside down   ....
2 to reduce the volume   ....
3 to arrive after a delay   ....
4 to reject   ....
5 to become   ....
6 to reverse direction   ....
7 to happen in a particular way ....
8 to disconnect something/
   to leave a road   ....

3 Complete each sentence with a suitable phrasal verb. Compare your answers with another student.

1 We watched the liquid .... a gas during the experiment.

2 They .... my idea and accepted Simon's proposal instead.

3 We .... and went home because we couldn't find their house.

4 He hurt his back when he .... in bed.

5 I .... the heating when I go on holiday.

6 Can you .... the TV? I'm on the phone.

7 The project .... OK in the end.

8 She missed the train, but she .... eventually.

1 You are going to read an article by the American writer, Bill Bryson. Before you begin, look at these phrases from the text. They have been divided into two parts. Match the two halves together. Read the article very quickly to check your answers.

1	computer	a	off
2	CD	b	ruin
3	snapped	c	in for
4	special	d	dealer
5	backs of seats	e	drawer
6	go	f	of guys
7	car	g	helpline
8	gadgets	h	promotion
9	bunch	i	and armrests
10	financial	j	and comforts

FCE Paper 1, Part 2

2 Now read the article and for questions 1-6 choose the answer (A, B, C or D) which you think fits best according to the text.

THE CUPHOLDER REVOLUTION

I am told that this is a true story.

A man calls his computer helpline complaining that the cupholder on his personal computer has snapped off, and he wants to know how to get it
5 fixed.

'Cupholder?' says the computer helpline person, puzzled. 'I'm sorry, sir, but I'm confused. Did you buy this cupholder at a computer show or was it a special promotion?'
10 'No, it's part of the standard equipment on my computer.'

'But our computers don't come with cupholders.'

'Well, pardon me, friend, but they do,' says the
15 man a little angrily. 'I'm looking at mine right now. You push a button on the front of the machine and it slides out.'

The man, it seemed, had been using the CD drawer in his computer to hold his coffee cup.
20 If you are not familiar with them, cupholders are little trays with holes for holding cups and other drinks containers, which are found in many places throughout every modern American car. Often they are fixed to the backs of seats or built
25 into armrests, but just as often they are hidden away in places you would never think of looking. Generally, in my experience, if you push an unfamiliar button in an American car, either it will

30 activate the windscreen wiper or it will make a cupholder slide out, rise up, drop down or otherwise magically enter your life.

It would be almost impossible to exaggerate the importance of cupholders in American cars these days. The *New York Times* recently ran a
35 long article in which it tested a dozen family cars. It rated each of them for ten features, such as engine size, boot space, handling, quality of suspension, and, yes, number of cupholders. A car dealer acquaintance of ours told us that they
40 are one of the first things people remark on, ask about or play with when they come to look at a car. People buy cars on the basis of cupholders. Nearly all car advertisements give them prominence in the text.

45 Some cars, like the newest model of the Dodge Caravan, come with as many as seventeen cupholders. Seventeen! The largest Caravan holds seven passengers. You don't have to be a nuclear physicist, or even wide awake, to work out
50 that that is 2.43 cupholders per passenger. Why, you may wonder, would each passenger in a vehicle need 2.43 cupholders? Good question.

There is a long tradition of filling the interiors of American cars with lots of gadgets and comforts,
55 and I suppose the surplus of cupholders is just part of that tradition. However, there is a limit to how many different features you can fit into a car. What better, than to fill it with cupholders, particularly when people seem to go in for them in
60 a big way? That's my theory.

However, not putting cupholders in a car is a serious mistake. I read a couple of years ago that Volvo had to redesign all its cars for the American market for this reason. Volvo's engineers had
65 foolishly thought that what buyers were looking for was a safe and comfortable car with a reliable engine, when in fact what they really wanted was little trays into which to insert their drinks. So a bunch of guys were put to work designing
70 cupholders into the system, and Volvo was thus saved from beverage embarrassment, if not actual financial ruin.

1 Why did the man phone the computer helpline?
   A His computer wasn't working properly.
   B He wanted to return his computer.
   C He had misused his computer.
   D He wanted a new part for his computer.

2 How did the man feel when he spoke to the helpline person?
   A confused
   B annoyed
   C puzzled
   D nervous

3 What does the writer say about cupholders in modern American cars?
   A There are far too many of them.
   B They are usually well-hidden.
   C They can confuse the driver.
   D There are more than you might expect.

4 What does the writer say about the Dodge Caravan?
   A It has more cupholders than people need.
   B It has more cupholders than any other car.
   C It carries more passengers than any other car.
   D It is scientifically designed.

5 In line 60, 'my theory' refers to the writer's view that
   A American cars have too many gadgets.
   B American cars have too many cupholders.
   C American cars are designed to suit the customers.
   D Americans give too much importance to cupholders.

6 Volvo redesigned its cars for the American market because
   A they were not safe or comfortable.
   B people didn't want to buy them.
   C their engines were not reliable.
   D they only had a few cupholders.

❸ Work with another student. Think of an object or invention which you think is unnecessary. Describe it and discuss which is the most unnecessary.

Speaking

❶ **Match the expressions in the box with their appropriate functions.**

1 What I meant was...
2 Let me think about that.
3 Do you mean...?
4 Could you say that again?
5 Let me put that another way.
6 Do you know what I mean?
7 If I can just finish...
8 I don't see what you mean.
9 Can I just say something?

a Repeat something you have said to make it clearer.
b Show someone has misunderstood you.
c Check you have understood.
d Show you haven't understood.
e Interrupt.
f Continue a discussion that has been interrupted.
g Ask someone to repeat what they have said.
h Check that someone has understood you.
i Give yourself time to think.

❷ **Here are some more useful expressions. Unfortunately, there is a mistake in each one. Correct the sentences.**

1 If I can go back what I was saying before...
2 I'm sorry, I'm no with you.
3 Are you say that...
4 Sorry, what you say?
5 Sorry interrupt but...
6 I haven't thought with that before but...
7 What I wanted say was...
8 Are you by me?
9 I'm sorry, that's not what am I saying.

❸ **Now match the expressions with their appropriate functions in question 1.**

FCE Paper 5, Parts 3/4

❹ **Work with three other students. Your teacher will give you each an opinion card. Write down at least four reasons why your opinions are correct. Have a group discussion. See if you can convince the other students to agree with you.**

UNIT 10

Use of English

1 With other students, discuss what each of the inventions below is for. Think of a name for each one and write it on the line under the photo. Would you buy something like this?

1 ....

2 ....

3 ....

4 ....

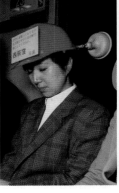

5 ....

6 ....

2 In fact, none of these inventions was designed to be of practical use. They come from Japan and their inventors are part of a club. Read about it below.

FCE Paper 3, Part 5

3 For questions 1-10, use the word given in capitals at the end of the line to form a word that fits into the space in the same line. There is an example at the beginning (0).

CHINDOGU

(0) Unlike.. many other Japanese arts, chindogu is not very | LIKE
old. In fact, it only dates back to 1986, when its (1)............, | FOUND
Kenji Kawakami, put his first pictures into a Japanese
(2)............ magazine as a joke. It is now a joke with | SHOP
worldwide (3)............ . The International Chindogu Society | POPULAR
has over 10,000 members and Kawakami's two books on
the subject are (4)............ from bookshop shelves across | APPEAR
the world.
Chindogu is ruled by strict principles. (5)............, the | BASE
object has to be (6)............ . If people can find any kind of | USE
use for it, your efforts have resulted in (7)............ . | FAIL
However, you do have to make your chindogu. An idea or
a (8)............ is not enough. It must have a real existence. | DRAW
But selling it is also (9)............ . If you accept money for | FORBID
one, you surrender your (10)............ . | PURE

4 Work with another student to see if you can invent a chindogu. Draw a picture of it and write a short description. Discuss your chindogu with another group. Decide which is the most useless chindogu.

Vocabulary

Science and technology

1 Name the things in the photos. Discuss the following questions with other students.

1 Which ones do you have?

2 Which ones do you use everyday?

3 Which one would you save from a burning house?

2 Discuss these questions with the other students in your group.

1 Do you use a computer? If so, how often?

2 What do you use it for?

3 How long have you been using a computer?

4 Do you use the computer for school work? If so, which?

5 How do you think you'll use a computer in the future?

6 What words and expressions do you know to talk about using a computer?

3 Match each verb with a suitable noun. Then compare your answers with another student.

1	to go into	**a**	a CD
2	to check	**b**	a film
3	to surf	**c**	a file
4	to buy	**d**	your password
5	to e-mail	**e**	the Net
6	to load	**f**	your e-mail
7	to create/edit/delete	**g**	the computer
8	to download	**h**	on-line
9	to turn on/off	**i**	your files
10	to type in	**j**	a Web site/ a program/ a chatroom
11	to back-up	**k**	someone
12	to insert	**l**	software

4 You are going to ask other students the questions below. But first write question 7. Now interview as many students as possible. If a student answers *yes* to a question, ask the second question.

1 Who checks their e-mail everyday? How many messages do they get?

2 Who sometimes shops on-line? What was the last thing they bought?

3 Who regularly backs-up their files? How often do they do it?

4 Who has downloaded music from the Web? What did they download?

5 Who has gone into a chatroom? Who did you meet?

6 Who surfs the Net for fun? What interesting things have they found recently?

7 ....

Prepositional phrases *on, in, at, by*

1 Match the opposites.

in general	in practice
at work	in pen
in theory	in particular
in public	on the phone
by cheque	in/during the day
in writing	in cash
by chance	on purpose
at night	in private
in pencil	on holiday

2 In each group of words, there is one word which can either use *in* or *out of* but cannot use both. Which one is it?

1	in/out of	control breath touch danger	2	in/out of	stock use date fashion
3	in/out of	luck place reach question	4	in/out of	debt print work advance

3 Complete each sentence with the best prepositional phrase.

1 Hats are .... at the moment. Everyone is wearing them.

2 I think we're .... They've got one DVD player left in the shop.

3 Mobile phones are very useful for keeping .... with people.

4 He hasn't got a job at the moment. He's ....

5 Camcorders are .... at the moment. We'll have to order you one.

6 This book is .... — you can't buy it anymore.

7 The car went .... and crashed into a bridge.

8 They think he's .... now and will make a full recovery.

In time/by the time/on time/at the time

4 Complete each sentence with the appropriate prepositional phrase.

1 We arrived .... for our appointment at exactly 9 o'clock.

2 We arrived five minutes early .... for our appointment.

3 .... the police arrived, the thief had disappeared.

4 I was with my parents .... of the accident.

5 Now match each one with its correct definition.

1 when one action clearly happens before or after another one ....

2 at the correct time ....

3 early ....

4 when two actions happen at the same time
....

UNIT 10
Grammar

❶ In Units 3, 7 and 8 we looked at different types of conditional sentences:

Type 1	*If I **see** her, I'll **tell** her.*
Type 2	*If I **saw** her, I'd **tell** her.*
Type 3	*If I'd **seen** her, I'd **have told** her.*

Look at the table below. Put a line through the information which is not true for each type. The first has been done for you.

	tenses/modals	time	probability
type 1	present/~~past~~ ~~past perfect~~	~~past~~/present/ future	higher
type 2	present/past/ past perfect	past/present/ future	zero/lower/ higher
type 3	present/past/ past perfect	past/present/ future	zero/lower/ higher

❷ For each question below, read the text. Then fill in the gaps in the sentences with an appropriate verb to make a type 1, 2 or 3 conditional sentence.

1 The man, it seemed, had been using the CD drawer in his computer to hold his coffee cup.
If you .... your CD drawer to hold your coffee cup, it ....

2 A man calls his computer helpline complaining that the cupholder on his personal computer has snapped off.
If computers .... cupholders, they .... stronger than CD trays.

3 However, not putting cupholders in a car is a serious mistake.
If this car .... cupholders, people .... it.

4 To be a chindogu, an object must be completely, or almost completely, useless.
If you .... something which people .... use, you .... to make a chindogu.

5 A chindogu cannot have a practical use, but you must make it.
If you .... it, it .... a chindogu.

6 Thousands of visitors at last year's event! Over 150 inventions from individual inventors.
If you .... to last year's event, you .... over 150 inventions.

7 John Montagu, the 4th Earl of Sandwich, was a compulsive gambler. In 1762 he ordered meat and cheese to be put between two slices of bread so that he could hold a meal in one hand while continuing with his game of cards.
If John Montagu .... a compulsive gambler, he .... the sandwich.

❸ There are a number of other words and phrases that have a similar meaning to *if*, though they are not exactly the same. Read the Theory Box below.

Theory Box

provided that/ providing that/as long as

We use these when we expect **something to happen**, and that this will lead to a **result**:

***Provided that** you use it correctly, your CD tray should work for years.*

Read this dialogue:

Dealer: What do you think of this Volvo?
Customer: Nice car, good engine. If it had some cupholders I'd be interested.
Dealer: This is the new model. It's got lots of cupholders.
*Customer: Well, **provided that** it's got cupholders, I'll have a look at it.*

unless

This has a similar meaning to **if** followed by a negative verb.

*Even a very good car won't sell **if** it **doesn't have** cupholders.*
*Even a very good car won't sell **unless** it **has** cupholders.*

However, look at these sentences:

***If** you use your CD tray as a cupholder, it **will** break.*
***Unless** you use your CD tray as a cupholder, it **won't** break.*

Is the second sentence true? No, it isn't — there are a number of other ways you might break your CD tray. You could drop a book on it, for example. **Unless** works when only **one** action will produce that result.

even if

We use this to indicate that the result of an action is **unexpected**, either positive leading to negative:

***Even if** a car **is** safe and reliable, it **won't** sell without cupholders.*

or the opposite:

***Even if** it **doesn't** have cupholders, **I'm** still **going to buy** it.*

4 Each of the inventions below was registered at the US Patents Office. With other students discuss what each invention is for and how it works — or why it won't work.

1 a This will work .... the wind is strong.

   b But you won't move .... the wind blows hard.

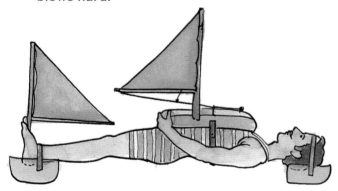

2 a It won't work .... you use a lot more birds.

   b .... it works, it's still cruel to the birds.

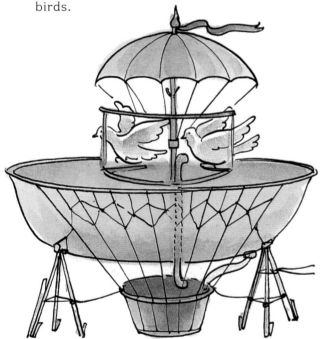

3 a This might work, ... it doesn't break in the middle.

   b It won't work. .... it doesn't break, it will bend.

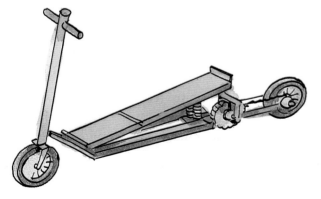

4 a .... you don't mind looking silly, it will keep you dry.

   b .... you don't mind looking silly, it's still a crazy idea.

5 a It could be fun, ... you don't roll downhill and turn into a snowball.

   b It might be dangerous to other people .... they were wearing them too.

5 Now complete the positive and negative sentences under each invention. Fill in the gaps with *provided/providing that*, *unless* or *even if*.

Writing

1 **Read the article below about clockwork radios. What does clockwork mean?**

The clockwork radio was developed by British inventor Trevor Baylis. He began to think about it in 1991 after seeing a television programme about AIDS in Africa. An AIDS worker said that advice about how to prevent the disease spreading could be broadcast if only radios and batteries were not so expensive.

Trevor had the idea of a radio that was powered by clockwork. If you turn a handle, it winds up a spring, which turns a wheel that produces electricity. There is nothing new in the basic technology. The Victorians used the same method to power toys. The difficulty was in adapting the process to make a radio work. More recent versions of the radio also have solar panels and play for an hour, twice as long as the original version.

Clockwork radios are now sold or distributed free in many developing countries. They are also proving popular in Europe and North America, partly for environmental reasons, because used batteries are almost impossible to recycle.

FCE Paper 2, Part 2

2 **Read these instructions:**

The company you work for has asked you to attend the UK Inventions Fair. They are looking for new ideas to develop. You see three inventions which look interesting. Write a report on them, describing their function, their possible advantages and disadvantages, and which one you think provides the best investment opportunity for the company.

Write 120-180 words in an appropriate style.

3 **Read the descriptions of the three inventions.**

Ultrasound walking stick

This sends out ultrasound waves. When these strike nearby objects they are reflected back to the handle and make it vibrate. The blind person using the cane can 'feel' when an object gets near.

Entertaining exercise bike

This isn't just an exercise bike with a game. If you pedal faster, you can move faster across the screen or shoot more effectively. The more you work, the more chance you have of winning the game.

Air jack

The power comes from the car battery. Air is pumped in and the jack lifts the car.
It can also blow up the tyre.

Vocabulary

by sight/at first sight/on sight/in sight

1 **Complete each sentence with the appropriate prepositional phrase.**

1 The police gave the order to shoot the terrorists ....
2 I know the manager .... but I've never spoken to him.
3 The ring looked like gold ....
4 Soon the station was .... and we could see our friends waiting there.

2 **Now match each one with its correct definition.**

1 know someone by looking at them ....
2 initially ....
3 visible ....
4 when you see someone immediately ....
....

at the end/by the end/in the end

3 **Complete each sentence with the appropriate prepositional phrase.**

1 Everything was okay .... and we met our friends.
2 She married him .... of the story and they lived happily ever after.
3 The film was so boring that we were all asleep .... of it.

4 **Now match each one with its correct definition.**

1 the conclusion (of a road, book, journey etc.)
2 finally
3 what is happening when something else has finished

Vocabulary

Cars and driving

1 Work with another student. What instructions would you give to someone to start a car?

2 Look at these instructions for starting a car. Put them in the correct order. Did you have the same instructions?

- [ ] Start the car.
- [ ] Put your foot on the clutch.
- [ ] Pull out.
- [ ] Put your seat belt on.
- [ ] Turn the steering wheel.
- [ ] Get into the driving seat.
- [ ] Let the handbrake off.
- [ ] Put the key in the ignition.
- [ ] Use your indicator.
- [ ] Put the car into first gear.
- [ ] Unlock the door.
- [ ] Look in the rear view mirror.

3 Read the conversation between a father and his son. Which things happened in the story? Tick the correct pictures. Then answer these questions with another student.

1 What happened?
2 Was it a minor or serious accident?
3 Did the son tell his father the truth at the beginning?

Father: Where have you been? I was getting worried.

Son: I had to fill up with petrol because I thought I was going to run out before I got home. Then I got held up because I had a little accident in the car.

Father: Not again! What happened this time? I hope you didn't try to overtake someone on a bend again.

Son: You know it's been raining all afternoon and when I came round the bend near the post office...

Father: Not the same place where you had the collision last time?

Son: I slowed down and suddenly I saw this sports car coming towards me so I put my foot on the brake and swerved.

Father: But you missed the other car, didn't you?

Son: Yes. I skidded and crashed into a tree.

Father: At least you're not hurt.

Son: The other driver is fine too and his car only has a little dent in it.

Father: And our car?

Son: I'm afraid it's a complete write-off. We'll have to buy another one.

Father: You mean that *I'll* have to buy another one!

4 Now find words or phrases in the conversation which mean:

1 a car which is completely destroyed in an accident
  ....

2 to put petrol in a car
  ....

3 to lose control of a car because the road is wet or icy ....

4 a car crash ....

5 to decrease speed
  ....

6 a small piece of damage when metal has been hit
  ....

7 to turn the steering wheel to avoid something ....

8 to have no more petrol in the car
  ....

9 to be delayed ....

10 to pass another car
  ....

UNIT 11
Eating and Shopping

Speaking

1 **Work with other students. Choose an answer to each question.**

1 Which is the most popular British takeaway food?
   a Doner Kebab   c Fish and Chips
   b Hamburgers   d Pizza

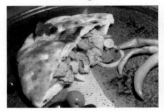 

2 Which of these is not a traditional English food?
   a Cornish Pasty   c Jellied Eels
   b Yorkshire Pudding   d Haggis

3 Which is the most popular British restaurant dish?
   a Chicken Tikka Masala   c Chop Suey
   b Steak and Kidney Pie   d Tagliatelle

4 Which is the most popular meal cooked by students?
   a Curry   c Fish and Chips
   b Roast Beef and   d Spaghetti Bolognese
     Yorkshire Pudding

5 Which is the most popular breakfast in Britain?
   a a cup of coffee   b bacon and eggs
   c porridge   d cereal and/or toast

6 Which country drinks the most tea?
   a Britain   b India
   c Ireland   d Turkey

7 Which of these would you recommend least?
   a British wine
   b English wine
   c Scottish wine
   d Welsh wine

8 Which factor first threatened farmhouse cheese production in Britain?
   a cheaper cheese from France
   b mad cow disease
   c the railway system
   d mechanised farming

Reading

1 Read the passages to check your answers.

FCE Paper 1, Part 1

2 Read the passage again. Choose from the list A-I the sentence which best summarises each part (1-7) of the article. There is one extra sentence which you do not need to use. There is an example at the beginning (0).

A An old industry makes a comeback.

B It is better to eat some food in the place it comes from.

C One foreign dish is not exactly what it seems.

D This is the only English meal which is really worth eating.

E Britain is no longer top of the table.

F The oldest variety is still the most popular.

G Production is affected by changing weather patterns.

H The traditional form is now very rarely cooked at home.

I Choice of food is sometimes affected by nostalgia.

0 | F |

Although you can get a takeaway hamburger or pizza from one of the big chains, these are usually located near the centre of towns and cities. They are not convenient for those who want a quick meal at home. You can have pizza delivered, but it is generally eaten in restaurants. Instead, Kebab shops are smaller and are found where people live. Kebabs have become very popular with younger people. However, fish and chips is still the favourite takeaway, as it has been for over 100 years.

1 | |

Very few British people will go out to a restaurant to eat British food. The most popular restaurants in Britain are those selling foreign food. The nation's favourite 'Indian' dish, Chicken Tikka Masala, was actually invented in Britain when a diner asked for a sauce to go with his Chicken Tikka (small pieces of marinated, grilled chicken with rice). Back in the kitchen, the chef added some spices to a tin of tomato soup and a new dish was born. The evolution of food is nothing new — Chop Suey, the popular Chinese dish, originated in the United States.

2 | |

As you travel through Britain, you can still find regional varieties of food: the Cornish Pasty in Cornwall, Jellied Eels in the East End of London, Yorkshire Pudding, as the name suggests, in Yorkshire in the north of England and the Haggis in Scotland. Although mass-produced versions of these are now available in any supermarket nationwide, local people are better at cooking traditional local food.

Eating and Shopping

3 | |

Many British students live away from home and cook for themselves. Takeaway fish and chips are quite popular. Roast beef is associated with memories of Sunday lunch with parents. In fact, many students now cook it for their friends because they feel homesick. However, on a daily basis, rice and pasta dishes are more common. Most students can cook curry, but the most popular dish is probably Spaghetti Bolognese, colloquially known as *spag bol*. The version produced is unlikely to have much in common with anything cooked in Italy.

4 | |

The full English breakfast includes bacon, eggs, sausages, mushrooms, tomatoes and black pudding, at the very least. It is very high in calories and cholesterol. It is now mainly found in hotels, guest houses and cafés. Scottish porridge, which is made by cooking oatmeal, is a healthy way to start the day, as is a bowl of muesli, but today most people have cereal and perhaps toast.

5 | |

The first advertisement for tea appeared in 1658 and by 1700 tea was on sale at more than 500 London coffee houses. As tea became cheaper and cheaper, it replaced ale and gin as the everyday drink of ordinary people. However, more recently sales have fallen as people turn to coffee and to fruit or herbal teas. Ireland is currently the top tea-drinking country with 1184 cups drank per person per year. Turkey comes second, having recently overtaken Britain. Indian consumption is close to the British level and is likely to pass it in the next few years.

6 | |

Wine-making was probably introduced to England by the Romans, and continued into the Middle Ages. However, summers later became cooler and it was no longer possible to grow grapes. In recent years, as temperatures have risen again, wine-making has returned to the south of England and Wales, and some reasonable table wines are produced. Scotland is still too cold for growing grapes, but some fruit wines are produced. 'British wine' means wine made from imported grape juice, which is lower in price, and in quality.

7 | |

Very good local cheeses have always been made in Britain, with many valleys in the countryside producing their own distinct varieties. But by the middle of the 19th century, Britain's railway network meant that it was more profitable to send milk into the cities than to make cheese on the farm. Then, during the Second World War, a new law gave farmers no alternative and locally-made cheese almost died out completely. However, in the past few years there has been a revival and more varieties are available once again.

Vocabulary

Food and cooking

1 Work with other students. Complete the mindmap below with as many words as you can.

fruit	vegetables

TYPES OF FOOD

meat	fish

2 Match the verbs for preparing food to the pictures.

1	to pour	6	to chop
2	to carve	7	to drain
3	to dress	8	to stir
4	to peel	9	to slice
5	to season/sprinkle	10	to grate

3 Work with another student. Discuss which ingredients you need to make a:

1 Spanish omelette   4 Spaghetti alla carbonara
2 Fruit salad   5 Hamburger
3 Roast lunch

4 Which verbs from question 2 could you use with the types of food below.

1	beef	4	an onion	7	soup
2	flour	5	bread	8	tomatoes
3	an apple	6	cheese	9	cream

5 Match the verbs for cooking with the pictures.

1 to fry

2 to boil

3 to simmer

4 to bake

5 to grill

6 to steam

7 to roast

Speaking

FCE Paper 5, Parts 1/4

❶ Interview three other students about their eating habits. Make notes so you can report your findings to the rest of the class.

Survey of students' eating habits

1 Who does the cooking in your house?
2 What do you eat for breakfast?
3 Which kinds of fruit do you like the most?
4 Which vegetables are the most boring?
5 Which kind of food could you live without?
6 What do you eat every day, once a month, twice a year?

7 Do you live to eat or eat to live?
8 What would you cook for friends if they came for dinner?
9 What is the strangest thing you have ever eaten?
10 How do you cook your favourite meal?

❷ This evening some friends are coming to dinner. Work with the other students in your group and decide what you are going to cook for them. Write out a menu. Remember you are students, you don't have too much money to spend!

❸ Your group has gone on holiday together to … (decide on the location). You are all hungry. In front of you there is an American restaurant, an Italian restaurant, a Thai restaurant and a Greek restaurant. Explain to the other students where you would like to eat and persuade them to come with you.

Listening

❶ Discuss the questions with another student.

1 Do you prefer eating at home or going out to restaurants?
2 What do you eat when you go out to a restaurant?
3 What kind of foreign food and drink have you tried?

FCE Paper 4, Part 3

🎧14 ❷ You will hear five people talking about food and restaurants. For questions 1-5, choose which of the opinions (A-F) each speaker expresses. Use the letters only once. There is one extra letter which you do not need to use.

Speaker

A I sometimes eat when I don't really need to. ☐ 1
B I try to find authentic foreign food. ☐ 2
C I think restaurants don't give value for money. ☐ 3
D When I go out to eat my choices are limited.
E The type of restaurant I like is improving. ☐ 4
F Restaurants don't sell the kind of food I used to eat. ☐ 5

Vocabulary

Adjectives for taste

1 Answer the questions about the adjectives of taste. Then compare your answers with another student.

1 The opposite of *sour* is ....
2 Does *bitter* mean *very sour* or *very sweet*?
3 The opposite of *ripe* is ....
4 Is *overripe* positive or negative?
5 Is Indian food quite *spicy* or *salty*?
6 Write these adjectives on the scale:
tasteless/tasty/bland/delicious
NO TASTE ....>..........................>
.................>........................> A LOT OF TASTE
7 Place these adjectives on the scale:
overcooked/cooked/raw/undercooked/rare
NOT COOKED ....>................>...........
.................> .... COOKED TOO MUCH
8 *Fresh* is a positive adjective to describe food which is ready to eat. *Stale, off, rancid, mouldy, rotten* are all adjectives to describe food which is bad. Which one would you use to describe the following?
.... bread   .... cheese
.... vegetables   .... butter
.... meat   the milk is ....
9 Are vegetables that are overcooked *crisp* or *soggy*?
10 Which water has gas in it, *fizzy* or *still*?

2 Work with another student. Ask them the questions below.

Student A
1 Can you peel bananas?
2 Does water simmer?
3 Is broccoli fattening?
4 Is an aubergine a vegetable?
5 Can you carve water?
6 Would you eat rancid cream?
7 Can milk be grated?
8 Do raspberries taste salty?

Student B
1 Can you peel strawberries?
2 Can you carve meat?
3 Can you slice lettuce?
4 Does fizzy water have a different taste to still water?
5 What happens when you chop onions?
6 Do you like eating stale cake?
7 What do you have to do with frozen prawns?
8 Do you like raw vegetables?

Grammar

Verbs followed by verb+ -ing or infinitive?

1 Some verbs are followed by verb+ -*ing*. Others are followed by an infinitive with or without *to*. For each sentence, decide if the verb in brackets should be an -*ing* form or an infinitive. Compare your answers with another student.

1 I don't dislike (*go*) to restaurants — but they're so expensive.
2 Did you mention (*have*) a meal together on Saturday?
3 If he's going to leave home he'll need (*learn*) to cook for himself.
4 I've avoided (*eat*) shellfish since I got sick about a year ago.
5 Why did you choose (*come*) to this place? The food's awful.
6 I didn't agree (*do*) all the washing up on my own.
7 When I finish (*shop*) I'm going to have a coffee.
8 Don't expect (*live*) long if you eat what Callum cooks.
9 Why does Kieran keep (*talk*) about food all the time?
10 James says that he enjoys (*cook*) more than his girlfriend does.
11 I hope (*find*) some unusual fish in the market today.
12 Could you ask Nathan (*pay*) his share of the bill?

2 There are some verbs which can be followed by verb+ -*ing* or an infinitive and the meaning of the sentence changes (C). Other verbs can be followed by verb+ -*ing* or an infinitive and the meaning of the sentence doesn't change (DC). With other students, decide if there is a change in meaning in the pairs of sentences below.

		C	DC
1a Chloe *started peeling* the apple.			
b Chloe *started to peel* the apple.		☐	☐
2a Georgia *went on working* in McDonald's.			
b Georgia *went on to work* in McDonald's.		☐	☐
3a Does he *like drinking* wine in the evening?			
b Does he *like to drink* wine in the evening?		☐	☐
4a I'd *prefer having* dinner later.			
b I'd *prefer to have* dinner later.		☐	☐
5a I'd *forgotten eating* lunch.			
b I'd *forgotten to eat* lunch.		☐	☐
6a She *tried losing* weight last year.			
b She *tried to lose* weight last year.		☐	☐

3 What is the difference in meaning?

4 Now look at these situations. Each verb has a different meaning depending on whether it is followed by verb + *-ing* or an infinitive. Choose the correct form in each case. Compare your answers with another student.

1a We forgot to get coffee in the supermarket so we stopped *buying/to buy* some on the way home.

b The doctor said she was too nervous so she stopped *buying/to buy* coffee.

2a Mum said I was sleepwalking last night. I walked into the kitchen to look for biscuits — but I don't remember *doing/to do* it.

b Mum asks me to buy some milk on the way home from school but I don't always remember *doing/to do* it.

3a Jake regrets *telling/to tell* Megan that her party was boring. She hasn't spoken to him since.

b I regret *telling/to tell* you that we have run out of pasta. We'll have to eat rice tonight.

4a I didn't mean *finishing/to finish* the chocolate cake but somehow it just disappeared.

b I'd like a curry but not if it means *walking/to walk* halfway across town.

5a I want to keep my weight under control so I like *running/to run* at the weekend.

b I like *running/to run* round the park before breakfast. Everything's so clean and fresh.

5 With other students, look at the four groups of verbs opposite, and write one of the four descriptions A-D in each box.

A Verbs which can only be followed by verb+ *-ing*.

B Verbs which can only be followed by the infinitive.

C Verbs which can be followed by either with a difference in meaning.

D Verbs which can be followed by either with no difference in meaning.

☐	☐	☐	☐
forget	avoid	agree	begin
go on	enjoy	ask	continue
like	finish	choose	hate
mean	give up	expect	intend
regret	keep	hope	attempt
remember	dislike	learn	love
stop	mention	refuse	prefer
try	miss	want	start

Turn to page 172 of the Grammar File for more information.

Vocabulary

Phrasal verbs/expressions with *put*

1 Choose the best definition to replace the phrasal verb in each sentence.

1 They want to put up the price of bread because it's too cheap.
   a increase
   b decrease

2 I didn't go to the concert because I was put off by the bad reviews.
   a discouraged
   b encouraged

3 Put yourself in my position. How would you feel if she never answered your e-mails?
   a imagine you are me
   b think about it

4 They're going to put the meeting off because everyone is away at the moment.
   a postpone the meeting
   b hold the meeting

5 She sent all her reports on time because she didn't want to put her colleagues out.
   a help her friends
   b inconvenience her friends

6 The fireman are finding it very difficult to put out the fire.
   a extinguish
   b control

7 You put your foot in it when you asked who wanted roast beef — they're all vegetarians.
   a said the right thing
   b said the wrong thing

8 Don't worry if the cake went wrong. Angela will put it right — she's a good cook.
   a fix
   b find

9 Could you put me through to the manager, please.
   a connect me
   b direct me

10 I can put you up for the night. I've got lots of space.
   a direct you to a hotel
   b give you a bed

11 I don't know how you put up with her behaviour. She's so rude and lazy.
   a accept
   b tolerate

12 I've put on so much weight since Christmas.
   a increased in weight
   b decreased in weight

2 Read each sentence below and decide if the phrasal verb is correct or incorrect. Correct the ones which are wrong. Then compare your answers with another student.

1 It took a long time for them to put off the fire.

2 I always put my foot in it when I'm nervous.

3 You shouldn't put on with her rudeness. Tell her how you feel.

4 I put in a lot of weight last year but I've lost it all now.

5 They put off the concert because the singer was ill.

6 They put up me when I visited them last year.

Use of English

1 You are going to read an article about buying clothes. Look at the title first and discuss what you think the article is about with another student.

FCE Paper 3, Part 1

2 For questions 1-15, read the text below and decide which answer (A, B, C or D) best fits each space. There is an example at the beginning (0).

0 A fast   **B** quick   **C** speedy   **D** sudden

One size fits all in McFashion

Our high streets are full of the same shops selling the same cheap fashion – the clothing version of McDonald's.

Fashion has begun to resemble (**0**).**A**. food: convenient, disposable, entertaining and much the (**1**)..... everywhere. Just as we can enter a McDonald's in London or Munich and order an identical meal, we can enter a Gap store in (**2**)..... cities and buy the same shirt. Just as McDonald's golden arches have become a (**3**)..... symbol, so too has Gap's simple blue sign.

Nearly every major retail chain today (**4**)..... McFashion. They may not carry exactly the same items, but they convey essentially the same (**5**).....: wear our clothes and you'll (**6**)..... in. McFashion is bland and down market, but it's also affordable and abundant. It lets us be part of certain social (**7**)....., but sometimes to the point at (**8**)..... our individuality disappears. McFashion (**9**)..... our wallets and leaves us little to hold on to in the long (**10**)..... .

McFashion, like its food (**11**)....., depends on speed. One of the realities of fashion is that we are easily taken in by a new trend, then (**12**)..... of it and begin to despise it. So we're stuck in an endless cycle, hurrying to be (**13**)..... . To make matters worse, the giant wheel of style continues to (**14**)....., so we grow weary of trends much faster than we (**15**)..... to.

	A	B	C	D
1	same	similar	better	alike
2	each	all	both	two
3	known	familiar	household	conventional
4	signifies	indicates	sells	shows
5	notice	theme	saying	message
6	fit	come	set	look
7	classes	groups	crowds	companies
8	when	which	where	that
9	pumps	lightens	draws	drops
10	life	day	run	time
11	equivalent	equal	parallel	twin
12	reject	exhaust	refuse	tire
13	cool	right	fashion	social
14	speed	turn	accelerate	spin
15	ought	used	want	have

3 Now read the information.

Big players in the high street

 Founded in Italy by Luciano, Guiliana, Gilberto and Carlo Benetton in 1965, the company has 5,000 stores in 120 countries around the world.

 Founded in San Francisco in 1969 by Donald and Doris Fisher, the company now has 4,250 stores worldwide.

 Established in Sweden in 1945, there are 840 stores in 17 countries, with another 110 due to open this year.

ZARA Owned by the Inditex group, the first store was opened in Spain in 1975 - there are now 1,228 stores in 44 countries.

4 Discuss the questions below with other students. Tell the others about your shopping habits and see if you can agree on what you think will happen in the future.

1 Do you have a favourite shop where you buy your clothes, or do you prefer to shop around?

2 Do you prefer chain stores or small local shops?

3 What are your favourite clothes?

4 Do you buy clothes because you like them or to fit in with a particular group?

5 What do you think the fashion of the future will be like?

6 Do you think that one day everyone will dress in a similar way?

Grammar

Expressing preferences

1 Put one of the words or phrases below into each space to make ways of expressing likes and dislikes or a preference.

have	keen	love	mind	stand	to have

1 I can't ....

2 I don't ....

3 I'd prefer ....

4 I'm not ....

5 I really ....

6 I'd rather ....

2 Now read the two conversations below.

A Which **would** you **prefer** — beef or lamb?

I'd **prefer** lamb.

Which **would** you **rather have** — beef or lamb?

I'd **prefer to have** lamb.
I'd **rather have** lamb.

B Which **do** you **prefer** — beef or lamb.

I **prefer** beef.

Theory Box

Expressing preferences

Question **A** is a specific question, the kind you **would** ask in a restaurant. You ask with **would** and answer with **would** or **'d**. Question **B** is a general question, the kind you can ask at any time. You ask and answer in the Present Simple. Of course, you could answer:

*I don't know — I like **both** of them.*
*I don't like **either** of them.*
*I don't know — **neither** of them is very appealing.*

And if there are three choices:

C Which **would** you **prefer** — beef, lamb or chicken?
Which **would** you **rather have** — beef, lamb or chicken?

*I don't know — I like **all** of them.*
*I don't like **any** of them.*
*I don't know — **none** of them really interests me.*

Note that **neither** and **none** are singular.

3 Work with other students. Imagine you are going for a meal at the restaurant below. Discuss what you'd prefer to have and get ready to order your meal.

EAT THE WORLD RESTAURANT

Menu

Starters
Chinese crab and sweet corn soup
French duck liver pate
Swedish smoked herring
Greek feta cheese in vine leaves

Main courses
Mexican chilli con carne with rice
Indian lamb curry with rice
Turkish aubergine with onion and tomato filling
Italian wild boar with polenta
Spanish seafood paella
Chinese crispy duck with pancakes

Sweets
American sticky toffee pudding with cream
English trifle
Austrian apple strudel with cream
Selection of cheese from many countries

Writing

FCE Paper 2, Part 1

❶ Your class is planning a celebration meal and you have to choose a restaurant. You see an advert for one which is different and decide to find out more. You phone the manager but the restaurant is so noisy, she suggests that you write an e-mail. Read the advert below and the notes you have made. Using this information and your own ideas, write an e-mail of 120-180 words to the manager covering all these points.

❷ But first think of ways to ask for information. In the letter, you need to be polite and formal. Some of the expressions below are appropriate for that style of letter. Others are not, because of the degree of politeness, the level of formality or grammatical correctness. With another student, see if you can separate them into two groups. Write 1-10 in one of the boxes below.

1   I wonder if you could let me know...
2   You have to inform me...
3   I'd also like to know...
4   I'd be grateful if you would tell me...
5   I really need to know...
6   Could you please tell me...?
7   It would be helpful if you could tell me...
8   It is necessary that you let me know...
9   I also wonder if it would be possible...
10 I'd also like to know...

appropriate	inappropriate

Hadleigh's Canal Boat Restaurant

Ship Inn Quay
tel: 05847 129865

How long?

Could they squeeze in 22?

- Experience a scenic cruise through glorious countryside while you enjoy our wonderful boat-cooked food.
- The *Catherine*, our traditional narrow boat, can seat up to 20 people in 5 tables of 4.

Ask for samples and prices

- Public cruises at weekends throughout the year. Private parties also catered for.

Which evenings?

- Our party menus suit all tastes and most pockets.
- Live musical entertainment on Saturday evening cruises (available to parties by request).

What kind of music?

Vocabulary

Confusing words *rise/raise*

❶ Read these sentences and decide which verb can be followed by an object and which one cannot.

1   The sun rises in the east.
2   I raised my hand to ask a question.
3   I hope they raise our salaries next year.
4   Taxi fares rose by 1% last year.

❷ Write the number of the sentence from question 1 next to the correct definition. Then complete the table with the correct forms of the verbs.

Infinitive	-*ing* form	Past Simple	past participle	definition	example sentence
to rise				to move in an upwards direction to increase	
to raise				to move something in an upwards direction to increase	

❸ Complete each sentence with the correct form of *raise* or *rise*. Then compare your answers with another student.

1   I'm going to .... the problem with my manager next week.
2   Ssh. He's .... to make a speech.
3   The temperature .... during the day because it was so hot.
4   The team .... the cup after winning the final match.
5   The price of petrol has .... three times this year so far.

❹ Write answers to the questions using the correct form of *rise* or *raise*.

1   What can you do if you want to ask a question in a meeting?
2   What does the moon do every evening?
3   What happens when inflation gets higher?
4   What does a cake do when you bake it in the oven?
5   What can companies do to pay their employees more?
6   What does a farmer do with his animals?

Confusing words *lie/lay/lie*

5 Look at the three pictures. Match the two parts of each sentence. Write the number of the completed sentences under the correct picture.

1	He lied	a	on the bed and went to sleep.
2	He lay	b	his clothes on the bed.
3	He laid	c	when he said his name was John.

6 Write the number of the sentence from question 5 next to the correct definition. Then complete the table with the correct forms of the verbs.

Infinitive	-ing form	Past Simple	past participle	definition	example sentence
to lie				to say something which is not true	
to lie				to put your body in a horizontal position	
to lay				to put something in a horizontal position	

7 Read each sentence below and decide if the verb is correct or incorrect. Correct the ones which are used incorrectly. Then compare your answers with another student.

1 He's been *laying* about his age for years.
2 I like *laying* on the beach and doing nothing.
3 She *lay* the table for six people for dinner.
4 The ship has *laid* at the bottom of the bay since it sank.
5 He *lied* when he said that he was working this afternoon.
6 We *lay* on the floor and watched TV all afternoon.

8 Complete the sentences with the correct form of the verbs *lie*, *lay* or *lie*. Then compare your answers with another student.

1 You don't look very well. Why don't you .... down on the couch?
2 She .... to him when she said she couldn't go to the cinema.
3 I .... on the floor listening to music when the phone rang.
4 They .... the baby in the bath.
5 I .... the newspaper on the table and we read the headlines.
6 Don't .... on the grass — it's wet.
7 She got off her motorbike and .... her helmet on the wall.
8 Those stones .... on that site for centuries.
9 He .... down on the grass staring at the clouds.
10 They were .... the table for dinner when I got there.

9 Match the three sentences.

She lay	about the meal	on the table.
She laid	all the food	and ate her ice cream.
She lied	on the sofa	being good. It was disgusting.

1 ....
2 ....
3 ....

UNIT 12
Global Warming

Speaking

FCE Paper 5, Part 4

1 Read the facts about the environment.

The amount of carbon dioxide in the atmosphere is increasing.

Global temperatures are rising and so are sea-levels.

Heatwaves, storms and flooding are becoming more common and more extreme.

The Polar ice caps are melting.

Malaria-carrying mosquitoes are spreading north and south from the tropics.

Some species of plants and animals can't adapt and are declining.

2 Decide which of these points of view you agree with. Think of evidence to support your ideas.

- [ ] The world has always gone through warmer and colder periods. At the moment we are just entering a warmer period. Global warming is part of a natural cycle.

- [ ] Global temperatures have never risen as fast as this before. The Polar ice caps are melting. We've never had such unpredictable weather patterns. The reason is pollution.

3 Work with another student who has a different point of view. Listen to their ideas and explain your own. Below there is a language box of phrases to use when discussing opinions.

> **Language Box**
>
> **Agreeing**
> *I completely agree...*
> *That's right/true...*
>
> **Partial agreement/disagreement**
> *That's a good idea but...*
> *I don't completely agree...*
>
> **Disagreeing**
> *I'm sorry, I don't agree with you...*
> *That's wrong/not right/true...*
>
> **Asking for confirmation/clarification**
> *Are you sure?*
> *Do you really think so?*

Reading

FCE Paper 1, Part 3

① You are going to read a report which gives two different views of global warming. Eight sentences have been removed. Choose from the sentences A-I the one which fits each gap (1-7). There is one extra sentence which you do not need to use. There is an example at the beginning (0).

Is global warming occurring?

Throughout history, major changes in temperature occurred at a rate of a few degrees over thousands of years. Man-made global warming is occurring much faster. **(0)...I...** .
Some regions have warmed by as much as 3°C. Scientists predict **that** in the next fifty years global warming will raise the average temperature by 1.5 to 6 °C.

ACCU-Weather, the world's leading commercial weather forecaster, states **that** global temperatures have shown an increase of about 0.45°C over the past century.
(1)........ . Interestingly, as the computer climate models have improved in recent years, the predicted increase in temperature has been lowered.

Are humans causing the climate to change?

The rapid build-up of atmospheric gases from coal, oil and gas is the source of the problem. We have increased levels of carbon dioxide, the primary global warming gas, in our atmosphere by 30% in the past 100 years. Scientists are already finding **that** the number and intensity of heatwaves, storms and flooding is increasing. **(2)........** . More than 36,000 km² of Antarctic ice have broken off and melted since 1995.

98% of total global greenhouse gas emissions are natural (mostly water vapour). **(3).........** . Although the climate has warmed slightly in the last 100 years, 70% of **that** warming occurred before 1940. **(4)........** . Many scientists feel **that** a slight rise in global temperature is not likely to lead to a massive melting of the earth's ice caps.

What are the consequences?

Plants and animals around the world are moving to new habitats in order to escape a changing climate. **(5)........** . Scientists project **that** as warmer temperatures spread north and south from the tropics, malaria-carrying mosquitoes will spread with them. **(6)........** .

Larger quantities of CO₂ in the atmosphere and warmer climates would lead to an increase in vegetation. **(7)........** . Experts believe **that** the spread of diseases is more linked to rapid urbanization, increased drug resistance, higher mobility through air travel and lack of insect-control programmes.

A This was before the great increase in greenhouse gas emissions from industrial processes.

B There has also been a rise in sea level of 10 to 25 cm in the past century.

C We can slow down and eventually stop global warming, but we must act today.

D They conclude *that* global warming will put as much as 65% of the world's population at risk — an increase of 20%.

E This may simply be due to normal climatic variation.

F Only 2% are from man-made sources.

G During warm periods in history vegetation flourished, at one point allowing the Vikings to farm in Greenland.

H Those *that* can't adapt to new condition go into decline. This is the case with many today.

I The average temperature of the planet has risen by about 0.5 °C in the last 100 years.

The environment

1 Which of the words in the box are the results (R) of global warming and which are the causes (C)?

carbon dioxide emissions   CS sprays
destruction of the rainforests   exhaust fumes
extinction of animal species   flooding
greenhouse effect   heatwaves
holes in the ozone layer   jet engines
pesticides   pollution   rising sea levels   storms

Global warming	
causes	results

2 Do the quiz to find out who is the most environmentally friendly student. Compare your answers with other students.

Always (**A**) Often (**O**) Sometimes (**S**) Never (**N**)

Do you: A O S N

1 separate your rubbish into metal, paper, plastic, bottles?
2 take your metal, paper, plastic and bottles to the recycling bins?
3 use CS sprays?
4 eat organic food?
5 use public transport?
6 ride a bike to get to school or work?
7 share car journeys with friends and family?
8 buy 'green' products?
9 take your holidays near home?
10 use solar/wind power?

Word transformation

1 Complete the table with the definitions.

1 the opposite of interested
2 when you want something to eat
3 when you want something to drink
4 when you know a lot about a subject
5 when you say one thing but think the opposite
6 the opposite of weak
7 the opposite of brave
8 the opposite of low
9 when you have good sense and judgement
10 when you are good at getting people to agree with each other

adjective	noun	definition
strong		
	wisdom	
bored/boring		
	hunger	
thirsty		
expert		
	diplomacy	
	hypocrisy	
cowardly		
high		

2 Write the missing words in the table. Compare your answers with another student.

3 Complete each sentence with the appropriate word from the table above.

1 I must have a drink — I'm so ....
2 We can't do this ourselves. We need the .... of a computer engineer.
3 They're both the same .... — 1m 80, I think.
4 The old woman was famous for her .... and people often asked her for advice.
5 I'm not very .... I always say the wrong thing at the wrong time.
6 He's so .... He says he likes the Strokes because I like them, but he doesn't really.
7 The girl showed no .... when she saved her brother. She was very brave.
8 You must eat more to build up your .... after your long illness.
9 I'm so .... — just give me something to eat.
10 School holidays can be very .... for children if they don't have anything to do.

Grammar

that clauses

1 There are nine examples of *that* in the reports on p. 123. Discuss the following questions with another student.

1 Which one could be replaced by *this* or *the*?
2 Which one could be replaced by *which*?
3 What type of word comes before all the other examples?

2 *That* is used to connect a verb to the rest of the sentence. But it only works after certain verbs. Read the sentences with *that* below. Decide which *five* sentences are incorrect. Compare your answer with another student.

1 Some scientists predict that global warming will continue.
2 If people go on that we live in this way, the planet may die.
3 They have found that the amount of severe weather is increasing.
4 In spite of the warnings we continue that we produce huge amounts of pollution.
5 Most experts conclude that the increase in malaria is due to global warming.
6 Others believe that there are many reasons for the spread of diseases.
7 Many people like that they have a lifestyle which consumes a lot of energy.
8 Some organisations advise that we should make more use of alternative energy.
9 Some feel that a slight increase in temperature is not important.
10 Experts want that we reduce the amount of carbon dioxide we produce.

3 Now read about clauses on pages 172-3 and rewrite the incorrect sentences. Note that some of the verbs will need a pronoun to explain who or what should do something.

Theory Box

that clauses

Some verbs can be followed by a clause beginning with *that*. Look at these two groups. The verbs are taken from the sentences above:

that clause **possible**	*that* clause **not possible**
believe	*advise*
conclude	*continue*
feel	*go on*
find	*like*
predict	*want*

How are the two groups different? We can say that the verbs on the left are to do with **reporting** what we have **discovered** or what we **feel**. They are also verbs which can be followed by a **subject** + **verb clause**. However, that doesn't explain why *advise* is on the right. We have to say:

  *I advise you **to do** it.*

Though it is possible to say:

  *I recommend **that** you do it.*

This is only a guide, not a rule. You really have to find out what each verb can do.

Vocabulary

Weather 1

1 Look at the different types of weather in the box and complete the mindmap. You can check the meanings of these words in a dictionary.

  breeze cyclone downpour drizzle fog
  gale hail mist shower sleet snow

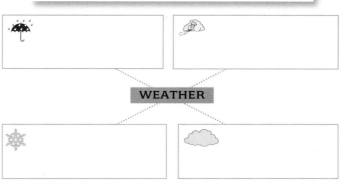

2 Which are the worst types of weather in each group? Which of the nouns in question 1 can you make into adjectives?

3 Complete the sentences with the best noun. Compare your answers with another student.

1 We've had lots of quick .... today. I got really wet each time.
2 I couldn't see when I was driving last night because of the thick ....
3 Quite a few trees came down last night in the ....
4 I don't think that's rain. I can hear it on the window. I think it's ....
5 It's not raining much — there's just a little bit of ....
6 The .... was very heavy and some rain got into the car.
7 Did you see that .... on the TV last night? It destroyed a town.
8 The .... is really bad today, it's difficult to breathe.

UNIT 12

Use of English

FCE Paper 3, Part 2

1 For questions 1-15 read the text below and think of the word which best fits each space. Use only one word in each space. There is an example at the beginning (0).

Tectonic Plates

The surface of the Earth is not continuous (0)...but... is broken into seven large pieces and a number of smaller ones. These are called plates and they are (1)......... moving in different directions and (2)....... different speeds (from 2 cm to 10 cm per year – about the speed at which your fingernails grow) in relation to (3)....... other. This means that they (4)......... crash together, pull apart or slide (5)......... their edges.

The place where the two plates meet is called a plate boundary and it is (6)......... that volcanoes and earthquakes occur.

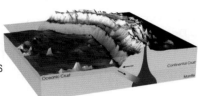

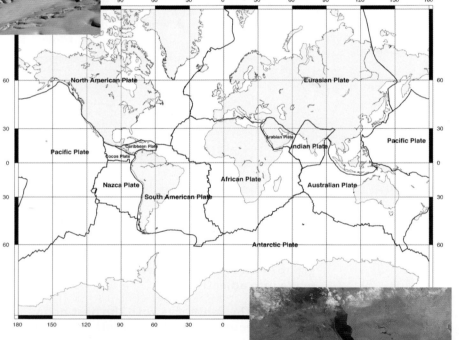

Where plates collide, mountains are formed. Examples of (7)....... are the Alps, the Rockies, the Andes and the Himalayas. (8)......... places where they are moving apart, the land between them drops down to form a wide valley (9)....... as the Rift Valley in East Africa and the Rio Grande in New Mexico. With the third type of boundary, where plates slide past each other, there are no spectacular geographical features (10)......... these areas can be just (11)......... unstable. Perhaps the most famous boundary (12)......... this type is the San Andreas fault in California. (13)......... Los Angeles is located on a different plate to the rest of North America, it is actually moving towards San Francisco (14)......... about 6 centimetres per year. It should arrive in the southern suburbs (15)......... about ten million years' time.

Listening

1 Look at the dangerous situations at the top of p. 127. What's the best thing to do if any of these things happen to you? Discuss your ideas with other students.

FCE Paper 4, Part 4

15 2 You will hear part of a talk about surviving dangerous situations. For questions 1-7, decide which of the statements are TRUE and which are FALSE. Write T for TRUE or F for FALSE in the boxes provided.

		T	F
1	You should try to hit a shark on the nose.	☐	☐
2	To avoid sharks, it's safer to go swimming in daylight.	☐	☐
3	When a car falls into water, wait till it reaches the bottom before trying to get out.	☐	☐
4	When a car is sinking, keep the car's windows closed as long as possible.	☐	☐
5	When a car is underwater, only wait inside the car if you can't open the windows.	☐	☐
6	Break down a door in the same way you see in films.	☐	☐
7	Tools can be useful for forcing a door lock open.	☐	☐

3 Work with another student. Have you ever been in any dangerous situations like these? Discuss your experiences.

Grammar

allow/permit/let

1 These words are similar in meaning. *Allow* and *permit* also have similar grammar, but *permit* is more formal. *Let* is the least formal of all three. Complete each sentence with *allow*, *permit* or *let*. Sometimes more than one is possible.

1 Please .... Samuel in — he's lost his key.
2 This school doesn't .... mobile phones in the classroom.
3 .... me get a chair for you.
4 People are not .... to swim here.
5 It is not .... to drive in this street.
6 They don't .... you to park here
7 My parents won't .... me stay out too late.
8 Will you .... me to buy you a drink?
9 Smoking isn't .... in bars in this city.

2 Write either *allow*, *let* or *permit* in each space.

1

	noun/pronoun +	*adverb*
	Alan/him	out.
	noun/pronoun +	*verb*
They won't	Alan/him	leave.
	noun/pronoun +	*verb + adverb*
	Alan/him	go out.

2

	pronoun	
	it.	
	gerund	
	smoking.	
They won't	*noun/pronoun* +	*infinitive*
	Alan/him	to go.
	noun/pronoun +	*infinitive + adverb*
	Alan/him	to go out.

3

	pronoun	
	it.	
	gerund	
	smoking.	
They won't	*noun/pronoun* +	*adverb*
	Alan/him	out.
	noun/pronoun +	*infinitive*
	Alan/him	to leave.
	noun/pronoun +	*infinitive + adverb*
	Alan/him	to go out.

4 They aren't .... to swim there — it's dangerous.
5 Are we .... to use dictionaries in the exam?

3 Imagine you are the ruler of your country. Think of six things you would allow or not allow. Write your laws and discuss them with the others in the group. Remember to use *allow*, *permit* or *let*.

1 What can you see in the two pictures? How are they similar? How are they different? Compare your ideas with another student.

2 Look at the article which accompanied the photos. What do you think the news report is about? Compare your ideas with another student.

3 Read the article. Did you guess correctly?

Despite frequent weather warnings, London was caught by surprise when 10 centimetres of snow fell in two hours this morning. Many Londoners tried to get to work, although they were asked to stay at home. In spite of the weather forecast, none of the roads had been gritted and there were thousands of minor accidents. The situation was very similar to the one almost two years ago. Londoners were quick to contrast their situation with Switzerland where the same amount of snow fell in Zurich. However, the situation there was completely different. While people struggled to get out of their houses in London, the Swiss made it to work on time. The Swiss services are much better prepared for severe weather conditions than the British ones, which is hardly surprising considering that they live with such conditions for much of the winter.

4 Read the passage again. Underline the expressions that are used to talk about contrast, similarities or differences. Write them in the appropriate column.

contrast	similarities	differences

5 Now write these expressions in the correct column. Compare your answers with another student.

> are exactly the same   one similarity is
> slightly different   the main difference
> they both show   whereas

6 Work with another student. Choose two pictures each to compare and contrast. Make sure you answer these questions when you talk about your pictures:

1 What do the pictures show? What's the linking theme?
2 What are the similarities and differences?
3 Remember to personalise what you say, tell your partner where you would prefer to go, which situation looks the most dangerous or the most fun, etc.

Vocabulary

Phrasal verbs/expressions with *bring*

1 Choose the best word to complete each sentence.

1 I need to bring the subject *up/on* at the next environmental meeting.
2 They're going to bring the meeting *up/forward* by a week.

3   The demonstration for clean water will bring *down/out* the military government.

4   I think we should bring this discussion *to a close/ to an ending* now and go on to the next point.

5   I'll bring it to his *view/attention* when I speak to him this afternoon.

6   It brought *in/back* memories of my childhood when I saw the photos of my family.

7   They're going to bring *up/in* a new law to control the level of petrol emissions from cars.

8   Her day job didn't bring *in/back* enough money and she had to work in the evenings too.

9   They're going to bring *out/in* another book on the greenhouse effect next year.

10 A lot of people want to bring *in/back* capital punishment because they think it will reduce the number of serious crimes.

2 Write the appropriate phrasal verb/expression next to the correct definition. Compare your answers with another student.

1   to introduce something ....

2   to mention something to someone ....

3   to make someone aware of something ....
....

4   to end something ....

5   to make a government lose its power ....
....

6   to remind someone ....

7   to reintroduce ....

8   to move an appointment etc. to an earlier time
....

9   to publish, to introduce for sale ....

10 to earn money ....

Grammar

Verbs and prepositions

1 Write one preposition from the box on each line below. Then choose the best way, a or b, to finish the sentence. Some prepositions can be used more than once. Compare your ideas with another student.

| about at for in on to with |

1   I don't agree ....   a   the important things
    Jade and I agree ....   but we still have rows.
                               b   using up the world's
                                   resources in this way.

2   Your shoes belong ....   a   so many environmental
    She belongs ....   groups that I've lost
                                   count.
                               b   the cupboard — not all
                                   over the floor.

3   Someone hit him ....   a   the nose right at the
    Don't hit a door ....   start of the match.
                               b   your shoulder — use
                                   your foot instead.

4   They laughed ....   a   his ideas for years,
    We can laugh ....   but they're accepted.
                               b   driving into the river
                                   now, but it was scary.

5   If you stop shouting .....   a   me I'll be able to
    We shouted ....   concentrate.
                               b   them to get out of the
                                   water.

6   Ryan threw the ball .... a   Ethan and he scored
    Luke threw the ball ....   inside a minute.
                               b   the referee and was
                                   sent off.

7   They need to work ....   a   his father since he left
    He's worked ....   school.
                               b   scientists to reduce
                                   pollution.

2 In two of the sentences, the preposition is followed by a verb. Which form of the verb is used?

Adjectives and prepositions

3 Fill each space in the sentences below with an appropriate adjective from the box. Then add a preposition. Use each preposition twice.

| accustomed   amazed   disappointed   impressed
    pleased   shocked
    similar   suspicious   terrified   useless |

| at   by   of   to   with |

1   Jessica's still .... how rude Charlie was to her mother.

2   You won't see me swimming here. I'm .... sharks.

3   I was .... how many e-mails I had when I got back from holiday.

4   I'm a bit .... this ticket. It says I've won a prize.

5   I don't know why they picked him — he's completely .... football.

6   Of course I'm .... the result but it was a boring game.

7   I spend most of the day in the swimming pool. I'm not .... heat like that.

8   We were all .... the way Sara handled such a difficult situation.

9   This is quite .... my old car so I find it easy to drive.

10 I was quite .... the film. I thought it would be funnier.

Writing

1 Read the leaflet below. With other students, discuss what you think can be done, either by governments or by individuals, to reduce pollution and create a cleaner world. Make a list of ten things you would recommend: five for ordinary people and five for the government.

Energy and pollution – some facts

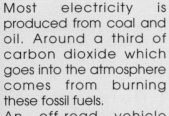
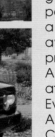

Most electricity is produced from coal and oil. Around a third of carbon dioxide which goes into the atmosphere comes from burning these fossil fuels.

An off-road vehicle produces 43% more global-warming pollutants and 47% more air pollution than the average car. A scooter produces less than either. A bicycle produces none at all.

Every year, drivers in Los Angeles and New York City waste over 2,700 million litres of petrol sitting in traffic – that's about 7.5 million tons of carbon dioxide in just those two cities.

Fluorescent bulbs last 10,000 hours longer than standard bulbs, and keep a lot of carbon dioxide out of the atmosphere during their lifetime.

Every year an area of rainforest the size of Italy is cut down.

This means that hundreds of millions of tons of carbon dioxide goes into the atmosphere, instead of being absorbed by the trees.

Forests are not cleared for their wood, but in order to keep cattle and grow coffee and rubber. Temperate forests are also being cut down. In Siberia alone, 25 million hectares are lost every year.

FCE Paper 2, Part 2

2 You have just attended a lecture where this leaflet was given out. Write a report which gives your opinion on the environment. Write your answer in 120-180 words in an appropriate style and use this title:

A cleaner world — the way forward

But first ...

1 Think of what kind of magazine you are writing for: general interest, student, environmental or...? Write a brief description here:

....

2 Now think of the readers. Are they students, people who are interested in the environment, the general public? Describe them here:

....

Remember these two ideas when you write your article. They will help you decide on the style to use.

Paragraph planning

Paragraph 1

You need an opening sentence. It needs to do these things:

a get the readers' attention.

b show what your article is going to be about.

When you write your article, you'll need to write two or three more sentences expanding on this point and connecting it to the next paragraph.

Paragraph 2

Now you need to give the readers some facts. Pick the major causes of pollution from the leaflet. Write them here, in your own words, 3 or 4 should be enough.

1 ....

2 ....

3 ....

4 ....

Later describe these in more detail.

Paragraph 3

Now you need to suggest solutions to these problems. Write them here:

1 ....

2 ....

3 ....

4 ....

Later you can expand on these.

Paragraph 4

You need to write a conclusion — but write your article first.

Vocabulary

Weather 2

① Work with another student. Discuss these questions.

1. Do you have four seasons in your country?
2. What's your favourite season?
3. Which types of weather are most common in the different seasons?
4. Which types of weather do you rarely or never have?
5. Which types of weather do you like?
6. Which types of weather do you dislike?
7. What kind of activities do you do in the different seasons?
8. What type of weather do you like when you go on holiday?

② Write the opposite of the weather words.

1. boiling ....
2. clear ....
3. gloomy ....
4. humid ....
5. chilly ....
6. dry ....
7. harsh ....
8. the same ....

③ Complete the conversation below with the opposite of the adjectives from question 2.

Angela: The weather here in Dubai is really hot, boiling in fact. What's it like in London?

Brian: Absolutely ¹................ . Yesterday was chilly but today the roads are all icy.

Angela: Really, it was ²................ here yesterday. And the sky was so clear.

Brian: The sky has been ³................ here for three days. It's so gloomy.

Angela: That's a shame because it's so ⁴................ here. And it never rains, so it's very ⁵................ .

Brian: Whereas it's quite ⁶................ here so I don't have to water the garden.

Angela: Well, I miss the rain. The weather here is always the same.

Brian: I wouldn't like that. It's so ⁷................ here. You never know what to expect. Although I don't like the winters. They're so harsh with all that snow.

Angela: I suppose so, the climate here is very ⁸................ but it's so boring!

④ Tick the adjective in each group which does not go with the noun.

1. gentle
    heavy
    torrential   rain
    strong
2. light
    strong
    high   wind
    low

3. light
    heavy   showers
    strong
    scattered
4. gentle
    warm   breeze
    strong
    light

⑤ Work with another student. Ask questions to get the following information.

Student A

1. Another word for a strong wind is a ....
2. A very heavy shower is a ....
3. The opposite of a heavy shower is a ....
4. The opposite of a warm breeze is a ....

Student B

5. Showers that happen from time to time during the day are called .... showers.
6. The opposite of light rain is .... rain.
7. If the rain is very heavy and there is a lot of it, it is .... rain.
8. Another word for light rain is ....

⑥ Match the extreme weather in the box to the picture.

1. blizzard
2. tornado
3. thunder and lightning
4. drought
5. typhoon
6. storm

1 Change the verbs in brackets into their correct form. Add _'ll/will_, _'d/would_ and _'ve/have_ where necessary.

1 If he .... (have) more sense, he wouldn't get involved.

2 If he .... (shout) at me I'll shout back.

3 She .... (look) better if her hair wasn't so short.

4 If he .... (move) quicker he would have scored.

5 If I knew more Swedish I .... (be) able to read this.

6 If Larry hears about this there .... (be) trouble.

7 I'd go out for a run if I .... (not feel) so bad

8 I'll have to speak to the manager if she .... (want) a discount.

9 I .... (recognise) him if he'd worn his normal clothes.

10 If you .... (go) to bed earlier you'd have slept better.

2 Put the two halves of each sentence together to makes types 1-3 conditionals.

1 If Charlie was here

2 Morag will let you see the letter

3 If I hadn't lost my temper

4 If Eric gets the job

5 I'd go on holiday

6 If he'd patented the idea

7 If you go into hospital,

8 We'd have got here earlier

9 If you whistle that tune again

10 If Kate had more sense

a he'd have been a rich man.

b it would never have happened.

c if I had more money.

d I'll hit you.

e he'd be able to help you.

f who'll look after the kids?

g she'd tell Alan to leave.

h if we hadn't missed the bus.

i he'll be a lot happier.

j if you ask her.

3 Write _provided that_ or _unless_ in each of the spaces below.

1 .... you look after it, this garment will last for years.

2 .... he apologises, I won't speak to him again.

3 He's going to have an accident .... he starts driving more carefully.

4 He'll be at home by now .... he's gone to the café.

5 We'll go walking .... the weather isn't really horrible.

6 .... you check it regularly, a smoke alarm is reliable.

7 We should still have some milk .... the kids have drunk it.

8 I'll talk to her on her mobile, ... she's got it switched on.

4 Write _if_ or _even if_ in the correct place in each of the incomplete sentences below.

1 the weather's beautiful, I'm not going out.

2 you want some food, help yourself to what's in the fridge.

3 I don't think we'd win half their team was injured.

4 I couldn't have helped I'd known about it earlier.

5 I mixed these two chemicals there would be an explosion.

6 It won't be any cheaper you book now.

5 In each sentence below, add either _to_ or _-ing_ to the verb in brackets. Remember that in some cases both are possible with no difference in meaning.

1 I hope .... (see) you again soon.

2 She doesn't enjoy .... (talk) about personal things.

3 Michael keeps .... (sing) odd bits of old songs.

4 I like .... (get) the car serviced every six months or so.

5 Did you remember .... (buy) some flowers for your mum?

6 It's a good idea but it means .... (find) some money.

7 We regret .... (tell) you that your appeal has been turned down.

8 I've agreed .... (work) the next three weekends.

9   Karen started .... (*watch*) the film after midnight.

10 Will she refuse .... (*do*) the extra work?

11 Does Cleo prefer .... (*eat*) late?

12 After he left IBM he went on .... (*start*) his own company.

13 Why did we choose .... (*go*) to that restaurant?

14 I try .... (*avoid*) offending people but I'll make an exception for him.

15 He was told to stop .... (*drink*) so much coffee.

6 Write *all, both, either, neither* or *none* in each of the spaces below.

1   .... David and Mo are Welsh.

2   We invited the Merton twins but .... of them could come.

3   She has a lot of friends and .... of them will be there.

4   .... of the present team is worth keeping.

5   .... of his six cousins live abroad now.

6   There are two roads. Take .... one — it doesn't matter which.

7   His parents .... grew up in Dublin.

8   .... he wants to do it or he doesn't. Which is it?

7 Write *about, at, for, in, on, to* or *with* in each of the spaces below.

1   Don't laugh .... him — he doesn't like it at all.

2   Ned's so awkward that I don't think I can work .... him.

3   That defender's a complete animal — he belongs .... a zoo.

4   Do you agree .... the rest of the committee about this?

5   I don't know whether to laugh .... this or cry.

6   The ball bounced off the wall and hit him .... the back of the head.

7   Just hold the dart like this and throw it .... the board.

8   Jake has been working .... this moment for years.

9   Throw that book over .... me, would you?

10 Somebody hit him .... a motorbike last week.

11 We agree .... the money but are still arguing over the details.

12 Who do these trainers belong ....?

8 Choose between the two prepositions in each of the sentences below.

1   He's terrified **by/of** losing his memory.

2   Jenny was shocked **about/by** his rudeness.

3   Larry's worried about the conference because he's useless **about/at** speaking.

4   I'm not accustomed **to/with** eating so early in the evening.

5   The police must be suspicious **of/with** that shop.

6   Though they're brothers, they're not similar **to/with** each other at all.

7   You'll be amazed **at/with** how much he's grown since you last saw him.

8   I wasn't at all impressed **about/by** how he handled the situation.

9   Are you pleased **of/with** your new house?

10 She's still a little nervous **about/by** the results.

9 Write *allow, let* or *permit* in each of the spaces below. Use passive forms where necessary.

1   They won't .... you to bring that into the country.

2   Would you .... me have a look at his notes?

3   This is a one-way street — you're not .... to drive this way.

4   If I can't pay for the meal at least .... me to buy the drinks.

5   The principal doesn't .... chewing gum in the school.

6   .... me give you some help here.

7   Her parents won't .... her to stay out after 11 o'clock.

8   Eating or drinking aren't .... in the library.

9   The doctor won't .... him out till he feels better.

UNIT 13
Free Time

Speaking

FCE Paper 5, Part 1

❶ **Work with other students and discuss these questions about the free time activities in the box.**

> chess computer games cycling dancing DIY gardening going out with friends hiking
> ice skating jogging keeping a pet keeping fit/going to the gym painting photography
> playing musical instruments skateboarding/rollerblading snooker/pool stamp collecting
> surfing the Internet swimming wind-surfing yoga

1 Which of these activities have you done?

2 Which of the activities would you like to try? Why?

3 Which of the activities do you think are boring? Why?

4 Which of the activities are old fashioned or uncool?

5 Do you know anyone who has an unusual hobby? What is it?

Writing

❶ **Work with another student and discuss this question.**

1 If you were forced to live without TV, would you miss it? What would you do?

❷ **Read this article, by Shwetha, who lives in the United Arab Emirates.**

Is There Life Without TV? Or A Real Life Horror Story

Life without television is impossible to imagine. Life without the television and the telephone as well is even worse. All because I stayed too long on the Internet and my mother said no television or Internet for two days. I couldn't believe it.
I didn't know how to survive. I went around the house not knowing what to do to. The boredom was killing me. I almost started to cry. The books in the house didn't interest me because I'd already read them. I didn't want to listen to music because I found it too depressing. My parents suggested various ways of passing the time, all of which were

ridiculous. Who could even think of *stamp collecting* or *playing chess* when you could be doing more interesting things? Then they suggested that I go for a walk. I told them that it was far too hot to go out.

Mum and Dad left the house in the evening. They said it was to do the shopping, but I knew better. They were tired of hearing me plead with them to lift my punishment. I couldn't switch the TV on once they were gone, because they'd removed the aerial.

So I sat at home, staring into space. I tried daydreaming, but didn't get very far. It wasn't that interesting. To make things worse, I was missing an episode of my favourite programme. That was so unfair.

3 Now, look at the items in the box. Tick (✓) the ones that you have, or have access to.

> TV   radio   video   computer
> computer with Internet connection
> cassette player   CD player   DVD player
> Playstation, GameCube or Xbox   mobile phone
> car   motor bike/scooter   bicycle

4 Choose the three that you would find it most difficult to live without. Discuss your preferences with other students.

5 Read this paragraph written by Bert Morton, an Englishman who grew up in the 1950s.

> **Nowadays** kids are surrounded by technology, but **when I was young** there was only the radio. We got a TV **later** but it was in black-and-white and there was only one channel. **At first** they had a different programme for kids every afternoon and as I remember they were rubbish.
> So what did we do the rest of the time? I read books – mainly boys' adventure stories **at that time**. And tons of comics too – not the magazines kids have **today**, but real comics with stories. It was **about then** that the first American comics appeared, and I can remember swapping Superman and Batman stories with my friends. I collected all sorts of stuff **at different times** like stamps and coins. I made models, everything from aeroplanes to cars to castles. **In those days** a lot of kids played instruments. All this was only after dark or **when the weather was bad**. The rest of the time we played outside.
> I sometimes think **today's kids** have more interesting things to do. **At the moment** I have a TV, a video, a PC, a CD player and so on. I'd find it just as difficult to live without them as any 16-year-old. It's funny, **these days** lots of older people will tell you life was more fun **back then**, but they all seem to have TVs and videos **now**.

6 Look at how the time expressions are used in the text. They all appear in the table below. Put a tick (✓) in the appropriate column against each one.

time expression	then	now
nowadays	....	....
when I was young	....	....
later	....	....
at first	....	....
at that time	....	....
today	....	....
about then	....	....
at different times	....	....
in those days	....	....
when the weather was bad	....	....
today's kids	....	....
at the moment	....	....
these days	....	....
back then	....	....

FCE Paper 2, Part 2

7 Write a composition, giving your opinions on this statement:

TECHNO KIDS
traditional hobbies are dead, today, technology is everything

Use a paragraph plan like this:

1 Introduction — indicate how much you agree with the statement.

2 Write about the hobbies people had in the past and the things they do now.

3 Make a comparison — what are the good and bad points of each.

4 Conclusion — decide if any older pastimes have a place in the modern world, or if technology has completely taken over.

Remember to use some of the time expressions you looked at. Write your composition in 120-180 words in an appropriate style.

Listening

1 Work with other students and discuss where you like to meet your friends or make new friends.

> at home   in a bar/café   at a disco   at a sports club
> in a bar   on trips   at sports events
> in school/college/at work

2 It's a rainy afternoon in the middle of winter after school. What would you do with your friends? Discuss your ideas with other students.

FCE Paper 4, Part 2

(16) **3** You will hear a teenager talking about where British teenagers meet their friends. For questions 1-10, complete the sentences.

School finishes in Britain at [_____] 1 o'clock.

Many families in Britain [_____] 2 between 5 and 6 o'clock.

The first British cafés were opened by [_____] 3 .

British cafés are used by workers and [_____] 4 .

Shops close in Britain at around [_____] 5 .

Pubs mainly sell coffee at [_____] 6 .

If young people order [_____] 7 in a pub, it won't please the pub landlord.

Evening begins in Britain at around [_____] 8 o'clock.

In Britain, teenagers often meet in [_____] 9 .

Some teenagers [_____] 10 and try to get into pubs.

4 Read about Emma's week. Complete the second calendar with what you will do this week, or what young people do in your country.

APRIL

Monday	Tuesday	Wednesday
Swimming practice	Study at Katie's house	Walk Mrs Jones's dog
Thursday	**Friday**	**Saturday**
Gym club	Youth meeting...	Party at Liam's
Sunday		
Go skate boarding		

Monday	
Tuesday	
Wednesday	
Thursday	
Friday	
Saturday	
Sunday	

5 With other students discuss the differences and similarities between the life of teenagers in Britain and teenagers in your own country. Say what you like and dislike about each way of life.

Reading

1 Read the introduction to the following article.

Perhaps for the first time in history, it is possible to get hold of things without leaving your own room – as long as you can connect to the Internet. This doesn't mean hacking into a bank's computer system and transferring money to your account. That can be done, but only by experts. But almost anyone can log into a music-sharing Web site and download tracks onto their own PC. It's very simple. It can also be – depending on the site you use – against the law.

2 Work with other students. Have any of you ever downloaded something from the Internet? Tell your group.

FCE Paper 1, Part 4

3 You are going to read an article in which six people talk about downloading music from the Internet. For questions 1-15, choose which person (A-F) is referred to. The people may be chosen more than once. When more than one answer is needed, these may be given in any order. There is an example at the beginning (0).

GETTING MUSIC FROM THE INTERNET
Six people talk about their attitudes to sharing music files on the Internet.

A **Max Morelli** is in his 4th year at secondary school. He says, 'Music is the main thing in my life – I play keyboards. I also download stuff that I want to listen to. It's not quite as simple as it used to be. The first big free site, Napster, was shut down by the record companies, but there are others. Sometimes it's a bit tricky – you download a file and find that it's been put there by the record companies and it's actually empty. I know it's illegal, but I haven't been caught yet. I haven't got much money and CDs are so expensive!'

B **Molly Turner**, a university student, says, 'I like listening to music but I can't afford to buy many CDs. I find file-sharing useful, and it's quite easy, really. You just type the title of the track you're looking for, or the name of the artist, into the search engine. If another member of the site is online and has that track, you can start to download it from their PC. It takes about half an hour, and most of the time it works. But you can spend time downloading a track and then lose the end of it because the person at the other end switches off their computer. But the site I belong to is legal so I don't have to worry about people knocking on my door.'

C **Khalid Aslam** left school last year. He says, 'Most of the music I listen to is modern Asian dance music. I've got a big collection at home and I work in clubs in the evenings, as a DJ. I don't make enough money to live on, but I hope to in the future. I'm very interested in the technical side of music. I've got a lot of equipment at home. I can take a track from the Internet and turn it into something completely different. As well as getting tracks I can also chat online with other people who like the same stuff. It's like being part of a community and you don't get that when you just go into a shop and buy a CD.'

D **Jasmine Lee** is a junior executive in a London record company. As you might expect, she disapproves of sharing music files. 'I think people who do this need to be aware of the consequences. In the US in April 2003 a student was caught running a music file-sharing site with 650,000 songs on it. The record companies took him to court and he ended up paying thousands of dollars. Since then they've started hundreds of similar court cases. We're taking this seriously. CD sales are falling and, apart from anything else, that affects the amount of money that the artists get paid. I mean, if nobody makes money, nobody is going to make music.'

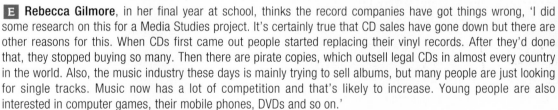

E **Rebecca Gilmore**, in her final year at school, thinks the record companies have got things wrong, 'I did some research on this for a Media Studies project. It's certainly true that CD sales have gone down but there are other reasons for this. When CDs first came out people started replacing their vinyl records. After they'd done that, they stopped buying so many. Then there are pirate copies, which outsell legal CDs in almost every country in the world. Also, the music industry these days is mainly trying to sell albums, but many people are just looking for single tracks. Music now has a lot of competition and that's likely to increase. Young people are also interested in computer games, their mobile phones, DVDs and so on.'

F **Sam Bailey** is a 20-year-old guitarist. He says, 'I suppose because I'm in the music business I should be against file-sharing, but I'm not sure. For a start, the record companies are always going on about how the artists lose money, but if anybody is an expert at taking money from artists, it's the record companies. I know some people in this business make a lot of money, but there are many working musicians who don't make very much at all. Musicians download stuff to see what other musicians are playing. You start by imitating others, then you try to develop your own style.'

Which person

- talks about the legal consequences of file-sharing? **0** **D**
- doesn't want to break the law? **1** ☐
- is mainly interested in one type of music? **2** ☐
- knows a lot about the record industry? **3** ☐
  4 ☐
- thinks musicians should be paid more? **5** ☐
- downloads tracks for professional reasons? **6** ☐ **7** ☐

- is opposed to file-sharing? **8** ☐
- talks about how much artists get paid? **9** ☐
  10 ☐
- uses music sites also to socialise? **11** ☐
- plays a musical instrument for pleasure? **12** ☐
- doesn't have much money at the moment? **13** ☐
- thinks music will be less popular in the future? **14** ☐
- admits he doesn't use legal sites? **15** ☐

④ **Have you ever bought a pirated CD or downloaded a track without paying for it? Look at the statements from the article below and tick the ones you agree with. Then discuss your views with others in a group.**

> I know it's illegal, but I haven't been caught yet. I haven't got much money and CDs are so expensive!

> ...the site I belong to is legal so I don't have to worry about people knocking on my door.

> It's like being part of a community and you don't get that when you just go into a shop and buy a CD.

> I mean, if nobody makes money, nobody is going to make music.

> It's certainly true that CD sales have gone down but there are other reasons for this.

> ...but if anybody is an expert at taking money from artists, it's the record companies.

Grammar

-ing forms

❶ **Read these sentences from the article. What kind of words come before the *-ing* forms?**

1 but you can spend time **downloading** a track and then lose the end of it...
2 As well as **getting** tracks I can also chat online...
3 ...a student was caught **running** a music file-sharing site with 650,000 songs on it.
4 ...people started **replacing** their vinyl records.
5 ...I should be against file-**sharing**, but I'm not sure
6 You start by **imitating** others, then you try to develop your own style.

Theory Box

Besides using the **-ing** form of the verb to make the Present Continuous:

She is dancing.

and other continuous tenses, we can use it in various other ways to describe activities:

1 It can follow some **prepositions**:
   Despite playing the guitar sometimes, he isn't really interested in music.

He's quite fond of listening to classical music.

2 It can follow **verbs**:
   *Would you **mind not going** to the concert on Friday?*
   *I **regret lending** Karen my violin.*

3 It can follow a **verb with preposition**:
   *I'm **looking forward to hearing** some good music tonight.*

4 It can follow a **verb with a pronoun and preposition**:
   *He **accused me of borrowing** his trumpet.*

5 It can follow **nouns**:
   *He spent **three weeks learning** to play that.*

6 It can follow a **noun with a preposition**:
   *I have no **intention of going** to a jazz club again.*

7 It can follow an **adjective** and **preposition**:
   *Who is **responsible for managing** this band?*

❷ **Rewrite each sentence. Use the examples from above as models. Change the word in bold to its *-ing* form, and make any other necessary changes. The first one has been done for you. Then compare your answers with another student.**

0 It will be good to **hear** her play live.
   I'm looking forward to hearing her play live.
1 I wish I hadn't **asked** him to sing.
   ....
2 He doesn't intend to **play** in the United States again.
   ....
3 Bob **organises** the band very well.
   ....
4 I'd rather you didn't **play** heavy metal in the house.
   ....
5 Although he **plays** the guitar very well, he doesn't make much money.
   ....
6 'Adam **took** my concert tickets,' she said.
   ....
7 Reece took a month off to **recover** from the tour.
   ....
8 She **works** all day then sings in a club for most of the night.
   ....

Vocabulary

Newspapers, magazines and television

1 **Work with another student. Discuss the following questions.**

1 How much TV do you watch? How often?
2 Which programmes do you watch?
3 How often do you read a magazine/ comic/ newspaper?
4 Which one do you read?
5 Which part do you read first/never read?

2 **Decide if the words in the box are connected with newspapers (N), television (T) or both (B).**

	N	T	B
1 caption	☐	☐	☐
2 channel	☐	☐	☐
3 chat show	☐	☐	☐
4 documentary	☐	☐	☐
5 dubbed	☐	☐	☐
6 editor	☐	☐	☐
7 gossip column	☐	☐	☐
8 headline	☐	☐	☐
9 review	☐	☐	☐
10 series	☐	☐	☐

3 **Complete the sentences with a word from question 2. Compare your answers with another student.**

1 If you want to listen to famous people talking about their lives, watch a ....
2 If you're interested in nature, watch a ....
3 To find out about a new play, read a ....
4 A cartoon is difficult to understand without its ....
5 There are hundreds of different .... on satellite TV.

6 If you want to find out about a famous person's private life, read a ....
7 The .... decides what goes into a newspaper.
8 You often look at the .... to quickly see what's in the news.
9 If a programme is .... the people speak in the language of the country where it is shown.
10 Is that .... still on? It's been on TV for years now.

Speaking

FCE Paper 5, Part 3

1 **You are the editor of a news programme for teenagers. Look at the list of possible news items to include in a five-minute broadcast. Work with other students and decide which five you should include and the order that they will go in.**

1 plane crash in China killing 200 people
2 1% increase in the price of petrol
3 the wedding of two international rock stars
4 government plans to reduce pollution
5 research into the effects of computer games
6 a man who kept 30 poisonous snakes in his flat
7 weather forecast for tomorrow
8 latest football results
9 how to win 1,000,000 euro
10 latest Hollywood release

2 **What pictures would you choose to go with your news stories? Discuss with the other students in your group.**

Entertainment

1 Circle all the words for people in the box. Then decide if they refer to books (B), plays (P), films (F) or concerts (C).

book	novel	director	scene	lines	trumpet
	storyline	flop	set	scenery	best seller
play	chapter	star	hit	character	musical
	credits	stuntman	backing vocals	producer	special effects
film	soundtrack	box office	on location	stage	screen
	script	guitarist	cameraman	photography	applause
concert	rehearsal	cast	soloist	guitar	violin
	audience	lead vocalist	plot	actor	conductor

2 Now do the same to the other words in the box. Then write the appropriate word next to the correct definition below.

1 The names and jobs of the people involved in a film
....

2 The opposite of a success
....

3 The list of names of people who acted in a film or play
....

4 The written form of the film or play ....

5 When the actors practise before a public performance
....

6 The words learnt by an actor in a film or play ....

7 The events in a book, play or film
.... or ....

8 A small section of a film or play
....

9 Beautiful countryside in a film or painted backgrounds in a play
....

10 The place where the film is shot or the play is acted
....

3 What do these questions refer to: a play, a film, or a concert? Then match each question to its answer.

1 Where's it on?
2 What's it about?
3 Who's it by?
4 Where's it set?
5 Where was it shot?
6 Who's in it?
7 Who's playing?
8 Who's the conductor?
9 Who's the support band?
10 When's it on?

a In a studio in Hollywood.
b Shakespeare, I think.
c At 7.30 this evening.
d The Philharmonic Orchestra.
e At the Odeon.
f The Libertines, I think.
g I don't know. Someone Russian.
h Two strangers who meet and fall in love on a train.
i Brad Pitt.
j In Rome, in the 1950s.

4 Work with another student. Think of a book, film or play that you have read or seen recently. Practise using the questions to find out about your partner's book, film or play.

Writing

FCE Paper 2, Part 2

1 You are going to write a review of the book, film or play you spoke about in question 4. Your review should include a summary of the plot, information about the writer, characters, director and actors, the good points and bad points. Finish your review with a recommendation: would you advise your friends to read this book, or see this film or play? Write your review in 120-180 words.

Grammar

get/have something *done*

1 Max is worried because none of the girls he knows are interested in him, and none of his friends want to spend any time in his room. He asks his older brother Jordan for some advice. Read their conversation.

Theory Box

get/have something *done*

I'll… . What is he going to do? He isn't going to cut his own hair. He'll go to the hairdresser's and **get his hair cut**, or **have it cut**. We use this structure when we talk about someone else doing something for us:

get/have + my hair/it + past participle

Get is less formal than **have**, and is almost always used for commands, like:

Get your hair cut!

2 Now fill in the missing words in the conversation below. Use *get* or *have* and the past participle of the verb in brackets.

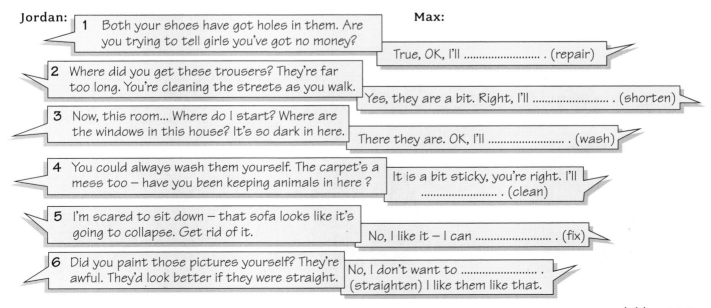

Jordan:

1 Both your shoes have got holes in them. Are you trying to tell girls you've got no money?

2 Where did you get these trousers? They're far too long. You're cleaning the streets as you walk.

3 Now, this room... Where do I start? Where are the windows in this house? It's so dark in here.

4 You could always wash them yourself. The carpet's a mess too – have you been keeping animals in here ?

5 I'm scared to sit down – that sofa looks like it's going to collapse. Get rid of it.

6 Did you paint those pictures yourself? They're awful. They'd look better if they were straight.

Max:

True, OK, I'll .... (repair)

Yes, they are a bit. Right, I'll .... (shorten)

There they are. OK, I'll .... (wash)

It is a bit sticky, you're right. I'll .... (clean)

No, I like it – I can .... (fix)

No, I don't want to .... (straighten) I like them like that.

Vocabulary

Shops and shopping

1 **Where can you buy these things? Match the item with the shop.**

You can buy		from a	
bread			baker's
cheese			butcher's
cough medicine			chemist's
fresh fruit			delicatessen
nails and screws			department store
pens			fishmonger's
prawns			greengrocer
sheets and towels			grocer's
steak			hardware shop
sweets			newsagent
tinned food			off licence
wine			stationer's

2 **What can go wrong? Use a word from the box to complete each conversation.**

fade   leak   refund   run   snap   shrink   stretch

1 I bought this sweater last week but when I washed it, it .... Look, it's half the size it was.

2 I bought this blouse last week but when I washed it, the colour .... Look how light it is.

Can I help you?

3 I bought these shoes last week but they .... in the rain. Look how wet they are.

4 I bought this sweater last week but when I washed it, it .... Look how big is.

5 I bought this dress last week but when I washed it, all the colours .... Look at the colours now.

6 I bought this comb yesterday but it's .... in two. Look at the two pieces.

7 I'm sorry. Would you like a new one or a ....?

3 **Complete each sentence with the correct name of the shop, business or service.**

1 She's gone to the .... to have her hair done.

2 Charlie's at the .... — he's having a tooth filled.

3 I'm taking the car to the .... to have the exhaust fixed.

4 I'll have to have this suit cleaned. Can you drop it off at the ....

5 I have to see the .... today to get these legal papers.

6 Dad's off to the .... to pick up some photos he had developed.

7 Could you take my watch to the .... and have it repaired?

8 He should go to the .... and have his blood pressure checked.

4 **Work with another student. Make a list of other things which can go wrong. Have you ever taken something back to a shop? Tell your partner what happened.**

Vocabulary

Phrasal verbs/expressions with *fall*

❶ Read the story and answer the questions.

1 Did Zoe have a lot of boyfriends? Why/why not?
2 Was Lewis happy at the beginning of the story? Why/why not?
3 Was Lewis happy at the end of the story? Why/why not?

Men found Zoe irresistible and they were always falling for her. They'd do anything to please her but she never fell in with any of their plans. She just wasn't interested in them. Then one day, she was walking home after work when she met Lewis. They fell into conversation, and she discovered he was an English student at university. He looked very depressed and he told her all his problems: he'd fallen behind with his work and had fallen out with his girlfriend. Next he had fallen for a con trick that he'd seen in the local paper and lost some money. Lastly his holiday in Spain had fallen through because his girlfriend had decided to go with someone else.

After telling Zoe his problems, he felt much better and they arranged to meet the next day. This was the beginning of their romance and this time Lewis had fallen on his feet because Zoe thought he was the love of her life!

❷ Read the story again. Underline all the phrasal verbs/expressions with *fall*.

❸ Now write the phrasal verb/expression next to the correct definition.

1 to be deceived ....
2 to argue ....

3 to agree to someone's suggestions ....
....
4 to fail to be completed...........
....
....
5 to fall in love with someone ....
....
....
6 to fail to meet deadlines.........
....
....
7 to be lucky, especially after a difficult time ....
....
8 to begin by chance ....
....

❹ Complete each sentence with the correct phrasal verb with *fall*.

1 She .... with her university exams.
2 The actor and the director .... about the script and didn't talk to each other for weeks.
3 He .... her the minute he saw her — it was love at first sight.
4 She .... his story and gave him £20. Then she saw him getting into a taxi.
5 They .... and were still chatting when they got onto the bus.
6 He .... her plans and agreed to go to the cinema.
7 He's really .... this time — his new girlfriend's taking him to Paris!
8 Unfortunately, the business deal has ....

❺ Choose five of the phrasal verbs/expressions. Write a sentence containing each one. Work in pairs and test your partner. Student A reads out their first sentence but says BEEP instead of the phrasal verb. Student B gives the correct phrasal verb.

143 >>>

UNIT 14
Work and Study

Vocabulary

Education

1 Work with another student and answer the following questions:

1 Which of the subjects in the table do you study?

2 Are there any other subjects which you study which are not in the table?

subject	person	adjective
mathematics	mathematician	mathematical
engineering		
biology		
chemistry		
physics		
history		
politics		
economics		
languages		
accountancy		
law		
statistics		
art		

2 Now write the name of the person who specialises in these subjects and the adjectives in the table.

3 Work with another student and discuss these questions:

1 Which subjects are necessary for a good education?

2 What is the purpose of education? To find a job, or to develop a student's character?

3 Which subjects would you choose between history or media studies? Latin or cookery? Art or film studies? French or music? Why?

4 Work with another student and decide what subjects the following people should study. You may want to suggest other skills which are necessary for each job.

1 Matthew plans to be a journalist. He would like to write about international politics.

2 Charlotte will own and manage the family business when she is older.

3 Joseph would like to work for an international finance company.

4 Lauren wants to be an archaeologist. She would like to work abroad.

5 William would like to work for an international charity as a fundraiser.

5 Which verb goes with which nouns? Tick the boxes.

	a course	a degree	a distinction	a test	an exam	university
attend						
do						
fail						
get						
pass						
resit/retake						
revise for						
study for						
take						

6 Interview the other students in the class.

Find someone who: name/s

1   has never had to retake an exam.   ....
2   likes doing tests.   ....
3   has taken a practical exam.   ....
4   attends a course outside school.   ....
5   has got/is planning to get a degree in an arts subject.   ....
6   doesn't mind failing tests.   ....
7   knows someone who studies for exams at the last minute.   ....
8   is going to do an exam this term.   ....

Speaking

FCE Paper 5, Part 3

1 Work with another student and match a job from the box to the correct picture.

artist   chef   dustman   hairdresser   lawyer (barrister)
librarian   lifeguard   mechanic   nurse   pilot
police officer   scientist   social worker   soldier
stockbroker   surgeon   traffic warden   vet

1   ....

4   ....

7   ....

2   ....

5   ....

8   ....

3   ....

6   ....

9   ....

2 Now choose two jobs from question 1. Think of one advantage and one disadvantage for each one and write them in the spaces below. You might choose from these topics or choose your own.

danger   holidays   hours
job satisfaction   pay
stress levels   working conditions

job	
advantage	
disadvantage	

3 Now, discuss your choices with other students. Explain which of these jobs you would like/dislike doing.

Vocabulary

Adjective and noun collocation with *poor, rich, long, short*

1 In each group of words, there is one noun that cannot be used with the adjective. Which one is it?

1	poor	hearing loser time eyesight
2	rich	people colour food memory
3	long	memory people hours time
4	short	notice supply building article

2 Which adjective/s from question 1 can you use with the following nouns?

1   .... soil
2   .... speech
3   .... sound
4   .... health
5   .... scent
6   .... speaker

Listening

1 **Look at the list of jobs with another student and answer these questions.**

1 Decide if these jobs have been traditionally done by men or by women and tick the box.

2 Decide which sex, if any, you think they *should* be done by and tick the box.

3 Work with another two students and compare and discuss your results.

	traditionally done by		should be done by		
	men	women	men	women	either
airline pilot	☐	☐	☐	☐	☐
au pair	☐	☐	☐	☐	☐
beautician	☐	☐	☐	☐	☐
coal miner	☐	☐	☐	☐	☐
nurse	☐	☐	☐	☐	☐
personal assistant	☐	☐	☐	☐	☐
builder	☐	☐	☐	☐	☐
priest	☐	☐	☐	☐	☐
primary school teacher	☐	☐	☐	☐	☐
secretary	☐	☐	☐	☐	☐
truck driver	☐	☐	☐	☐	☐

FCE Paper 4, Part 3

🎧17 **2** **You will hear five people talking about work. For questions 1-5, choose from the list (A-F) what each speaker says. Use the speaker letters only once. There is one extra letter that you do not need to use.**

A I'm often mistaken for someone else. Speaker 1 ☐

B In this job you have to be trustworthy. Speaker 2 ☐

C I only do this job for the money. Speaker 3 ☐

D I only work at certain times of the day. Speaker 4 ☐

E I felt I had to earn some money. Speaker 5 ☐

F I've done a number of different jobs.

Grammar

Relative clauses

1 **Read these sentences and decide on the correct interpretation, a or b.**

1 Politicians who are dishonest should be put in jail. ☐

2 Politicians, who are dishonest, should be put in jail. ☐

a All politicians are dishonest and they should all be put in jail.

b Some politicians are dishonest and these should be put in jail.

2 **How do the commas in the second sentence make a difference in meaning? Discuss your ideas with another student.**

Theory Box

Relative clauses (1)

*Politicians **who are dishonest** should be put in jail.*

This sentence says that dishonest politicians should be put in jail. **Who are dishonest** begins with a **relative pronoun**. It indicates which politicians we are talking about. We call it a **defining relative clause**.

*Politicians, **who are dishonest**, should be put in jail.*

This sentence says that **all** politicians should be put in jail — because they are all dishonest.

Who are dishonest, doesn't indicate which politicians. It simply gives us **extra information** about all of them. We call it a **non-defining relative clause** and we show that it is separate from the main message of the sentence by using commas.

Note that the relative pronouns are **who, whom, which, whose, where** and **that**.

3 With another student, discuss the differences in meaning between these sentences with relative clauses.

1a Alex's sister who works in Brazil is a photographer.

b Hannah's brother, who works in Argentina, is an engineer.

2a The player who scored the goal is a defender.

b The goalkeeper, who let it in, should be sacked.

3a The assistant referee who said he was offside should get his eyes tested.

b The referee, who disagreed with him, made the right decision.

4a The bridge over the River Tyne which was opened in 2000 is called the Millennium Bridge.

b The bridge over the River Humber, which was opened in 1981, is known as the Humber Bridge.

5a When most people think of Paris, they think of Paris which is the capital of France.

b However, this film is set in Paris, which is also a town in Texas.

4 Decide if the sentences below are defining or non-defining relative clauses. Do they need commas or not? Compare your answers with another student.

1 The job which he got meant him moving to Manchester.

2 The course which involves a lot of study starts next week.

3 My boss who doesn't like me at all is a nasty little guy.

4 Connor was dreading the interview which actually went quite well.

5 The exam which I sat was easier than this one.

6 I'm going for a drink with my colleagues who are a nice bunch.

7 The factory where I worked was some distance from the town.

8 The people who work hardest don't always get promoted.

9 The office which I work in is small and overheated.

10 Michael whose idea it was seemed pleased that we liked it.

5 Now write the names of four of your family or friends here. Write two pieces of information about each one to make a sentence with a relative clause. Don't forget to use commas if necessary.

0 *My mother, who comes from Mexico, rarely speaks Spanish.*

1 My ....
....

2 My ....
....

3 My ....
....

4 My ....
....

6 Now tell another student about your friends and family. Be prepared to answer any additional questions they may have.

❶ Read the introduction to the article. Work with other students and discuss which qualities are necessary to become a successful entrepreneur.

		yes	no
1	energy	☐	☐
2	creativity	☐	☐
3	arrogance	☐	☐
4	intelligence	☐	☐
5	ruthlessness	☐	☐
6	love of money	☐	☐
7	self-confidence	☐	☐
8	good education	☐	☐
9	ability to take risks	☐	☐
10	good social skills	☐	☐

Who wants to be a millionaire?

An entrepreneur is someone who can start a business from nothing, make it work successfully and perhaps make millions. Do you have the qualities necessary to become a successful millionaire? And what are these qualities? A recent TV series in Britain tried to find out, and you can read about their conclusions later in this article. But first, what do you need to be a millionaire?

FCE Paper 1, Part 3

❷ Compare your ideas with those in the article. Eight sentences have been removed from it. Choose from the sentences A-I the one which fits each gap (1-7). There is one extra sentence which you do not need to use. There is an example at the beginning (0).

He lay in the chair. His mouth hung open. When people spoke to him, he responded with grunts. His bleached hair hung over his face. He looked like a typical rebellious, couldn't-care-less teenager. (**0**)...C... . Along with four others he recently featured in the TV series, *Mind of a Millionaire*, which investigated the type of personality you need to become very rich. So what is it that distinguishes these self-made entrepreneurs from the rest of us?

'They are delightful, they are fascinating, they are fun, creative, stimulating and inspirational, but you wouldn't want to spend much time alone with one of these guys,' said Dr Atkinson, a business psychologist. (**1**)........ .

There were five millionaires on the programme, and three other people to compare them too. The idea was to see if millionaires are different from the rest of us. What it showed was that successful entrepreneurs are highly energetic, extremely self-confident, self-centred and have a love of gambling. (**2**)........ Educational qualifications are not necessary, neither do you need to be able to get on with people, but a bit of ruthless arrogance helps. And it's probably a good thing to come from a poor background. The millionaires have all the characteristics of the criminal. In fact, as one of the participants in the programme suggested, it isn't unreasonable to see criminals as failed entrepreneurs.

Dominic made his money from fold-up scooters. When he was 13 he noticed a fold-up silver Viza scooter on the Internet. (**3**)........ . This kept him quite busy, and being at school became a major inconvenience. He was frequently absent. (**4**)........ . 'Dominic doesn't need a safety net,' he said. 'He believed in himself to a degree that most people find quite irritating.' Dominic agreed. 'You have to be confident in yourself. If you're not, you aren't going to succeed.'

So he left school early – like the other millionaires taking part in the programme. Dominic was particularly negative when he spoke about the value of education. 'Being out there making money, travelling the world, interacting with businesses, doing deals, doing legal work, for a 14-year-old, that is a better education than going to school,' he said. (**5**)........ . 'I don't think I'm bright,' he said. 'I think I'm focused. I'll make an admission: I've never read a book.'

Since his success with scooters, Dominic has moved on. He once said that from the age of two music was the thing he only ever wanted to do. (**6**)........ . He hates the typical boy bands out there at the moment and is eager to introduce his 'alternative' band to the world.

'For me it's never been about the money,' Dominic said. 'Have you ever heard of a 13-year-old wanting millions? I set up my first company when I was just eight! The money just proved I was successful.'

(**7**)........ . He's moved into his own West London flat, a property once owned by John Lennon. Anyone who feels inferior to Dominic can take comfort in the fact that there's something which makes him like the rest of us. What does his mum thinks about all of this?

'She just wants me to move back home!' he admitted.

A 73% of them don't notice or care what other people think of them.

B On one occasion his headmaster noticed that he was playing truant when he saw him on TV in Japan discussing the possibilities of importing Japanese toilets.

C This was Dominic McVey, 18 years old and a millionaire since the age of 15.

D He knew these would be popular, and arranged with the Americans to import them into Europe through a company that he set up with his mother.

E But he does make some use of his money.

F Now he's making music, in a way, as the manager of a new boy band called Most Wanted.

G However, he doesn't have a high opinion of his academic ability.

H He should know — he's a millionaire himself.

I Although he's made a large amount of money, he hasn't spent it on anything significant.

3 Did you choose the correct qualities to be a millionaire?

4 What do you think of Dominic? Write down your reactions to the article. Compare your ideas with another student.

Writing

Narrative tenses: Past Simple, Past Continuous, Past Perfect

1 Work with another student. Read these two sentences and answer the questions about them.

I arrived. Jacob left.

Combine them into one sentence and change one tense to make the meaning the same as:

1 Jacob left before I arrived.
When ....

2 Jacob left after I arrived.
When ....

3 Jacob started to leave before I arrived.
When ....

2 Choose the best tenses for these sentences.

While Ben .... (*drive*) to the office he .... (*have*) an accident. He .... (*be*) quite badly hurt because he .... (*forget*) to fasten his safety belt.

3 In this sentence the order of events is shown by the numbers, but this isn't clear from the text. Which verb do you need to change to the Past Perfect to make this clear?

$$\overset{1}{\text{Jamie got up}} \text{ and } \overset{2}{\text{had a shower. He}} \overset{4}{\text{watched the news}}$$

when he $\overset{3}{\text{ate}}$ his breakfast.

4 Now answer these questions:

1 Which tense do we use to show that an action began before another action and continued at least until the second action happened?

2 Which tense do we use to show that an action happened before another action, *when the order of events is unclear*?

FCE Paper 2, Part 2

5 Write an answer to this question:
You have decided to enter a short story competition. The competition rules say that the story must begin or end with the following words:

It was Maria's first day in the building, and she had never felt so strange.

First, think about what you are going to write. Discuss your answers to these questions with another student.

1 Who is Maria?
2 What does she do?
3 What does she look like?
4 What is the building?
5 Why is Maria there?
6 Why is it strange?

Write 120-180 words and use what you have learned about the narrative tenses.

Grammar

Defining and non-defining relative clauses

❶ Work with other students and answer the questions about each sentence.

1 Alice's brother who lives in London is an electrician.
   a Is this sentence correct? What does it tell you about my family?

2 Alice's father who lives in London is an electrician.
   a Is this sentence correct? Why/why not?

Theory Box

Relative clauses (2)

In **defining** relative clauses, it is common to replace **who** or **which** with **that**. So we can say:

                    that
The first job ~~which~~ I got was filling shelves in a supermarket.

We can't do this in **non-defining** relative clauses. So we can't say:

                    ~~that~~
The pay, **which** was very low, hardly covered my rent.

❷ Complete each sentence below with a job from the box. Then replace *who* or *which* with *that* if it is possible.

> bookmaker   bouncer   plumber   receptionist
> midwife   technician   undertaker   vicar

1 If there's a problem with your water supply which you can't fix yourself, call a ....

2 When Eleanor had her baby, the ...., who she knew quite well, did a fantastic job.

3 The official name for the job is *doorman*, but people who don't work in the club call him a ....

4 The keys which the .... gave us were for the wrong room and we had to go down to the ground floor again.

5 The ...., who doesn't like paying us money when we win, was annoyed when my horse came first at 100-1.

6 A priest who works in the Church of England is usually known as a ....

7 When the video broke down in the middle of a lesson, I called the ...., who is normally very helpful. But he was too busy to come.

8 He was offered a job as an ...., but he didn't want to be known as a guy who works with dead people.

Theory Box

Subject pronouns in relative clauses

1 *The job **which/that she took** was in a restaurant.*

2 *The job **which/that really interests** her is in television.*

Both of these sentences include **defining relative clauses**, so we can use **which** or **that**. However, in sentence 1 there is another possibility:

   1 The job she took was in a restaurant.

We can leave out the relative pronoun. But we can't do this in sentence **2**.

   2 The job really interests her is in television. ✗

Why is this? With another student, look at sentences 1 and 2. Decide why **which/that** can be only be left out of sentence 1. How has **the job** changed in the two sentences?

❸ Choose the correct word to complete each gap in the text.

In sentence 1, the subject of the sentence is **1**................... (*she/the job*) and the object is **2**................... (*she/the job*). In sentence 2, the job is the **3**................... (*subject/object*) of the sentence. In **4**................. (*defining/non-defining*) relative clauses, if the relative pronoun, *who*, *which* or *that*, refers to the **5**................... (*subject/object*) of the sentence we can leave it out.

❹ Read these sentences. Make each pair into one sentence with a defining or non-defining relative clause. If it is possible to leave out the relative pronoun, do so.

1 One of the millionaires was Dominic McVey. He was in the TV series.
   One of the millionaires ....

2 He set up the company with his mother. It imported fold-away scooters.
   The company ....

3 Plumbing can be a dirty job. It is well-paid.
   Plumbing ....

4 I look after the cats. They belong to people on holiday.
   The cats................................

5 My mum is a single parent. She couldn't give me any more pocket money.
   My mum ....

6 I did the work during my gap year. It was quite varied.
   The work ....

Theory Box

who and whom

Whom can be used instead of **who** if it is the **object** of the verb in a relative clause:

*Of all my colleagues, the one **whom** I like most is Lucia.*

*His mother, **whom** I know quite well, is boss of the company.*

However, **whom** is only used in **formal** English. When speaking or writing **informally**, there is nothing wrong with using **who** as the object of the clause.

Use of English

❶ **Work with other students. Imagine you have been given enough money to take a year out from study or your job — without losing your place in school, college, or university, or your salary. Would you:**

1 travel or stay at home?
2 do nothing, or try a different type of work or study?
3 do things for your own benefit, or help others?
4 have a rest, or try to make some money?

FCE Paper 3, Part 4

❷ **For questions 1-15, read the text below and look carefully at each line. Some of the lines are correct and some have a word which should not be there. If a line is correct, put a tick (✓) beside it. If a line has a word which should not be there, underline this word. There are two examples at the beginning (0 and 00).**

0	..✓.. School is nearly over — so what are you going to do next? More
00	..of.. and more of young people in the UK are choosing to take a gap year
1	.... – a year off between high school and university. This approach
2	.... even has the royal approval. In 2000, Prince William spent part of
3	.... his gap year as a volunteer in Chile, while just in 2003 his younger
4	.... brother Harry himself learned to work with cattle in Australia. Gap
5	.... years can take up many forms. Some students choose to prepare for
6	.... their university course by getting some practical and experience or
7	.... learning a relevant language. Some want to help others, and get
8	.... involved with voluntary projects. Both of objectives can be followed
9	.... either at home or overseas, while some who simply choose to travel,
10	.... working as they move around all the world. For many, of course, the
11	.... gap year is a more serious business, either a chance to work and make
12	.... some money to help them through their coming university course. In
13	.... general, universities are in favour of the gap years. At the end of it they
14	.... get a more mature student with a better idea of the outside world and
15	.... a more informed idea of which this course they want to study.

❶ **Work with your partner. Think of an idea for making money — something you could build, or sell, or import/export. Think of the kind of company you would set up in order to make your idea work. Decide how much money you will need to borrow from a bank to get your company started. Fill in the business plan below.**

Standard Commercial Bank
Business loan application

Name of company: ....
....

Name(s) of company directors: ....
....

Description of product: ....
....

Type of activity (tick as applicable)

Manufacturing	☐
Wholesale*	☐
Retail**	☐
Import	☐
Export	☐

notes: * selling to shops ** selling to the public

Amount of money you require to borrow: ...
....

Period of loan: ....
....

❷ **Work in a group of four. You are going to roleplay the meeting between the entrepreneurs and the bank managers. Choose which role you want to play. Your teacher will give you the roleplaying cards.**

UNIT 14
Vocabulary

Phrasal verbs for education

1 Choose the best answer to replace the phrasal verb in each sentence.

1 How are you *getting on* in English?
 a studying
 b progressing
 c enjoying

2 I find it very difficult to *keep up with* the teacher and the rest of the class.
 a fully understand
 b continue at the same speed
 c like

3 Although I went to the lecture, I didn't *take in* much of what he said.
 a write down
 b hear
 c understand

4 If I *get through* my final exam, I'll be very happy.
 a pass
 b take
 c miss

5 The lecturer gets angry if you *hand in* your homework late.
 a start
 b give
 c write

6 It's very useful when the teacher *goes over* the homework in class so that I can understand my mistakes.
 a explains
 b gives
 c marks

2 Now read the conversation between two students and check your answers. Can you explain the meaning of the three *phrasal verbs*?

Amy: How are you getting on in English?
George: Not bad. At first I couldn't keep up with the teacher.
Amy: Well, maybe he thought that you were taking everything in.
George: Yes, when we said we didn't understand, he *slowed down* and I started to learn quickly.
Amy: Is he a good teacher?
George: Yes, he is. He's quite strict — he won't mark our homework if we hand it in late. But he *puts his ideas across* clearly and it's useful when he goes over our homework in class after he has corrected it.
Amy: Have you missed any lessons?
George: No, it would be very difficult to *catch up with* the rest of the class if I missed anything.
Amy: Well, you've got your final exam in a week, haven't you?

George: Yes, but I should get through it if I get down to a bit of work now!
Amy: Well, good luck.
George: Thanks.

3 Complete each sentence with the correct phrasal verb from questions 1 and 2.

1 He couldn't .... the other students and had to move to an easier class.

2 The lecturer couldn't .... clearly and the students didn't understand anything.

3 He found it difficult to .... what she was saying because it was very confusing.

4 I hope I .... the end-of-term exams because I don't want to resit them.

5 She was ill for three weeks and had to .... all the work when she went back to school.

6 Could you .... please. You're speaking too fast.

7 She .... her essay at the end of term and went on holiday.

8 I'm not .... very well with my English at the moment. I'm the worst student in the class!

4 Choose the best word to complete each sentence.

1 .... is responsible for running a school.
 a A head teacher
 b A principal
 c A chancellor

2 Students have to pay .... to study at university.
 a grants
 b fees
 c scholarships

3 Eton is a very expensive and famous .... school in England.
 a comprehensive
 b public
 c state

4 In the exam, there are five ....: A, B, C, D and E.
 a marks
 b scores
 c grades

5 He got a .... to show his employer that he had completed the course.
 a diploma
 b certificate
 c degree

6 Their daughter goes to a .... school. She only goes home during the holidays.
 a co-educational
 b boarding
 c day

7 Her three-year-old son has just started .... school.
- **a** primary
- **b** secondary
- **c** nursery

8 The pupil was given .... for being rude to a teacher. He had to do some extra work at school.
- **a** a detention
- **b** a suspension
- **c** an expulsion

Name: Joe Healy
Sex: male
Age: 28
Qualifications: none
Experience: 3 years with major company but sacked.
Notes: Good, knows the business. Maybe a bit unstable.

Speaking

FCE Paper 5, Parts 3-4

❶ You work for a small independent record company. You have recently signed a new teenage band called Skorch!!! and they have recorded their first CD. Unfortunately, your marketing manager has just left the company. You urgently need to hire a new one to promote the band and have interviewed four candidates. Read the information about them below.

Name: Damien Donahue
Sex: male
Age: 19
Qualifications: Nothing formal.
Experience: Has already managed a band.
Notes: Keen. Came across well at interview.

Name: Charles Farnham
Sex: male
Age: 33
Qualifications: BA Marketing, MBA
Experience: Has worked with a number of record companies.
Notes: Too conventional for this kind of band?

Name: Fran Paton
Sex: female
Age: 29
Qualifications: BA Music
Experience: Limited – was a singer until 2 years ago.
Notes: The band liked her.

❷ Work with another student and match each language function 1-7 to a language sample A-G.

1. Starting the discussion.
2. Asking for the other person's suggestion.
3. Making a suggestion.
4. Agreeing with a suggestion.
5. Disagreeing with a suggestion.
6. Making another suggestion.
7. Summing up a decision.

A Yes, that's a good idea.
B Well, I think we should seriously consider ....
C Why don't we start by looking at the kind of person we really need?
D I don't think we should appoint him/her. He/she isn't really qualified/doesn't have the right experience/wouldn't be good with this band.
E Who do you think we should appoint?
F So we all agree that we should appoint ....?
G It might be a good idea to look at .... first. What do you think of him/her?

❸ Work with your partner to choose a new marketing manager for your record company. Follow these instructions:

1. Discuss the qualities and skills the new marketing manager will need.
2. Each of you should choose a different candidate for the job.
3. Discuss your choice. Use the language samples above to convince your partner that your candidate should get the job.

❹ When you have chosen the best candidate for the job, answer these questions with your partner:

1. Do you like teenage bands like Skorch!!!? Why/why not?
2. What kind of music do you like?
3. Who are your favourite bands/singers?
4. Would you like to work in the music business? Why/why not?
5. What job would you like to do?

UNIT 15
Britain and the World

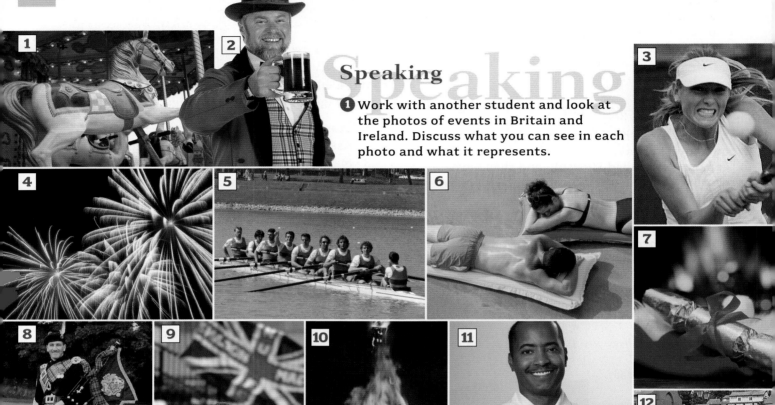

Speaking

1 Work with another student and look at the photos of events in Britain and Ireland. Discuss what you can see in each photo and what it represents.

2 Match each festival in the list (A-L) with the correct photo (1-12).

A	☐	New Year Celebrations/January
B	☐	St Valentine's Day/February
C	☐	St Patrick's Day, Ireland/March
D	☐	The Boat Race, London/April
E	☐	FA Cup Final, London/May
F	☐	Wimbledon Lawn Tennis Championships, London/June
G	☐	Summer holidays/July
H	☐	Royal National Eisteddfod, Wales/August
I	☐	Highland Gathering, Braemar, Scotland/September
J	☐	The Goose Fair, Nottingham/October
K	☐	Bonfire Night, England, Scotland, Wales/November
L	☐	Christmas Day/December

3 Now make a list of equivalent events in your country with your partner. Think of one for each month of the year. Then compare your lists with other students.

1 January ....
2 February ....
3 March...
4 April...
5 May ....
6 June...
7 July...
8 August ....
9 September ....
10 October...
11 November...
12 December ....

Reading

FCE Paper 1, Part 4

1 You are going to read a magazine article about the experiences in Britain of people from other countries. For questions 1-13, choose from the people (A-E). The people may be chosen more than once. When more than one answer is required, these may be given in any order. There is an example at the beginning (0).

Which person or people

- travelled part of the way to Britain overland? **O** **A**
- has stayed in Britain for the longest? **1** ☐
- failed to do what they wanted to in Britain? **2** ☐
- spent time with relatives in Britain? **3** ☐
- has a relationship which started slowly? **4** ☐
- has parents from different countries? **5** ☐
- speaks English less fluently than their parents do? **6** ☐
- came to Britain to work? **7** ☐ **8** ☐
- learned to do something because of a parent's influence? **9** ☐
- come from a background which mixes cultures? **10** ☐ **11** ☐
- mentions the weather in Britain? **12** ☐
- wanted to study in England but was unable to? **13** ☐

LIFE IN BRITAIN

A Christmas and New Year

Ellie Fraser, a 19-year-old New Zealander, visited Britain with her boyfriend, Craig.

It's normal for young people from New Zealand and Australia to travel round the world, either after school or university. Well, Craig and I both had summer jobs and so we set off in September. We flew to Calcutta then went through India, Pakistan, Iran and Turkey into Europe and got to Britain in December, just in time for Christmas. In New Zealand Christmas comes in summer, so I wanted to have one with log fires and snow and all that stuff. Which we did – it even snowed a bit. We stayed with Craig's cousins in the Lake District. Then we'd heard that for New Year Scotland was the place to be, so we went to one of my mother's cousins in Inverness. It was great, but very cold.

B St Valentine's Day, St Patrick's Day, the FA Cup Final.

Marco Cecutti is 18 and comes from Italy.

My family owns a small factory – we make kitchen equipment. Last year my father sent me to work in a similar factory in Manchester, to learn the job and improve my English. Manchester isn't a very beautiful city, but it's fun – especially Manchester United. I have a girlfriend now, Susan. She's from Dublin and she's a student here. I sent her a card on St Valentine's Day and after that went out once or twice. But on another saint's day, St Patrick's Day, we went to an Irish pub and we had a really great night. I was hoping United would get to the FA Cup Final this year and we could go to London together, but we got knocked out. Still, we won the league so it wasn't all bad.

C The Boat Race and the Goose Fair

Arnold Kreuzer is an American Pilot based in England.

I've been in England for about five years now so I must like the place. When I get some leave, rather than just hanging around the base like a lot of the guys seem to do, I like to travel around. I've been in London a few times, though not for a while. The last time was for the Boat Race back in April. I used to row at Harvard and had the idea of going on to Oxford to do a master's but things didn't work out. Anyway, it was a great race and Cambridge won, which I liked because Cambridge is just down the road and I know it fairly well. Last week me and some of the guys went over to Nottingham for the Goose Fair. This is quite simply the biggest fair you're ever going to see. It's been going for about 700 years and it was just mind-blowing. All the colours and lights and the smells – I loved it.

D Wimbledon Lawn Tennis Championships and the National Eisteddfod

Moreen Thomas is a 16-year-old from Argentina.

I come from Argentina, but my name is Welsh because my grandfather emigrated from Wales to Patagonia in the south of Argentina to look after sheep. They still speak a dialect down there which mixes Welsh and Spanish so even I know a few Welsh words. So that's me, Welsh, English and Spanish-speaking. However my Spanish is obviously much better than my English. That's true of most of us younger members of the community now. Also, I play tennis and last year I was invited to Wimbledon. I went with my mother and father – my father's also my manager. I got through the first round but was knocked out in the second round by a Czech girl. I was really disappointed, but after that we spent the summer in Britain and in August we went to Wales for the Eisteddfod – it's a big celebration of Welsh language and music.

E Braemar Highland Games

Diego MacAuley Alvarez is 19 and comes from Spain.

I'm from Spain, but my father is Scottish. He came to Spain to work, met my mother and he's still here. We live in Galicia, in the north-west of Spain, and there's still some Celtic tradition there in the music, although the old language has gone. We have a local type of bagpipes and I learned to play these when I was younger, and my father encouraged me to learn the Scottish bagpipes. So when I came to Edinburgh to study English, I had to go to a Highland Games. There's all sorts of athletic events, and throwing big things like hammers and trees, and of course, lots of bagpipes. I went to the Braemar Games, which is the biggest, and the Queen always goes there. I saw her, but the music was my main interest.

UNIT 15

Vocabulary

Money

1 Tick [✔] the words that mean you have enough money. Compare your answers with another student.

> affluent   badly off   broke   hard up   in debt   poor
> prosperous   rich   short (of)   wealthy   well off

2 Some of the words have very similar meanings. Answer the questions and compare your answers.

1 Which word means you have more money, *wealthy* or *well off*?
2 Which word is the opposite of *rich*?
3 Which word is almost the same as *prosperous*?
4 Which word means you have less money, *broke* or *short*.
5 Which word is long-term, *badly off* or *short*?
6 Which word is short-term, *hard up* or *broke*?
7 Which expression means you owe money to someone?
8 Which word is similar to *poor*?

3 Now place them on the scale below.

no money >...
....> a lot of money

4 Match the word from the box to the correct picture.

> a note   bank statement   cash
> cash machine/cash point   cheque   coins/change
> credit card   debit card/switch

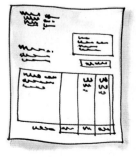

5 Complete these sentences with the correct word.

1 I'd like to pay .... cash.
2 I'd like to pay .... cheque.
3 I'd like to pay with a ....
4 Have you got any .... for the phone?
5 Do you take ....?
6 The .... isn't working.

6 Read the sentences. Are the words in italics good news or bad news?

1 My bank account is *in credit*.
2 My bank account is *overdrawn*.
3 My bank account is *in the red*.
4 My bank account is *in the black*.
5 My bank account is *in debit*.

7 Complete the sentences with a phrasal verb that means the same as the *verb*.

1 Money is *deposited* in a bank account. = Money is .... a bank account.
2 Money is *withdrawn* from a bank account. = Money is .... of a bank account.

8 Complete the sentences with an appropriate word.

1 Switzerland and Japan are .... countries.
2 I haven't got any money. Could you lend me five pounds? I'm ....
3 Have you got any .... for the phone?
4 This machine only accepts .... — it doesn't accept notes.
5 My salary is .... in my bank account at the beginning of every month.
6 I need to go to the bank to .... some money because I want to go shopping.
7 My bank account is .... by £200. I'll have to pay bank charges on it.
8 I'm a bit .... of money at the moment. Could you lend me twenty pounds?
9 I can't pay by .... because I haven't got any money in my account.
10 If the bank's closed, I can get money from the ....

Listening

❶ You are going to hear a conversation between three people from different countries — Argentina, Australia and India. Look at the words in the table. You will hear all of them on the recording. Work with other students and decide in which of the three countries you would be most likely to hear them. For each word, tick one of the boxes.

			Argentina	Australia	India
1	*alcanzar*	to be enough	☐	☐	☐
2	*arvo*	afternoon	☐	☐	☐
3	*barbie*	barbecue	☐	☐	☐
4	*basura*	rubbish	☐	☐	☐
5	*beaut*	good, nice	☐	☐	☐
6	*box-wallah*	businessman	☐	☐	☐
7	*bueno*	good	☐	☐	☐
8	*busy-body*	busy person	☐	☐	☐
9	*qué*	what	☐	☐	☐
10	*cloth piece*	piece of cloth	☐	☐	☐
11	*cobber*	friend	☐	☐	☐
12	*goondaism*	hooliganism	☐	☐	☐
13	*journo*	journalist	☐	☐	☐
14	*key bunch*	bunch of keys	☐	☐	☐
15	*police-wallah*	policeman	☐	☐	☐
16	*Pommy, Pom*	British person	☐	☐	☐
17	*press-wallah*	journalist	☐	☐	☐
18	*strides*	trousers	☐	☐	☐
19	*water bottle*	bottle of water	☐	☐	☐

❷ Each speaker has a different experience of English, and the English they speak has developed in different ways. Discuss these questions with another student:

1 Do you know how English is used in these countries? Is it spoken:
   a as a first language by most of the people?
   b as a second language but also used for official purposes?
   c as a first language by some people but not used officially?
   d only as a second language and not used officially?

2 Which languages have influenced English in each of these countries?

❸ Now listen and check your answers to questions 1 and 2. Write the names Dev, Isabel and Mike against the name of the countries they come from.

1 Argentina ....
2 Australia ....
3 India ....

FCE Paper 4, Part 4

❹ Now listen to the conversation again. For questions 1-7 write D for Dev, I for Isabel and M for Mike in the spaces provided.

1 Who isn't a native-speaker of English? ☐

2 Who has the most negative attitude to the British? ☐

3 Who comes from a community where English is declining in use? ☐

4 Whose grammar isn't influenced by another language? ☐

5 Who complains about an aspect of English grammar? ☐

6 Who uses words which combine elements from different languages? ☐

7 Who uses words from another language without changing them? ☐

Phrasal verbs/expressions with *look*

❶ Work with another student and match the sentences to make ten conversations.

- [ ] 1 I'm looking for my purse. Have you seen it?
- [ ] 2 Hello, Zoe. Where's Simon?
- [ ] 3 Is *practise* spelt with a *c* or an *s*?
- [ ] 4 What are you doing over the weekend?
- [ ] 5 Looking back, I should have asked him before I borrowed his car.
- [ ] 6 I think business is looking up now.
- [ ] 7 Look after yourself — don't work too hard.
- [ ] 8 When will you hear about your computer?
- [ ] 9 Does she get on well with her father?
- [ ] 10 Look out. There's a car right behind you.

A They're looking into what went wrong and they'll be in touch by the end of the week.

B Oh well, we all make mistakes!

C Yes, it's on the kitchen table.

D Oh dear. Too late!

E Yes, we've almost paid off our overdraft and our customers are happy.

F I don't know. I'm just really looking forward to having a rest.

G Oh yes. She's always looked up to him and listened to his advice.

H Oh, he's having a look at a car that we're thinking of buying.

I I will, don't worry.

J I don't know — look it up in a dictionary.

❷ Underline the phrasal verbs/expressions with *look* in question 1. Write each one next to its correct definition below.

1 to anticipate something with pleasure
....

2 to improve
....

3 to examine something
....

4 to investigate
....

5 to find information in a book
....

6 to take care of yourself
....

7 to be careful
....

8 to respect someone
....

9 to remember something in the past
....

10 to search for something
....

❸ Complete each sentence with the appropriate phrasal verb/expression. Compare your answers with another student.

1 If you don't know the meaning of a word, you should .... it .... in a dictionary.

2 Can you help me .... my glasses? I can't find them.

3 .... You're going to fall.

4 Can you .... the DVD player? It's stopped working again.

5 My mother often .... to the days when she was young — it can be very boring.

6 The nurses .... her really well when she was in hospital.

7 I'm .... the weekend because it's my birthday.

8 Things are .... financially now and we're no longer in debt.

9 I didn't .... any of my teachers at school. I thought they were useless.

10 The shop has promised to .... my complaint about the poor service I received.

Grammar

Theory Box

Reported speech (2)

When we report speech, a number of things can change, for example the time and place. If we report it soon afterwards, we might use a present tense instead of a past tense because the reported speech is still true:

Bill	**says**	that he **wants** to go to Rome	**now.**
	is saying		**tomorrow.**
	has said		**next week.**

If we report it later, we may change the time reference:

Bill **said** that he wanted to go to Rome | **then.**
| | | **the next/following day.**
| | | **the following week.**

If we report it in a different place, for example, in Rome, we might say:

Bill said that he wanted to **come** to Rome...

❶ Now use the information on time and place in the table on page 159 to report these statements. Pay particular attention to the changes in time and place between the direct speech and reported speech.

	direct speech	said			reported	
		by	when	where	when	where
1	'I'm moving to a new flat on Monday.'	Martin	Saturday		Monday	
2	'I want to go home now.'	Heather	now	across town	2 minutes later	across town
3	'Jodie's having a party tomorrow night.'	Liz	Thursday		Saturday	
4	'I'll get some new clothes tomorrow.'	Jonny	last week		a week later	
5	'The music shop is over there.'	Will	2 minutes ago	across the street	now	where he pointed to
6	'Pierre's going back to Paris next week.'	Clara	last week	London	a week later	Paris

1 ....

2 ....

3 ....

4 ....

5 ....

6 ....

Theory Box

Reporting verbs

Besides *say*, *ask* and *tell*, a number of other verbs are used to report speech. These are followed by different structures.

		(pro)noun	(that)	clause	preposition	gerund	infinitive
1	verb +						
2	verb +						
3	verb +						
4	verb +						
5	verb +						
6	verb +						

1	She **agreed** to go out with him.
2	He **admitted** stealing the money.
3	Bill **apologised** for insulting her.
4	He **admitted** (that) he had stolen the money.
5	The doctor **advised** me to lose weight.
6	Anne **accused** Joe of cheating.

❷ Decide which of the groups A-F below goes with each of the structures above. Note that some verbs appear in more than one group. Write 1-6 in each of the boxes.

- [ ] **A** *insist*
- [ ] **B** *blame congratulate*
- [ ] **C** *deny recommend suggest*
- [ ] **D** *decide offer promise refuse threaten*
- [ ] **E** *encourage invite recommend remind warn*
- [ ] **F** *agree decide deny explain insist promise realise recommend reply suggest*

❸ Now complete these sentences by putting the verb into an appropriate tense or modal. Compare your answers with another student.

1 *extended present*
   Andrew admitted that he sometimes .... (*go*) home early.

2 *earlier past*
   She agreed she .... (*buy*) too much food.

3 *future in the past*
   Dr Marsh recommended that I .... (*stop*) drinking coffee.

4 *present*
   Fiona denied that she .... (*go out*) with Alan.

5 *past*
   Bert explained that he .... (*lose*) the letter on the way home.

6 *future*
   They've decided that they .... (*have*) the meeting next week.

Theory Box

Reporting verbs and tenses

In group 4 of the reporting verbs, where the verbs are followed by clauses, various tenses and modals can be used:

earlier past	*He admitted that he **had stolen** the car.*
past	*Alison agreed she **made** a mistake.*
future in the past	*He insisted that he **could afford** a bigger car.*
	*Max promised he **would repay** the money.*
present	*His sister realised that she's **studying** too hard.*
extended present	*George denied that he often **gets** impatient.*
future	*Alan replied that he'**ll see** you as soon as possible. The boss has decided that we **must finish** this today.*

UNIT 15
Speaking

1 Work with another student. Read about the festivals below. Write one letter A-F below the name of each country.

    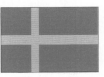

☐ Brazil   ☐ China   ☐ Greece   ☐ Mali   ☐ South Korea   ☐ Sweden

A People believe that during this month, ghosts wander the earth looking for food, so they cook meals for the ghosts to bring good luck. Other kinds of things are offered to dead relatives. Fake bank notes are burned. Some people also burn paper models of houses and cars – even television and radio sets.

B The cattle are brought to the river and driven across. For a few days families are reunited before the cattle are moved on again. On the first day the unmarried men and women dress up and parade through the streets. There is also a competition to judge which cattle are fattest and best looked-after.

C Over the two days of this festival there are many events, including lantern-making contests, martial arts displays, plays and traditional songs and dances. At dusk on the second day, thousands of people parade through the streets carrying lanterns, many of them in the shape of lotus flowers. The celebration ends with a group dance and a fireworks display.

D On this day women don't do any work but instead they spend the day relaxing with friends in cafés. The men have to stay at home, do the housework and look after the children. In some villages, if a man is found away from his home, he will be stripped and soaked with cold water.

E At dawn on December 13th, the eldest daughter in each family puts on a white dress and a head-dress, holding four burning candles. She carries coffee, buns and cookies to her parents. Her sisters and brothers follow, also dressed in white, with the girls carrying burning candles. They then sing the traditional song, Santa Lucia.

F People worship Lemanjá, the goddess of the sea, by dancing and launching small boats and baskets filled with presents, especially her favourites – perfume, mirrors, combs and watermelon. It is believed that if she accepts the gifts they will be carried out to sea. If not, they are washed back onto the shore.

2 Choose the correct name from the box for each festival in question 1.

> Crossing of the Cattle   Reveillon
> Lotus Lantern Festival   Midwife's/Women's Day
> Santa Lucia   The Hungry Ghost Festival

3 Now work with another student. Read the descriptions below of three of the festivals. Underline the words or phrases which are used to introduce or join together the different ideas in each passage.

A Despite Saint Lucia being from far-away Sicily, she is greatly respected in Sweden. Since her feast day, December 13th, is the longest night of the year in the old calendar, she may represent the return of the sun. She might also be important simply due to the fact that her name itself means light. Furthermore, this festival involves candles and white clothes – things which are light, so that people can remember the long dark nights will not last forever.

B For over 350 years, ships carried African slaves to Brazil, and today it has the largest black population outside Africa. These slaves brought their African gods with them. In addition, the Portuguese families usually employed an African woman as a nanny for their children so this tradition became known to the rest of the population. Today, although Brazil is a Catholic country, most people see celebrations like Reveillon as a part of their culture.

C The Fulani people who live in Mali make their living by looking after cattle. The cattle are then sold in the countries to the south, where cattle cannot survive long because of the tsetse fly. However, the grass in Mali is so poor that the cattle must be moved continually, therefore the men can be away from their homes for long periods. This festival brings families together and allows the young people to meet in order to arrange future marriages.

4 Now read these facts about another of the festivals.

- Around 40% of Korea's population is Buddhist.
- Buddha's birthday is on the eighth day of the fourth lunar month.
- A lunar date will fall on a different day every year of the solar calendar.
- Currently this date is in late May.
- Lanterns have always been a popular art-form in Korea.
- Many lanterns are made in the shape of the lotus flower.
- In Buddhism, this flower shows that beauty can come from dirt, just as Buddhists can rise above lower human instincts.

FCE Paper 5, Part 4

5 Now work with another student. Use the words from question 3 to connect these facts into a description of the Lotus Lantern Festival and the reasons why Koreans celebrate in this way.

6 Think about a festival that you know about, either in your own country, or in another country. Write some notes on what people do and why they do these things to explain to another student. Then think of some questions to find out about your partner's festival.

7 Now take it in turns to ask each other about your festivals.

Britain and the World
Vocabulary

Prepositional phrases *for, from, to, under*

1 Choose the correct preposition for each sentence.

1　I think I'll have tea instead of coffee *for/from* a change.
2　I saw a beautiful house *for/to* sale in the newspaper.
3　I visit my cousins *for/from* time to time.
4　We've had fifty phone calls about the new product *for/to* date.
5　It's illegal to buy alcohol *from/under* age.
6　*For/From* my point of view, I think we should ask her what she thinks.
7　What a waste of time. We did all this work *for/to* nothing.
8　I'm not going to phone her *from/for* now on. She can call me.
9　I think people should get married *for/to* life.
10　I agree with you *for/to* some extent but not completely.

2 Underline the prepositional phrase in each sentence in question 1. Then write the expressions which go with each preposition in the table.

for	from	to	under

3 Now choose the correct preposition for these expressions. Write them in the chart.

a change　a while　bad to worse　control
discussion　good　guarantee　hand　hire
lunch　morning to night　my surprise　repair
sale　some degree　your advantage

4 Work with another student. Student A says a prepositional phrase but without the preposition. Student B replies by using the prepositional phrase in a sentence. For example:

Student A: a change

Student B: Last night we went to a Chinese restaurant for a change.

UNIT 15
Vocabulary

American and British English

1 Look at the pictures. What do we call these things in American and British English?

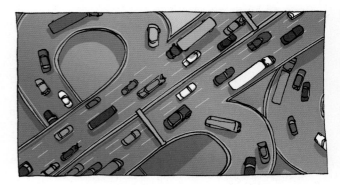

2 Do you know any other words which are different in American and British English?

3 Work with another student and match the British and American words. Check your ideas in a dictionary.

British	American
1 biscuit	a fall
2 handbag	b line up
3 pavement	c restroom
4 queue	d subway
5 sweets	e schedule
6 tap	f garbage
7 timetable	g mail
8 trousers	h cookie
9 underground	i purse
10 autumn	j vacation
11 public toilet	k candy
12 holiday	l faucet
13 post	m pants
14 rubbish	n sidewalk
15 city centre	o cheque
16 bill	p downtown

4 There are also some grammatical differences between American and British English. Read the sentences below. Can you guess which are British English and which are American English?

1a	She just went out of the room.	American
b	She has just gone out of the room.	British
2a	He has already done that.	....
b	He already did that.	....
3a	I'm going to stay home.	....
b	I'm going to stay at home.	....
4a	I'm going to meet him.	....
b	I'm going to meet with him.	....
5a	He's gotten much taller.	....
b	He has got much taller.	....
6a	He isn't going to help.	....
b	He ain't gonna help.	....
7a	They gotta go now.	....
b	They have got to go now.	....
8a	I work Monday to Friday.	....
b	I work Monday thru Friday.	....
9a	What did you do on the weekend?	....
b	What did you do at the weekend?	....

5 Underline the differences between the two sentences. Which ones are differences between tenses/verbs (V) and which ones are differences between prepositions (P)?

Writing

1 Read the statement and then work with other students to answer the following questions.

Within the next few years, American English will become the world's standard language.

1 Decide if you agree or disagree with the statement.
2 Make some notes — write a list of reasons why you do or don't agree.
3 Discuss your ideas with the other students.
4 Decide on a paragraph plan for your answer.
5 Write your answer.

FCE Paper 2, Part 2

2 Write your answer in 120-180 words in an appropriate style.

3 When you have written your answer:

1 swap your composition with another student.
2 comment on your partner's composition and tell them:
   a how interesting it is.
   b how much you agree or disagree with what they say.
   c if it has influenced your ideas.

Vocabulary

Verb and noun collocation with *earn*, *win*, *gain*, *lose*, *spend*

1 Read the sentences and write each *verb* next to its correct definition below.

1 I *spent* all my money on a beautiful dress for the party.

2 I have *gained* so much weight that I can't fit into my clothes.

3 She *won* first prize in the travel competition.

4 I have *lost* my diamond ring — have you seen it?

5 He *earns* a lot of money as bank manager.

a To be successful in a game, war etc., to receive a prize as a result of something. ....

b To work for money or something. It also suggests you deserve what you have worked for. ....

c To obtain something which can be wanted or not. It is not connected with money. ....

d To give out in payment (especially money), to pass one's time. ....

e To no longer have something. ....

2 Which nouns in question 1 can be used with the following verbs?

earn	gain	lose	spend	win

3 Which nouns from the box can be used with the verbs from question 2?

a bet   a place   a race   a salary   a war
an argument   an election   confidence
experience   interest   the advantage
the weekend   time   your job
your temper   your way

4 Interview the other students in the class to find out who has done these things. Make the questions to ask who:

1 has won a prize?

2 has spent a weekend in Paris?

3 has gained valuable experience in their life?

4 has won an election?

5 lost or gained weight recently?

6 lost their temper recently?

7 won an argument recently?

8 earns a high salary?

9 has won a bet?

5 If a student answers *yes* ask another question to find out more information.

6 Complete each sentence with the appropriate verb. Compare your answers with another student.

1 My money .... high interest in a savings account at the moment.

2 Twenty workers .... their jobs when the company closed.

3 The speaker .... confidence when he saw that his audience were listening to him.

4 He .... a place at Oxford University by studying for six months before the entry exam.

5 The two companies are competitors, but the larger one is now .... the advantage over the smaller one.

6 He .... a lot of experience when he worked as a trainee with the company.

7 I .... my way in the dark and had to stop to look where I was on the map.

8 He .... a lot of time deciding what to wear to the job interview.

Use of English

FCE Paper 3, Part 5

1 Read the text below. Use the word given in capitals at the end of each line to form a word that fits in the space in the same line. There is an example at the beginning (0).

DIVIDED BY A COMMON LANGUAGE

In 1877 the linguist Henry Sweet made the
(0)...*prediction*... that within 100 years, British
and American English would be (1)..................
unintelligible. This hasn't happened but mainly
because of British (2)................. to American
English. When the first talking films made their
(3)................. in Britain in the 1920s, people
were heard to complain that the actors were
(4)................. .
Well, it seems their (5)................. developed
quickly enough, but even today, US film and TV
companies are cautious about a British
production (6)................. any form of accent
except RP. (7).................., the traffic in words
across the Atlantic is almost (8)................. in one
direction. Forms like *radio* and *truck* have largely
replaced the British equivalents of *wireless* and
lorry, and we (9)................. use words like
teenager and *baby-sitter* without (10)................
that they originated across the Atlantic.

PREDICT
MUTUAL
ADJUST
APPEAR
COMPREHEND
UNDERSTAND
INVOLVE
MEAN
EXCLUSIVE
CHEERFUL
CARE

1 Choose the correct form of the verb in each sentence below.

1 As well as tennis she **plays/playing** some badminton too.

2 Who is in charge of **feed/feeding** the goldfish?

3 I'd rather we **had/having** more time to think about it.

4 As well as **he works/working** in the office he has an evening job too.

5 I'm looking forward to **see/seeing** that film when it comes out.

6 Despite **he lives/living** beside the sea he has never learned to swim.

7 Although they **work/working** closely together they aren't good friends.

8 I regret **I spend/spending** so much time in the café.

9 She accused me of **I cheated/cheating** in the exam.

10 Whose responsibility is it to **clean/cleaning** this room?

11 Would you mind **feed/feeding** the cats while I'm away?

12 I have no intention of ever **speak/speaking** to him again.

2 Say what you'll do to improve these situations. Use the example to guide you.

0 The car isn't running properly.
get/fix
.....I'll get it fixed.....

1 Your hair's a mess.
get/cut

....

2 The printer isn't working.
have/see to

....

3 The theatre has some tickets for you.
have/pick up

....

4 There's a leak in the pipe here.
get/repair

....

5 It's cold in here. Is the heating off?
have/turn on

....

6 These trousers are too loose.
have/take in

....

7 These doors are a mess.
get/paint

....

3 Put commas into the sentences below where they are necessary.

1 She took great care of her teeth which were beautiful.

2 Sarah whom I've known for years can be short-tempered.

3 The thing which she most wants is a car.

4 He hated doing his military service which lasted six months.

5 The books which sell most copies are written by celebrities.

6 The lecturer who taught me most about it was Tony Allison.

7 I want a computer which has more memory.

8 I'll leave this town which I hate as soon as possible.

9 The novel which I'm most fond of is *Crime and Punishment*.

10 The best horse he owned which was leading suddenly fell.

4 In the sentences below, replace *who/which* with *that* where this is possible.

1 The band which he plays in is quite good.

2 His mother, who comes from Brazil, taught him to speak Portuguese.

3 She isn't very keen on the present which he gave her.

4 The job which he wants would involve him moving to Newcastle.

5 His bike, which wasn't worth much, was stolen last week.

6 The dog, which was old and fat, lay snoring in front of the fire.

5 In these sentences, cross out *who*, *which* or *that* where this is possible.

1 The man that he met was Russian.

2 The woman who met him was Bulgarian.

3 The car which they finally chose was a Toyota.

4 The first film that she starred in was a failure.

5 His speech, which was quite long, was interesting.

6 The thing that I want most now is a cup of coffee.

6 Report the sentences below, following the notes on time and place.

1 'I want to see Jill in Milan on Thursday,' Brian said.
Report this in Milan on Thursday.
....
....

2 'Chris will arrive in an hour,' her mum said.
Report this an hour later.
....
....

3 'I'm starting the new job on Monday,' Bob said.
Report this on Sunday
....
....

4 'The Post Office is at the top of the road,' Sue said.
Report this at the top of the road
....
....

5 'Mr McLean might be able to see you next week,' his secretary said.
Report this two weeks later
....
....

6 'We're moving to the new house in two months,' they said.
Report this a month later
....
....

7 Chose the correct form to follow the reporting verbs in the sentences below.

1 Ned promised **to send/sending** me the money.
2 They suggested **to see/seeing** a specialist.
3 Maria invited me **to help/that I help** myself to the food.
4 Kevin explained **for losing/that he lost** the notebook.
5 They blamed the Foreign Minister **for causing/that he caused** the crisis.
6 She insisted **to come/on coming** along tonight.
7 Her uncle threatened **to close/closing** down the company.
8 He realised **leaving/that he'd left** his books on the bus.
9 Alison recommended **to add/adding** some raisins to the recipe.
10 She encouraged me **to learn/learning** Greek.
11 Cheri apologised **for shouting/that he shouted** at her sister.
12 I congratulated him **on having/that he had** the book published.

8 Change the verbs in brackets below using one example of each of these forms:

Present Simple/*will* + Present Simple/*should* + Present Simple/Present Continuous/Past Simple/Past Perfect.

1 **present**
Marlene denied that she .... (*have*) problems at home.
2 **extended present**
Joe agreed that he .... (*spend*) too much time watching TV.
3 **past**
Ethel insisted that she .... (*need*) some time off work.
4 **earlier past**
Mary admitted that she .... (*make*) a big mistake.
5 **future in the past**
Harry recommended that we .... (*try*) the new bistro.
6 **future**
They promised that they .... (*come*) and fix it soon.

Grammar File

Index

1 Verb tenses, active

1.1 Present Simple

Form: see Appendix 1, Active Tense Structures

These are the most common uses of the Present Simple:

a For permanent situations:
*The sun **rises** in the east.*
*George **lives** in a very small flat.*

b For events which happen repeatedly (often with time expressions like **always, occasionally, often, seldom, sometimes, never, usually,** etc.):
*She always **goes out** on Saturday nights.*
*Larry never **drinks** tea.*
*The Manchester coach **leaves** at 8.30.*

c For short actions that happen at the moment of speaking, for example when you are describing a procedure:
*I **take** three eggs, **break** them in the bowl and **add** a little milk.*

d For actions in the future that are seen as facts:
*Liverpool **play** Arsenal on Saturday.*
*The next train **leaves** in an hour.*

e In situations where we perform the action by saying it:
*I **promise** to tell the truth.*
*I now **declare** this bridge open.*

f For telling jokes and stories:
*A man **goes** to the doctor and **says**, 'Doctor, I think I'm a pair of curtains.' So the doctor **says**, 'Come on — pull yourself together.'*

1.2 Present Continuous

Form: see Appendix 1, Active Tense Structures

The Present Continuous is used:

a To make **long actions** seem more **limited** in time. Compare:
*She **works** for the BBC.*
and:
*She's **working** for the BBC.*

b For temporary actions around the moment of speaking:
*I'm **having** lunch now.*
*The phone's **ringing**.*

c Or for longer, but still temporary actions, which may not be happening at the moment of speaking:
I'm studying a lot these days.

d To make very short actions seem longer or repeated. Compare:
The phone rings as he opens the door.
and:
The phone's ringing as he opens the door.

e When used with **always**, the Present Continuous can make a statement sound more emotional or more like a complaint:
He's always making a fool of himself at parties.
She's always buying me presents.

f For arrangements in the future:
I'm meeting him at 4.00.

This might only be an arrangement with yourself, as long as you made the decision before the moment of speaking:
I'm not going out tonight.

> **Note** that the Present Continuous is not normally used with state verbs like **believe**, **belong**, **cost**, **know**, **mean**, **own**, **realise**, **resemble** and **understand**. These verbs express things which we can't easily control, involuntary states, or facts, we don't make them temporary. See **Appendix 3** page 180. There are also some verbs which have more than one meaning. Whether they take the continuous or not depends on the meaning:
>
> *I think you're wrong.*
>
> Here **think** = **believe**. We can't change this.
>
> *I'm thinking about my family.*
>
> Here **think** refers to an action.
>
> *I see him.*
>
> He's just across the street. We can't control what we see.
>
> *He's seeing his girlfriend tonight.*
>
> Here **see** = **meet**. This can be changed.

1.3 Present Perfect

Form: see Appendix 1, Active Tense Structures

The Present Perfect is used for actions in the past that are relevant to the moment of speaking. The main uses are:

a For actions that began in the past and are still in progress. Note that the Present Perfect doesn't tell us whether the action is going to continue into the future:
I've been a student for three years and I've got one more year to do.
She's lived there for a long time but now she's moving.

b For actions in the past where the time is not stated. We use the Present Perfect because

something is important at the moment of speaking:
I don't want to see that film — I've already seen it twice.
I've been to Beijing so I can tell you something about it.

c For actions that have happened very recently, exactly how recently depends on the situation:
Give me a cloth. Fred's dropped his coffee cup on the floor.
You won't see Linda for a while, she's gone to Australia.

> **Note** that a number of words are closely associated with the Present Perfect:
>
> **a** **since** to say when the action started:
> *I've been here since six o'clock/Thursday/ August.*
>
> **b** **for** to say how long the action has been in progress:
> *She's known him for years.*
>
> **c** **just** to say that the action happened a short time ago:
> *Leroy's just left.*
>
> **d** **yet** to say that we expect something to happen:
> *Has the prime minister arrived yet?*
>
> **e** **already** to say that something happened before we expected it:
> *They've already scored a goal.*
>
> **f** **ever/never** to say that we are talking about all the time available:
> *Has Jo ever been to France?*
> *The Olympics have never been in Manchester.*

1.4 Present Perfect Continuous

Form: see Appendix 1, Active Tense Structures

The difference between the Present Perfect and the Present Perfect Continuous depends on the type of verb:

a With long-time verbs like **live** or **work**, in most cases there is no significant difference:
I've lived / been living here for six months.

However, if we are talking about a permanent situation, the Present Perfect Continuous isn't suitable because the continuous form makes the permanent action seem more temporary:
His granny has lived in Bristol all her life.
Not *has been living.*

b With shorter time verbs, we can use the Present Perfect Continuous to make the action seem longer:
I've spoken to Richard.
I've been speaking to Richard.

Or repeated:
*The students **have arrived**.*
*The students **have been arriving**.*

c When we are talking about a recent activity and don't include the details, the Present Perfect Continuous makes it seem more significant:
*'What have you done today?' 'I**'ve been studying**.'*
***Have** you **been crying**?*

1.5 Past Simple

Form: see Appendix 1, Active Tense Structures
We use the Past Simple:

a For actions in the past where the time the action happened is stated or understood by the listener:
*Clara **was** born in 1985.*
*How **was** the film?*
(I know you went to the cinema last night.)

b For actions in present or future time which are unreal. These include:

1 Wishes:
*I wish you **were** here.*
*If only **I had** more time.*

2 Suggestions:
*It's time we **went**.*

3 Preferences:
*I'd rather you **didn't tell** her.*

4 Second conditionals:
*If **I knew**, I'd tell you.*
(See also Section 6.2.)

5 Hypotheses:
*Suppose you **were** rich. What would you do?*
*Imagine you **were** on a desert island — would you survive?*

6 Polite enquiries:
***Did** you **want** something?*
*I thought you **had** some free time tonight.*

7 Polite requests:
*I **wondered** if I could borrow some money.*

In unreal situations, when we want to indicate more formality, we can use **were** instead of **was**:

*I wish she **were** here.*
*If only he **were** richer.*
*Suppose Isabel **were** here now.*

1.6 Past Continuous

Form: see Appendix 1, Active Tense Structures
The Past Continuous is used:

a To make actions in the past seem longer in time. This can signal that they were in progress when another action happened:
*She **was speaking** to Danny when I came in.*
*She **started speaking** to him before I came in.*

b Sometimes to make long actions seem shorter:
*His father **worked** in London.*
*His father **was working** in London at the time.*

c For future events seen from a point in the past:
*She got her hair done because she **was starting** a new job the next day.*

d Like the Past Simple, the Past Continuous is used for unreal events in present or future time:

1 Wishes:
*I wish he **was working** now.*
*If only I **was** still **seeing** her.*

2 Suggestions:
*It's time we **were going**.*

3 Preferences:
*I'd rather you **weren't going out** with him.*

4 Second conditionals:
*If I **was going** to a party I'd dress better than that.*
(See also Section 6.2.)

5 Hypotheses:
*Suppose she **was living** here.*
*Imagine you **were working** in Hollywood.*

6 Polite enquiries:
***Were** you **looking** for someone?*
*I thought we **were** going out tonight.*

7 Polite requests:
*I **was wondering** if I could borrow your car.*

> **Note** that a request with the Past Continuous, e.g. **was wondering**, is seen as more polite than one with the Past Simple.

1.7 Past Perfect

Form: see Appendix 1, Active Tense Structures

When used for real events, the Past Perfect works in an area of time we call **past-in-the-past** or **earlier past time**. We can use it in the following ways:

a To place one event before another in the past:
Compare:
*Alberto **left** when the film started.*
and:
*Alberto **had left** when the film started.*

> **Note** that the Past Perfect is only necessary when there might be some confusion about the order of events. We don't need it here:
> *He **woke up** and **got out** of bed.*
> It's unlikely that he would get out of bed before he woke up.

b To place one event further before another event in the past. Compare:
*When the film **finished** she **went** out.*

and:

*When the film **had finished** she **went** out.*

The Past Perfect suggests more time passed between when the film finished and she went out.

c   For unreal events in past time. These are the main types:

1   Wishes:
*I wish he**'d told** me this yesterday.*

2   Preferences:
*I'd rather you **hadn't eaten** all the biscuits.*

3   The third conditional:
*If I**'d known**, I would have told you.*
(See also Section 6.3.)

4   Hypotheses:
*Suppose she**'d stayed** in Paris, what would have happened?*
*Imagine you**'d married** Joanna.*

1.8   Past Perfect Continuous

Form: see Appendix 1, Active Tense Structures

Like the Past Perfect, this tense is also used for real events in **past-in-the-past** or **earlier past time**. We can use it in the following ways:

a   To make events seem longer. Compare:
*He**'d spoken** to Moira before I arrived.*
and:
*He**'d been speaking** to Moira before I arrived.*

b   To make events seem more significant. Compare:
*When I came in I saw that she**'d cried**.*
and:
*When I came in I saw that she**'d been crying**.*

c   With 'short-time' verbs, to suggest that the event was repeated:
*The guns **had fired** earlier.*
*The guns **had been firing** earlier.*

d   For future in the past when the event is placed before a later event:
*He**'d been thinking** of leaving her before she won the lottery.*

e   Like the Past Perfect, it can be used for unreal events in past time:

1   Wishes:
*I wish she **hadn't been working** for John when it happened.*

2   Preferences:
*I'd rather he**'d been playing** for Chelsea.*

3   The third conditional:
*If I**'d been sitting** in the front seat, I would have been killed.*
(See also Section 6.3.)

4   Hypotheses:
*Just suppose you**'d been sailing** on the Titanic.*
*Imagine she**'d been wearing** that dress.*

Verb tenses, passive   2

Form: see also Unit 5, page 54

While there are eight active tenses, there are only six passive ones. The **Present** and **Past Perfect Continuous** use the **Present** and **Past Perfect** passive forms. If the active voice focuses on the actions the passive focuses on the result:

		present	past
Simple	active	*people tell stories*	*they invited him*
	passive	*stories are told*	*he was invited*
Continuous	active	*they're following me*	*she was fixing it*
	passive	*I'm being followed*	*it was being fixed*
Perfect	active	*I've eaten them*	*they'd built it*
	passive	*they have been eaten*	*it had been built*
Perfect Continuous	active	*I've been eating them*	*they'd been building it*

Only transitive verbs (verbs that take an object) can take passive forms. Sentences like the following can't be changed to the passive:

He lives in Ireland.
He died in 1967.
We arrived late.

There are a number of reasons for using a passive rather than an active form of the verb. These are the most important:

a   When we don't want to mention the subject of an active sentence:
*This castle **was built** between 1296 and 1320.*
Who by? Well, the builders, presumably.

*This game **is played** in the Basque country.*
Who by? The people who play it.

*The photocopier **was broken** last night.*
Who by? Actually, I broke it, but I don't want to say so.

b   When we'd prefer to put the active subject at the end of the sentence. The active subject is now called the **agent** and is joined to the rest of the sentence with **by**:
*The cat **was chased by** a big dog.*
*This bridge **was opened** last year **by** the prime minister.*

c   Active and passive forms are used together to give variety:
*The first goal **came** in the 13th minute and it **was scored** by Martin. Ten minutes later young Mike Gregory **got** the second and early in the second half another one **was added** when a high ball from the left **was headed** in by Anderson.*

d   In informal use, **get** can be used to make the passive instead of **be**:
*His leg **got broken** in a skiing accident.*
*Bob's car **got stolen** last night.*

Grammar File

3 Modal auxiliaries

Any one of the English modals or semi-modals can come before any of the present tenses, like this:

will		
would		
shall	*win*	Present Simple
should		
can	*be winning*	Present Continuous
she *could*		
may	*have won*	Present Perfect
might		
must	*have been winning*	Present Prefect Continuous
has to		
's going to		

a   Modals are always followed by the main verb, so the Present Continuous:

She **is** winning.	becomes	She should **be** winning.
She **has** won.	becomes	She should **have** won.

b   We can't put a modal in front of a past tense:
She may won. ✗

c   For past time we use one of the Present Perfect forms:
*She may **have won**.*
*She may **have been winning**.*

3.1 'Present' modals

The main meanings of these are:

shall	intention	When **shall** we **arrive**?
will ('ll)	intention judgement	When **will** you **leave**? He**'ll be** at home now.
can	ability permission possibility	He **can swim** quite well. You **can go** if you want to. Strange things **can happen**.
may	permission possibility	You **may come** in now. This **may happen**.
must	internal obligation logical deduction	You **must see** a doctor. The answer **must be** wrong.
going to	intention judgement	What **are** you **going to do**? It**'s going to** rain.
have (got) to	external obligation logical deduction	You **have (got) to** stop here. She **has (got) to** be joking.
need	necessity	You **needn't** bother.
should/ought to	obligation	You **ought to** be careful.

Note that although we call them 'present' modals, all of these can work equally in **present** or **future** time. In fact, we don't know which time is being referred to unless we know the context. The questions:
Who'll get the job?
And:
Who's that at the door?
Can both be answered by:
It'll be Jack.

---

a   **will/shall**
Shall expresses more sense of choice than **will**:
*What time **will** we arrive?*
This question asks for the listener's judgement, and might be said to the ticket collector on a train.
*What time **shall** we arrive?*
This question suggests there is a choice of times. You might say this to a companion in a car.

b   **will/going to**
Will expresses intention from the moment of speaking, **going to** from before the moment of speaking.
*I'm not sure what to do tonight — I think I**'ll** just **stay** in and watch TV.*
*I have to get this work finished because I**'m going to go** out tonight.*

With judgement, **will** expresses a personal opinion or feeling. **Going to** asks the listener to look at the evidence.
*I don't think they're right for each other. They**'ll** probably break up soon.*
*They have rows every day — they**'re** not **going to** stay together much longer.*

c   **may**
These days **may** is only used in very formal situations, to express permission.

d   **must**
When used for obligation, the negative can be either **mustn't** (negative obligation), or **don't have to/needn't** (no obligation). The negative, when used for logical deduction, is **can't**:
*You **mustn't** smoke in the building.*
*You **don't have to** do your homework.*
*That answer **can't** be right.*

e   **have (got) to**
Unlike the others, this has a past form: **had to**, which also functions as a past version of **must**.
*I **had to finish** the job.*

f   **need**
There is also a full verb, **to need to**, used in sentences like:
*Do I **need to** do it?*

Need as a modal is mainly used in questions and negatives like:
Need *I ask?*
*You **needn't** bother.*

However, in the past there is a difference between **need** and **need to** in the negative. Compare:
I needn't have gone to the library.

In this sentence, I went to the library and found out that it was not necessary to go.

I didn't need to go to the library.

In this sentence, I knew it wasn't necessary to go to the library. The sentence doesn't say whether I went or not.

3.2 'Past' modals

The meanings of **should**, **would**, **could** and **might** correspond to **shall**, **will**, **can** and **may**. The only difference is that when we change **shall** to **should**, we get a meaning like **obligation**:
I should do it.

This sentence means that I know I have an obligation — but I may or may not have the intention of doing it.
There are two main areas of use of 'past' modals:

a   In unreal present/future time:

I *shall* do it.	I *should* do it but I don't want to.	obligation
What *will* you do? This *will* work.	What *would* you do if you had time? Let's suppose this *would* work.	intention judgement
I *can* do it. You *can* park here. Strange things *can* happen.	I *could* do it tomorrow if I wanted to. You *could* park here if they allowed it. Things *could* go wrong if we're not careful.	ability permission possibility
You *may* eat now. It *may* be OK.	*Might* I suggest you try the beef? It *might* be OK but I doubt it.	permission possibility

b   And in real past time:

I *shall* see him.	I knew that I *should* see him.	obligation
We *will* go out. It *will* happen soon.	In those days we *would* go out most nights. I knew it *would* all go wrong.	intention judgement
Jess *can* speak German. You *can* smoke in here. There *can* be another way.	I *could* speak German when I was young. You *used to be able* to smoke here. There *could* be more options at that time.	ability permission possibility
Jill *may* leave now. Anything *may* happen now.	The boss said that Jill *might* leave. Anything *might* happen then.	permission possibility

c   When modals are used with the Present Perfect or Present Perfect Continuous, their meaning doesn't change. However, now, instead of referring to:

real events in present/future time:
It may go wrong.

or unreal events in present/future time:
It might go wrong.

or real events in past time:
We knew it might go wrong.

they refer to unreal events in past time:
It might have gone wrong but it didn't.

We don't know what *may have happened.*	possibility
They *might have gone away* for the weekend.	possibility
She *could have been* here but I'm not sure.	possibility
You *must have eaten* too much.	deduction
You *can't have felt* very well.	negative deduction
You *should have told* me. Why didn't you?	unfulfilled obligation
If he had been here, I *would have seen* him.	intention

used to, would, be used to, get used to   **4**

4.1   *used to* and *would*

Used to and **would** are both used for repeated actions in the past. However, by choosing **would** you also suggest that the action was voluntary. Because of this, **would** isn't used for actions which you can't affect in the short term. Both **used to** and **would** are followed by the basic verb:
He used to live in Birmingham but he would return to Wales whenever he could.

4.2   *be used to* and *get used to*

Be used to means **be accustomed to**. **Get used to** means **become accustomed to**. Both of these are followed by:

a   A noun:
Pablo's used to/is getting used to the British weather.

b   A gerund:
She still isn't used to/hasn't got used to driving to work.

c   A pronoun:
He was a difficult guy, but she was used to/got used to him.

d   A noun clause:
Bob should be used to/getting used to what they eat in India.

Grammar File

5 Clauses

5.1 Verbs + infinitive (to + verb) or gerund (verb + ing)?

a Verbs which can only be followed by the gerund:

> admit appreciate avoid consider deny
> dislike enjoy face finish forgive
> give up imagine involve keep mention
> miss practise risk suggest understand

b Verbs which can only be followed by the infinitive:

> afford agree appear arrange ask care
> consent decide expect fail happen hope
> learn need offer prepare pretend
> promise refuse seem swear want wish

c Verbs which can be followed by either with no difference in meaning:

> attempt begin continue hate
> intend love prefer start

d Verbs which can be followed by either, but with a difference in meaning.

> forget go on like mean
> regret remember stop try

> **Notes**
>
> **forget:** *He **forgot to tell** her.*
> This means he didn't tell her because he forgot.
> *He **forgot telling** her.*
> This means he told her but then forgot he had done so.
>
> **go on:** *She **went on to write** novels.*
> This means she did something else first, then became a novelist.
> *She **went on writing** novels.*
> This means she continued writing novels.
>
> **like:** *I **like to swim** before breakfast.*
> This means I prefer to do it at this time.
> *I **like swimming** before breakfast.*
> This means I enjoy the activity.
>
> **mean:** *He **meant to visit** his aunt.*
> This means he intended to visit his aunt.
> *He **meant visiting** his aunt.*
> This means he was talking about visiting his aunt, but perhaps you misunderstood him.
>
> **regret:** *I **regret to tell** you.*
> This means I'm going to tell you but I'm sorry I have to do it.
> *I **regret telling** you.*
> This means I'm sorry that I told you.

> **remember:** *I **remembered to send** the e-mail.*
> This means I didn't forget to send it.
> *I **remembered sending** the e-mail.*
> This means I had a memory of sending it.
>
> **stop:** *She **stopped to drink** coffee.*
> This means she stopped what she was doing and drank coffee.
> *She **stopped drinking** coffee.*
> This means she didn't drink any more coffee.
>
> **try:** *He **tried to lose** weight.*
> This means he went on a diet, which was a difficult, or impossible, activity for him.
> *He **tried losing** weight.*
> This means he lost weight as an experiment.

5.2 Other ways of using -ing forms

The most common are:

a After a preposition:
***Despite being** so young, he's good at the job.*
***As well as swimming**, she likes jogging and tennis.*

b After a verb + preposition:
*I'm **looking forward to seeing** you.*
*She's **thinking of leaving** home.*

c After a noun (sometimes with an optional preposition):
*She spent two **months painting** that picture.*
*You'll have no **difficulty (in) finding** it.*

d After a pronoun + preposition:
*Alison accused **her of stealing** her boyfriend.*
*The injury prevented **him from playing** for months.*

e After an adjective + preposition:
*Who's **responsible for checking** these figures?*
*She's very **good at avoiding** work.*

f After a preposition + (pro)noun:
*The bus left **with him running** behind it.*
*The game ended **without either team scoring** a goal.*

g After a noun + preposition + (pro)noun:
*There's no **point in you telling** me what to do.*
*There has to be **a reason for things being** so difficult.*

5.3 Verbs + that clause

a Some verbs can be followed by a clause beginning with **that**:
*I recommend **that** you do it.*

b Other verbs can't do this. We have to say:
*I advise you **to do** it.*

verbs which are followed by a *that*-clause:

> agree believe conclude expect explain
> feel find forget hear hope know
> learn predict pretend regret reply say
> suggest think understand write

c A *that*-clause can also be the subject of a sentence:
That the job would be difficult was something I expected.
That the price had risen so much came as a surprise.

5.4 *have/get* + object + past participle

a We use this structure to talk about someone else doing something for us, like a service:
*I must **have the TV fixed** this week so we can watch the match on Saturday.*
*I can't get online. I need **to get this modem checked**.*
*She isn't here. She's **getting the car washed**.*
*He only **had his hair cut** because of the interview.*

Have or **get** can take any tense or modal. We often use the infinitive followed by **need, want, would like**, etc. The difference between the two verbs is that **get** is less formal than **have**:
*I **need to get the car serviced**.*
*They **want to have the new carpet fitted**.*
*They **would like to have a washing machine fitted**.*

b We can also use **get** to mean finish doing something:
*Once I **get my homework done**, I'm going to go out.*
*He's a bit slow but he always **gets the job done**.*

5.5 Relative clauses

a There is a difference in meaning between these two sentences:
The students who worked hard were given an afternoon off.
The students, who worked hard, were given an afternoon off.

Each of them contains a relative clause — a clause introduced by a relative pronoun, in this case **who**. However, in the first sentence, the clause tells us *which* students were given an afternoon off — the ones who worked hard. So we call **who worked hard** a **defining relative clause**. In the second sentence, the relative clause is separated from the rest of the sentence by commas. This tells us that the meaning of the sentence is that all the students were given an afternoon off. The relative clause, **who worked hard**, just gives us some extra information about them — that all of them worked hard. We call this a **non-defining relative clause**.

b Relative clauses can also be introduced by other relative pronouns, such as **which, whose** and **where**:
*The workers **whose break-time was over** left the canteen.*
*The workers, **whose break-time was over**, left the canteen.*
*The house **where Marta grew up** was in the country.*
*The house, **where Marta grew up**, was in the country.*

c In defining relative clauses it is possible to replace **who** or **which** with **that**. We can't do this in non-defining clauses. It is possible to say:
*The students **that worked hard** were given an afternoon off.*
*The film **that I liked** was a detective story.*

But not:
*The students, **that worked hard**, were given an afternoon off.* ✗
*The film, **that I liked**, was a detective story.* ✗

d Also, in defining relative clauses **only**, it is possible to leave out the relative pronoun **if the sentence starts with an object**:

S   V   O
He bought the trainers. They were the most expensive.

      O   S   V
The trainers ~~which~~ he bought were the most expensive.

> **Note** that if the sentence begins with a subject, the relative pronoun has to stay:
>
> S   V   O
> *He bought the trainers **which** were the most expensive.*

Conditionals   6

The three basic types of conditional sentence are:

Type 1/First	*If it's too expensive, I won't buy it.*
	If + Present Simple, *will* + verb
	For more probable events in present or future time.
Type 2/Second	*If it was too expensive, I wouldn't buy it.*
	If + Past Simple, *would* + verb
	For less probable or impossible events in present or future time.
Type 3/Third	*If it had been too expensive, I wouldn't have bought it.*
	If + Past Perfect, *would have* + past participle
	For events in past time which didn't happen.

However, other forms are possible.

Grammar File

6.1 Type 1/First Conditionals

The **if**-clause can come after the result clause (**a, d, j**). The other 'present' modals can be used in either clause (**b-e**). We can use no modals at all (**f**). The imperative can be used in the result clause (**g**). The other present tenses, Continuous, Perfect and Perfect Continuous, can be used in either clause (**h-k**).

a *I'll take the bus home **if I finish early.***

b *If you're hungry, I **can** make you a sandwich.*

c *If she's here, I **must** talk to her.*

d *I **won't** speak to you if you**'re going to** get angry.*

e *If he **has to** be there early, he **may** take the train.*

f *If it snows, I don't go out.*

g *If you want to enter the competition, **ring this number.***

h *If he**'s gone** home, I'll speak to him tomorrow.*

i *If she**'s coming** to the party, I may stay at home.*

j *He'll be tired if he**'s been working** since six o'clock.*

k *If he**'s told** me, I**'ve forgotten** all about it.*

6.2 Type 2/Second Conditionals

The **if**-clause can come after the result clause (**a, c**). The other 'past' modals can be used in either clause (**b-d**). The Past Continuous can also be used in either clause (**d, e**).

a *I'd help him **if I knew what to do.***

b *If I **could** run a business, I might give it a try.*

c *He **could** walk straight into that job if he wanted it.*

d *If she **was studying** now, she'd be in the library.*

e *If he was leaving tomorrow, he**'d be getting ready** now.*

6.3 Type 3/Third Conditionals

The **if**-clause can come after the result clause (**a, e**), the other 'perfect' modals can be used in either clause (**b, c**) and the Past Perfect Continuous can also be used in either clause (**d, e**).

a *I would have done it if I**'d had time.***

b *If I'd had enough money, I **might have lent** him some.*

c *If you **could have seen** it, you would have laughed.*

d *If I'd read that book, I **would have been** wasting my time.*

e *I would have known about it if she**'d been seeing** him.*

Note that while we use Type 3 Conditionals to talk about events in the past which didn't happen, it is also possible to talk about events which did. The **Real Past Conditionals** can have the same form as a Type 2 Conditionals:

*If the river **rose**, the people **would leave** their homes.*

Or it can use two past tenses:

*If I **saw** him, I always **spoke** to him.*

6.4 Mixed Conditionals

We can begin a conditional sentence with one type and finish it with another. Any combination is possible, but the most common ones are:

a **Type 1 > Type 2**, to indicate reduced probability in the result clause:
   If they trust you, maybe I could.
   If I get tired I might have a nap.

b **Type 3 > Type 2**, to indicate a move from past to present/future time:
   If he'd married Clara, he'd be a happier man today.
   If you hadn't made so many mistakes, you might not be in such a mess.

c **Type 2 > Type 1** which uses **should** in the *if*-clause. This indicates a higher probability than a normal Type 2. This form is commonly used in safety instructions:
   If a fire should break out, break the glass and push the alarm button.

   But it also has other uses:
   If you should meet Bill, tell him I want to see him.

   The speaker considers it a strong possibility that he will meet Bill.

Note that it is also possible to have a sentence with the same form as a Type 1, but which does not actually express a condition:

If you don't need something to eat, there's still a shop at the corner.

There's still a shop at the corner, even if you don't need something to eat.

6.5 Other ways of expressing conditions

Apart from **if**, we also use a number of other words to express conditions:

a **providing (that)/provided (that)/as long as**
   These indicate a single condition which is necessary to get the result:
   ***Providing (that)** you remember to switch it on, it will work.*
   *You'll pass the text, **provided (that)** you remember to turn up.*
   ***As long as** you go on taking these pills, you'll feel fine.*

b even if
We use this to indicate an extreme condition:
Even if you ask me nicely, I won't cook for you again.
I'm going to speak to him, even if he doesn't want to see me.

c unless/providing (that)/provided (that)/as long as
These refer to a single necessary condition which will produce the result. However, **they** work in the opposite way:
You'll get the job, provided you pass the medical.
You'll get the job, unless you fail the medical.
You'll get the job, if you pass/don't fail the medical.

7 Reported speech

1   Statements can be reported in the same tenses that are used by the speaker, especially if they are reported soon afterwards and/or the statement is still true. Reporting verbs like **say** and **tell** can also be used in the present tense:
'I'm going to London soon.' →
She says (that) she's going to London soon.

2   Later, and/or if the statement is no longer true, the tenses change in reported speech:

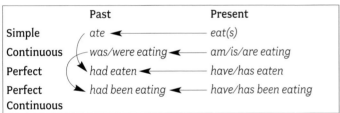

	Past	Present
Simple	ate ◄────	eat(s)
Continuous	was/were eating ◄──	am/is/are eating
Perfect	had eaten ◄────	have/has eaten
Perfect Continuous	had been eating ◄────	have/has been eating

Any statement made in the Past Perfect or Past Perfect Continuous has to be reported in the same tense — there is nowhere else to go:
'I'd known for some time.' →
He said (that) he'd known for some time.

Modals change to their equivalent past form:
'I can do it later.' →
She said (that) she could do it later.

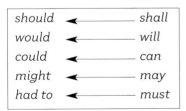

should ◄────	shall
would ◄────	will
could ◄────	can
might ◄────	may
had to ◄────	must

Past modals don't change:
'It might happen at any time.' →
He said (that) it might happen at any time.

3   Yes/no questions are reported using **if** and word order changes to the usual order for statements:
'Are you having fun?'
He asked (me) if I was having fun.

4   **Wh**-questions use the question word and word order also changes to the usual order for statements:

'Where are you going?'
He asked me where I was going.

5   Commands use **tell** and **to/not to**:
'Stop making a fuss.'
She told me to stop making a fuss.
'Don't break it.'
She told me not to break it.

6   If speech is reported later, **time words** in statements may change:

'I want to see her now.'	*He said (that) he wanted to see her then.*
tomorrow	the next/following day
	yesterday / today
next week	the following week
	last week /this week

7   If the speech is reported in a different place, references to movement and location also change.
'I want to go and see him there.'
She said she wants to come and see you here.

8   Often when we report speech, we don't simply reproduce the words spoken; we use a reporting verb and make a summary. So instead of reporting:
'You stole my girlfriend.'
as:
He said that I had stolen his girlfriend.
we might say:
He accused me of stealing his girlfriend.
The reporting verbs fall into 6 groups, each with its own grammar:

1   **agree, decide, offer, promise, refuse** and **threaten** are followed by an **infinitive**:
'I'll tell the police.'
He threatened to tell the police.

2   **admit, deny, recommend** and **suggest** are followed by a **gerund**:
'I think you should speak to Bernie.'
He suggested speaking to Bernie.

3   **advise, encourage, invite, recommend, remind** and **warn** are followed by a **noun** or **pronoun** and an **infinitive**:
'Remember to tell Joe.'
He reminded me to tell Joe.

4   **apologise** and **insist** are followed by a **preposition** and a **noun, pronoun** or **gerund**:
'I'm sorry I said it.'
She apologised for saying it.

5   **accuse (of), blame (for)** and **congratulate (on)** are followed by a **noun** or **pronoun**, a **preposition** and usually another **noun, pronoun** or **gerund**:
'It's all your fault.'
She blamed me for everything.

6   **explain, promise, realise** and **reply** are followed by optional **that** and a **clause**:
'I was at home that day.'
He explained (that) he had been at home that day.

A number of verbs in groups 1-5 above can also work in this way. These are **agree, decide, deny, insist, promise, recommend** and **suggest**. For a fuller list of verbs in each group go to page 159.

Grammar File

8 Nouns

8.1 Countable and uncountable

Uncountable nouns don't have a plural form and take a singular verb. Forms used with these are:

countable	uncountable
a drink	*some* milk
very few pencils	*very little* paper
a few potatoes	*a little* rice
another book	*some more* paper
fewer storms	*less* rain
not many problems	*not much* trouble
many/a lot of jackets	*a lot of* clothes
too many pictures	*too much* furniture

8.2 Singular and plural

a Singular countable nouns which don't change in the plural:

> barracks   crossroads   deer   headquarters
> salmon   series   sheep   species   aircraft
> Swiss   Chinese   Japanese

b Countable nouns which can be either singular or plural:

> family   team   government   staff   group
> (political) party   class   union   committee
> club   jury

c Uncountable nouns which look like plurals:

> athletics   billiards   binoculars   draughts
> jeans   mathematics   measles   news
> pants   pyjamas   scissors
> spectacles/glasses   trousers

d Plural uncountable nouns which have no singular:

> police   cattle   goods   groceries   manners
> savings   stairs   thanks   the English
> the French   the Spanish

Adjectives 9

9.1 Order of adjectives

When putting a number of adjectives in order, we move from the more subjective and temporary towards the more objective and permanent adjectives. The order given here can be varied a little but is a useful guide:

quality > size > age > shape > colour > origin > material > purpose

a nice big old narrow brown French wooden kitchen chair

> **Note** that when writing, you usually use a maximum of three adjectives with a noun.

9.2 Comparatives and superlatives

Form: see Appendix 2, Comparative and Superlative.

9.3 Adverbs: comparative and superlative

Adverbs generally form comparatives and superlatives with **more** and **most**:
He ran **more quickly** than his friends.

However, those adverbs which have the same form as adjectives use **-er** and **-est**:

	adjective	adverb
early	*I have an **earlier** start tomorrow.*	*She arrived **earlier** than usual.*
fast	*E-mail is **faster** than the post.*	*He drove **faster** than usual.*
hard	*It's **harder** work than her last job.*	*She's working **harder** these days.*
high	*The temperature is **higher** today.*	*Let's climb just a little **higher**.*
late	*Have you seen the **latest** news?*	*This is the **latest** he's ever worked.*
low	*He got the **lowest** mark for maths.*	*He came **lowest** in the class for maths.*
long	*Who's been here the **longest** time?*	*Who do you think will stay **longest**?*
near	*Where's the **nearest** post office?*	*John came the **nearest** to winning.*
soon	*His birthday is **sooner** than I thought.*	*Could he come **sooner** than Tuesday?*

Some forms are irregular:

badly	*worse*	*worst*
little	*less*	*least*
much	*more*	*most*
well	*better*	*best*

Far uses **farther**, **farthest** for distance:
*Who ran **farthest**?*

and **further**, **furthest** both for distance and for the meaning of additional/extra:
*Let's develop this idea **further**.*

10 Articles

Articles — *the*, *a/an* or no article?

10.1 *the*

In general, we use **the** when it is obvious to the listener what the speaker is talking about. To communicate effectively, we need to share the same **frame of reference**.

a If there is only one item of its type in the frame, we can use **the**.
In a room we can say:
*Shut **the door**, will you?*
Talking about our local area we can say:
*I saw **the doctor** today.*
***The sea** looks cold.*
If we talk about our country we can say:
***The government's** in a mess.*
and:
***The railways** are expensive.*
Talking about the world we can say:
***The North Pole** is warming up.*
and:
***The moon** looks red tonight.*
Talking about the universe we can say:
*Our future is in **the stars**.*

b Geography

We use **the** with	
oceans	*The Atlantic*
seas	*The Mediterranean*
mountain ranges	*The Alps*
island groups	*The Bahamas*
rivers	*The Tiber*
deserts	*The Gobi*

c Frames of reference can also work in terms of time:
*How was **the party**?*
and:
*Did you enjoy **the holiday**?*
and:
*Will you pass **the exam**?*

We can talk about events in someone's past and we can also do this with well-known events:
*He died in **the war**.*
and:
*They lost **the election**.*

d We can also have a grammatical frame of reference:
*...**the biggest house** in town...*
*...**the first man** on the moon...*
*...**the next film** I see...*
*...**the last chance** you have...*
*...**the same problems**...*
*...**the only thing** I want...*

e There are other ways we can refer to a noun, to let the listener know what exactly we are talking about. We can talk about it for the second time:
Yesterday I read a book and saw a film.
*Let me tell you about **the book**.*

We can indicate which one we mean:
*David Beckham — **the guy** I work with, not the footballer... .*
and:
*David Beckham — not **the** David Beckham — I mean a guy I work with who has the same name.*

f We also use **the** where we are talking about a group of things in general.
*Who invented **the computer**?*
*We need to save **the whale**.*
*She's learning **the guitar**.*

10.2 *a/an*

a We use **a/an** to identify a noun by saying that it is part of a group:

Is it a bird?    Is it a plane?

No — it's Superman!

b We use **a/an** to describe people's jobs.

c We can pick out one item from a group and describe it individually:
***A good shirt** can be quite expensive.*
*Have you got **a jacket** that would fit me?*

10.3 No article

When we talk about everything that exists of one type, there is no need for an article:
*One day we're going to run out of **oil**.*
***Computers** are coming down in price.*

Compare this with:
*Who invented **the computer**?*

When we use **the** we are thinking of a **type** or **group**. When we use no article we are thinking of **individual examples**:
***Computers** in the shops.*

Grammar File

We don't use **the** with names of countries — *France*

villages, towns and cities unless they contain an adjective — *Newcastle*
The *United Kingdom*
The *Vatican City*

or are plural — **The** *Netherlands*

We don't use **the** for the names of mountains: — *Kilimanjaro*

We also use no article when someone attends a school, college, university, hospital or church **for the intended purpose.** Compare these sentences:

*She's **in class** — the lesson will be finished in half an hour.*
*She's the only Chinese student in **the class**.*

*He's still **at school**. He won't leave for another year.*
*My husband's at **the school**. He works late on Monday nights.*

*Is your daughter **at college** or university?*
*Beth lectures at in **the college** during the day and two evenings at the university.*

*Damon's **in hospital**. He crashed his car yesterday.*
*Sheila doesn't like working at **the hospital**. She prefers the clinic.*

*My mother's **at church**. She tries to go every Sunday.*
*My mother's at **the church**. She's helping arrange the flowers.*

We use no article in these expressions:

in town	at home	at work	at sea
by day	at night	by car/bus/plane/train	
by phone	mail	e-mail	

11 Question tags

Normally, if the statement is positive, the question tag is negative:
*He's here, **isn't** he?*

If the statement is negative, the question tag is positive:
*He **isn't** here, **is** he?*

However, we can put a positive tag after a positive statement to express surprise, suspicion, worry, etc.
*He's here, **is** he?*

Negative statements can't be followed by a negative tag:
*He **isn't** here, **isn't** he?* ✗

You form the question tag with the auxiliary of the appropriate tense:

Present Simple:	*You **live** here, **don't you**?*
Past Simple:	*She **arrived** yesterday, **didn't she**?*
Present Continuous:	*You**'re coming** to the party, **aren't you**?*
Present Perfect:	*She**'s gone** home, **hasn't she**?*

Note that **be** takes **are** with **I** in the negative, rather than the regular **am**:
*I'm here, **aren't** I?*

And **have**, when used to express states, can use **have** or **do**:
*They have a nice house, **haven't/don't they**?*
*She had some problems then, **hadn't/didn't she**?*

If a modal comes before the verb, this forms the question tag:
will *You'll see him tomorrow, **won't you**?*
can *He can play on Saturday, **can't** he?*

Note that **nobody** and **everybody** use **they** rather than **he** or **she**. **Nobody** is followed by a positive tag:
*Nobody's here, **are** they?*

And ***everybody*** by a negative one:
*Everybody's here, **aren't** they?*

We use **will you?**, **won't you?** and **would you?** either to invite or tell people to do things. In an invitation, **won't** is more polite than **will**, and **would** is the most polite:
*Come in, **will** you?*
*Come in, **won't** you?*
*Come in, **would** you?*

In a command, **won't** is stronger than **would**, and **will** is the strongest:
*Get out, **would** you?*
*Get out, **won't** you?*
*Get out, **will** you?*

1 Appendix

Active Tense Structures

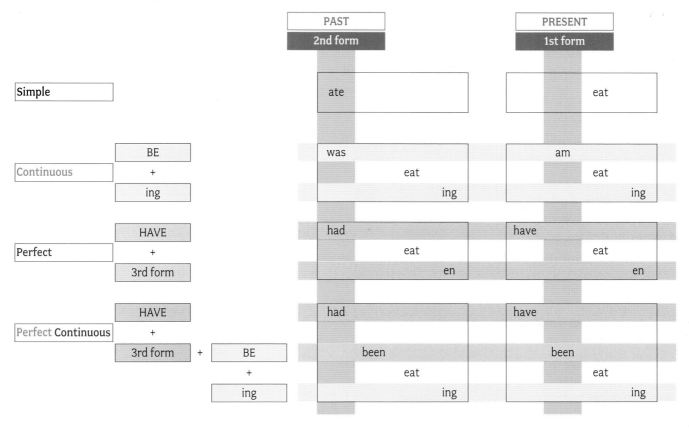

	PAST	PRESENT
	2nd form	1st form
Simple	ate	eat
Continuous — BE + ing	was eat ing	am eat ing
Perfect — HAVE + 3rd form	had eat en	have eat en
Perfect Continuous — HAVE + 3rd form + BE + ing	had been eat ing	have been eat ing

2 Appendix

Comparison — Adjectives, Adverbs and Determiners

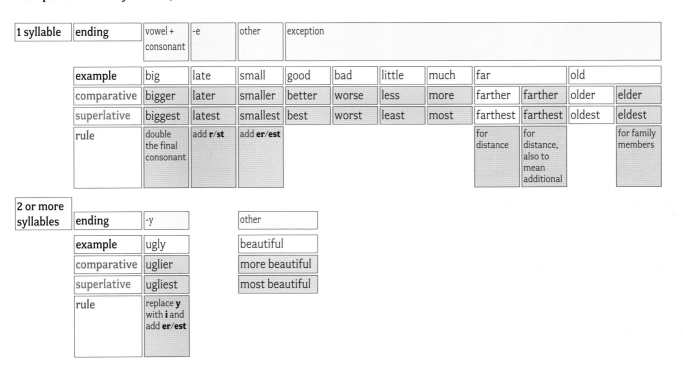

1 syllable	ending	vowel + consonant	-e	other	exception							
	example	big	late	small	good	bad	little	much	far		old	
	comparative	bigger	later	smaller	better	worse	less	more	farther	farther	older	elder
	superlative	biggest	latest	smallest	best	worst	least	most	farthest	farthest	oldest	eldest
	rule	double the final consonant	add **r/st**	add **er/est**					for distance	for distance, also to mean additional		for family members

2 or more syllables	ending	-y	other
	example	ugly	beautiful
	comparative	uglier	more beautiful
	superlative	ugliest	most beautiful
	rule	replace **y** with **i** and add **er/est**	

Grammar File

3 Appendix

Verbs not used in the Continuous

These verbs don't appear in any of the four continuous tenses — the Present, Past or Present/Past Perfect Continuous — except in the special meanings indicated.

appear   unless used to mean playing a part in the theatre:
He's appearing in Hamlet *in the West End.*

be   except where it means temporary behaviour:
He's being very silly.

believe, belong, concern, consist

cost   except where something is changing in price over a limited period:
Fish are costing more and more these days.

depend, deserve, dislike, doubt

feel   where it means think/believe; not where it means physical sensation:
I'm feeling a bit unwell.
Or touching:
He was feeling the bump on his head.

fit

forget   unless it refers to a knowledge of a subject:
I'm slowly forgetting my French.
Or to make a point, politely, in a discussion:
You're forgetting that we've already decided this.

guess   where it means feel/believe:
I guess that's so.
Not where it means actively trying to decide something:
I'm just guessing — is he Swedish?

hate

have   where it means own/possess, not where it means do:
He's having lunch.

hear   unless used for a medical/psychological condition:
He says he's hearing voices in his head.
Or where it means receiving a message on the radio:
I'm hearing you loud and clear.
Or in a legal sense:
They're hearing the case tomorrow.

hope   except in the polite use:
I'm/was hoping we might meet soon.

imagine   where it means think:
I imagine she may be right.
Not where it means an illusion:
You're imagining things.

impress, include, involve, know, lack, like, love

matter   unless used with expressions like **more** and **more/less** and **less**:
This is mattering less and less as I get older.

mean

measure   when used to mean the size of something:
The field measures about 150 metres.
But not where someone is checking it:
They're measuring him for a suit.

need, owe, prefer, realise, recognise, remember

resemble   unless used with expressions like **more** and **more/less** and **less**:
She's resembling her mother more and more.

see   unless where it means meet:
I'm seeing the doctor tomorrow.
Or for temporary medical/psychological condition:
I'm seeing stars.

seem

smell   unless it means an activity:
The cat's smelling the flowers.

sound

suppose   unless it indicates a temporary assumption:
If we're supposing that he's right — what are the consequences?

taste   unless it means checking the taste of something:
Wait a second — I'm just tasting the soup.

know

think   where it means feel/believe, not where you are actively using your mind:
What are you thinking about?

want   except in the Present/Past Perfect Continuous:
I've been wanting to speak to you for ages.
Or in the Past Continuous for a polite enquiry:
What were you wanting?

weigh   unless it means checking the weight of something:
She's weighing the ingredients for the cake.

wonder   except in the Present/Past Perfect Continuous:
Yes, I've been wondering about that.
Or in the polite use of the Past Continuous:
I was wondering if you could help me.

know, understand

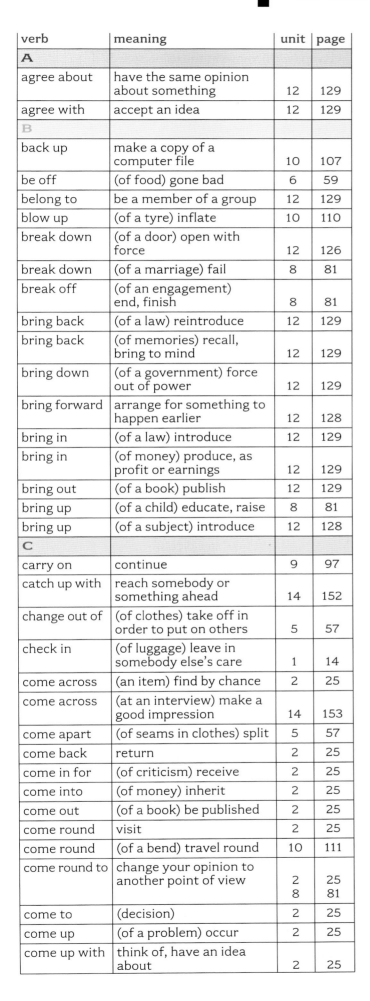

verb	meaning	unit	page
A			
agree about	have the same opinion about something	12	129
agree with	accept an idea	12	129
B			
back up	make a copy of a computer file	10	107
be off	(of food) gone bad	6	59
belong to	be a member of a group	12	129
blow up	(of a tyre) inflate	10	110
break down	(of a door) open with force	12	126
break down	(of a marriage) fail	8	81
break off	(of an engagement) end, finish	8	81
bring back	(of a law) reintroduce	12	129
bring back	(of memories) recall, bring to mind	12	129
bring down	(of a government) force out of power	12	129
bring forward	arrange for something to happen earlier	12	128
bring in	(of a law) introduce	12	129
bring in	(of money) produce, as profit or earnings	12	129
bring out	(of a book) publish	12	129
bring up	(of a child) educate, raise	8	81
bring up	(of a subject) introduce	12	128
C			
carry on	continue	9	97
catch up with	reach somebody or something ahead	14	152
change out of	(of clothes) take off in order to put on others	5	57
check in	(of luggage) leave in somebody else's care	1	14
come across	(an item) find by chance	2	25
come across	(at an interview) make a good impression	14	153
come apart	(of seams in clothes) split	5	57
come back	return	2	25
come in for	(of criticism) receive	2	25
come into	(of money) inherit	2	25
come out	(of a book) be published	2	25
come round	visit	2	25
come round	(of a bend) travel round	10	111
come round to	change your opinion to another point of view	2 / 8	25 / 81
come to	(decision)	2	25
come up	(of a problem) occur	2	25
come up with	think of, have an idea about	2	25

verb	meaning	unit	page
cut down	(of trees) cause to fall by cutting	12	130
cut down on	reduce the amount consumed	5	59
cut out	stop eating	5	59
D			
deal with	be involved with	3	26
do up	(of a button) fasten	5	56
do up	(of a room or house) improve	7 / 9	74 / 97
drive up	(of prices) cause to rise	9	94
drop off	leave something or somebody somewhere	13	142
F			
fall behind	be left behind by others	13	143
fall for	(of a person) fall in love with	13	143
fall for	(of a trick) believe in	13	143
fall in with	(of a plan) agree to	13	143
fall out	quarrel	13	143
fall through	(of a plan) fail to be completed	13	143
fill in	(of a form, etc.) write what is necessary	1 / 2	6 / 17
fill up	fill	10	111
find out	discover	13	139
finish with	(of a person) end a relationship	3	32
fit into	put in place inside	10	104
G			
get by	continue in spite of difficulties	4	41
get down to	(of work) begin to give serious attention to	14	152
get into	(of a space, a vehicle) enter	10 / 13	111 / 143
get on	(of a person) have a good relationship with	8 / 14 / 15	81 / 148 / 158
get on	advance or make progress	14	152
get out	leave or escape	2 / 12	18 / 125
get over	recover from	5	59
get through	(of an exam/competition) move through, pass	15 / 14	155 / 152
get to	arrive at	15	155
get up	(of bed) rise from	14	149
give away	give free of charge	6	62
give back	return	6	62

verb	meaning	unit	page
give in	concede	6	62
give in	return something used	6	62
give off	(of a smell) produce	6	62
give out	distribute	6	62
give up	stop taking	5	59
give up	stop trying	6	62
go down	(of sales) decrease	13	137
go for	choose	7 7	73 79
go in for	take an interest in	10	104
go off	(of an alarm) begin to ring	7	73
go off	(of food) start to decay	7	73
go off	leave	7 8	76 84
go on	do something after doing something else	11	116
go on	happen	7	73
go on	continue	7	73
go on about	talk about, sometimes at length	7 13	73 137
go out (with)	have a romantic relationship	7 8 15	73 81 155
go over	check	14	152
go through	check or search	1 7	14 73
go through	experience or suffer something	12	122
grow up	become an adult	8 9	81 92
grow up	increase in size or importance	6	62
H			
hack into	use a computer to see data illegally	13	136
hand in	give in	14	152
hang around	wait or be present	1 15	14 155
have (got) on	(of clothes) wear	9	95
have done with	finish	9	95
have on	have something arranged to do	9	95
have out	(of a tooth) cause to be removed	9	95
have sth. against	have negative feelings about	9	95
hold up	delay	10 1	111 14
K			
keep on	continue	4 6	47 59

verb	meaning	unit	page
keep up (with)	move at the same speed as	14	152
knock down	(of a building) demolish	9	97
knock out	force out of a competition	15	155
L			
laugh about	be amused by something	12	129
laugh at	be amused by something, make fun of	12	129
let down	(of clothes) lengthen	5	57
let down	cause somebody to be disappointed	8	81
let off	(of a brake) release	10	111
let out	(of clothes) make bigger	5	57
lie in	stay in bed in the morning	7	75
live on	support with money	13	137
log into	enter a Web site giving our user name, etc.	13	136
log on	begin using the Internet	8	83
look after	take care of	15 15	155 158
look back	think about something that happened before	15	158
look for	search	15	157
look forward to	hope to enjoy something in the future	13 15	138 158
look into	investigate	15	158
look out	take care	15	158
look sth. up	check in a dictionary, etc.	15	158
look up	improve	15	158
look up to	admire	7 15	74 158
M			
make up	be friends again after a quarrel	8	81
meet up with	meet	1	14
mess up	make dirty or untidy	3	32
move back	(of a place) return	14	148
P			
pass down	(of a family) continue through generations	8	82
pass on	send from person to person	3	27
pay by	pay using a cheque, credit card, etc.	15	156
pay in	pay using cash, etc.	15	156
pay off	repay an overdraft or loan	15	158
pick up	collect	1 13	14 142
pull down	(of a building) demolish	9	97
pull out	(of a car) move away from the side of the road	10	111
pull up	stop while driving	2	18

verb	meaning	unit	page
put across	(of an idea) explain successfully	14	152
put off	discourage	11	118
put off	postpone	11	118
put on	(of a CD) start playing	7	79
put on	(of clothes, etc.) dress in	5 / 10	57 / 111
put on	(of weight) gain	6 / 11	59 / 118
put out	(of a fire) extinguish	11	118
put out	(of a person) inconvenience	11	118
put through	connect	11	118
put up	(of a person) give a bed to	11	118
put up	(of a price) increase	11	118
put up	(of hands) raise	2	18
put up	(of a building) construct	9	97
put up with	tolerate	8 / 11	81 / 118
R			
run out (of)	(of material, food, etc.) be finished	7 / 10	74 / 111
S			
sell out (of)	sell all available	5	52
send out	transmit	10	110
send over	send to another person or place	5	49
set in	(of a book, film) put the story in a time and place	14	147
set off	(to a journey) start	15	155
set off	(of an explosive) cause to explode	2	22
set off (from)	start a journey	1	14
set out	start a journey	1	8
set up	start an organisation	3 / 14 / 14	27 / 149 / 150
settle down	live in a stable situation	8	81
shout at	shout in a hostile way	12	129
shout to	shout a warning	12	129
sign up	sign an agreement	1	13
slow down	move more slowly	10	111
snap off	break	10	104
speak up	speak louder	4	47
split up	(of a couple) stop being together	7 / 8	74 / 81
switch off	(of a machine) stop from working temporarily	13	137
switch on	(of a machine) start working	13	135

verb	meaning	unit	page
T			
take after	(of a parent/grandparent) resemble	8	81
take in	(of clothes) tighten	5	57
take in	cause to believe something false	11	118
take in	understand	14	152
take off	(of an aeroplane) begin to fly	1	14
take off	(of clothes) remove	5	57
take over	take responsibility	2	23
take part in	join	1	6
take up	(of a sport or hobby) start doing	5	59
take up	(of clothes) shorten	5	57
think of	have an opinion	10 / 14	108 / 149
throw at	throw intending to hit somebody	12	129
throw to	throw so somebody can have the object	12	129
touch down	(of an aeroplane) land	1	14
try on	(of clothes) try wearing	5 / 6	57 / 64
turn back	stop travelling and begin to return	10	103
turn down	(of volume) reduce	5	57
turn down	(of an idea, job application) reject	9 / 10	97 / 103
turn into	convert	10	103
turn off	(of a road) leave	10	103
turn off	(of a machine) stop from working temporarily	10	107
turn on	(of a machine) start working	10	107
turn out	(from a house) evict	9	97
turn out	(of a person, situation) become, develop or end	10	103
turn over	(of a car) roll onto its roof	10	103
turn up	arrive	3 / 10	32 / 103
W			
wake up	awaken	3	34
wind up	(of a spring) to tighten	10	110
work for	be employed by	12	129
work out	(of a situation) work well in the end	15	155
work out	calculate	1 / 10	7 / 104

Exam Writing Reference

In the FCE exam, you have to answer two questions, as follows:

Part 1   Question 1   Transactional letter

Part 2   Questions 2-4   Informal letter
                               Formal letter
                               Discursive composition
                               Story
                               Article
                               Report

               Question 5   Descriptive composition on one of the set books.

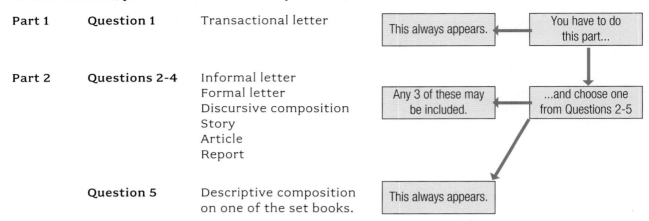

You have to write **120-180** words for each answer. If you write fewer than 120 you will lose marks. If you write more than 180, the examiner may not read them.

In the exam, you answer on a page with lines 174mm long. Draw a few lines this size and write something on them. Work out how many words, on average, you write on each line. This will save you time in the exam.

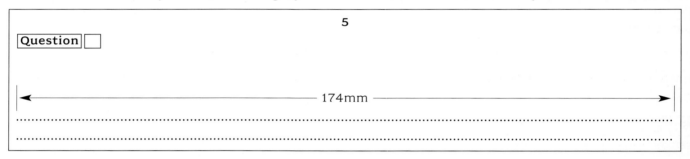

Part 1: Transactional letter

You and a friend have decided to go on a horse riding holiday in the Scottish Highlands. You have found an advertisement for pony trekking — travelling from place to place on a pony and you decide to find out more about it.

Read carefully the advertisement below, on which you have made some notes. Then, using this information, write a letter to the company covering all your points. You may add other relevant information of your own.

Write a letter of between 120 and 180 words in an appropriate style on the next page. Do not write any addresses.

Model answer

language points   layout points   structural points

You don't have a name to write to so start like this.

Begin all lines on the left of the page.

Use a new paragraph for each point you want to cover...

...unless they are closely related.

Think of different ways of saying 'please'.

Normal way of closing after Dear Sir/Madam,

Remember the capital letter.

Tell the person why you are writing to them.

Leave an empty line between paragraphs.

Think of ways of ordering your paragraphs.

Finish by telling the person what you expect them to do.

Standard closing sentence.

Full stop here.

Comma here.

Dear Sir/Madam,

I recently saw your advertisement for pony trekking in the Scottish Highlands and I'd be grateful if you would send me some additional information.

First of all, I would appreciate a price list covering the full range of your treks.

I am also rather worried since I am a complete beginner. In fact, I've only been on a horse once in my life. Could you tell me how much tuition I might need in order to join a trek?

You also say that accommodation is in youth hostels. I'd appreciate it if you could tell me how many people will share each room and also, who does the cooking. In other words, do we have to cook for ourselves, or are meals provided?

Finally, I would like to know which parts of the Highlands your treks visit? I have never been to the Scottish Highlands before and am interested in seeing which parts I can go to.

Thank you for your help in advance. I look forward to hearing from you soon.

Yours faithfully,
Laura Amento

Part 2: Informal letter

Question

This is part of a letter you receive from a pen friend.

I have studied English for some time and I do a lot of work but feel I am making no progress. Your English is better than mine – what do you suggest?

Write a letter, giving advice to your pen friend. Write 120-180 words in an appropriate style. Do not write any addresses.

language points   structural points

Begin with a general comment, an apology for not writing sooner or both.

Divide the main part of your letter into paragraphs and cover 2-3 points in each.

Dashes are quite appropriate in informal style.

Start a new paragraph where the subject changes a little.

At the end, say something about your current situation and make an excuse to stop writing.

Make up a name. Don't start with *Dear Friend/Pen friend*

Say something about the last letter you received.

Refer to the part of her letter that you want to write about.

Invent details where necessary.

Try to avoid repeating the same words.

Use contractions.

Use exclamation marks now and again – but don't overdo it.

Finish with an informal expression.

Dear Maria,

I'm sorry it has taken so long for me to answer your last letter. Things have been busy here recently. Anyway, it was good to hear from you again.

Do you remember that you asked me for advice about improving your English? Actually, I remember that when I was at your level I felt much the same. So the first thing I'd say is don't worry – lots of students feel this way when they get to Intermediate.

Also, you said in your letter that you do a lot of 'work'. Maybe this is the problem. Perhaps you should do other things, like reading or watching English videos and films. I also find that the Internet is very useful, and great fun. Give it a try – get out of the study!

I have to go now – my sister will be home in a minute and I know she'll want to talk to me about her new boyfriend – again! Hope everything goes well and that you feel your English is improving again soon.

Love,
Claudia

Part 2: Letter of Application

Question

You are interested in spending the summer in Britain and have just read the following advertisement.

> **Looking for summer work?**
> Busy restaurant needs waiters/waitresses. No experience necessary but good knowledge of English essential. Many of our customers are tourists so knowledge of other languages an advantage.
> Apply to: Matthew Roberts, PO Box 143

Write your letter of application in 120-180 words. Do not include any addresses.

language points   structural points

Begin with the job you are applying for.

Invent the name of a publication if necessary.

Keep the language formal – don't use contractions.

Refer to some contact details – but don't actually write them on the letter.

Use this, unless you began with Dear Sir/Madam,

If you don't know the name of the person, use Dear Sir/Madam, and end with Yours faithfully,

In this paragraph say something about yourself. Make it relevant to the advert.

Go on to include other relevant experience. If you don't have any, use your imagination.

This is fairly standard. Either use it or practise an alternative.

Print your name underneath your signature.

Dear Mr Roberts,

I would like to apply for the job of waitress in your restaurant, which I saw advertised in Summer Work in Britain.

I am 18 years old and in my final year of secondary school. I have been learning English for five years and am in a class at Higher Intermediate level. This means that my English is good enough to use in many jobs and I am sure I would be able to talk to your customers without difficulty. Besides English, my native language is Italian. I also speak quite good Spanish and some French.

I have some experience of this type of work because for the past year I have been employed as a waitress in a restaurant here at weekends.

I can be contacted either at my address or by e-mail, both of which appear at the top of this letter.

I hope you will consider my application favourably and look forward to hearing from you.

Yours sincerely,
Francesca Valvona

FRANCESCA VOLVONA

Remember

- Why are you writing?
- Where did you see the advert?
- Who are you?
- What can you bring to the job?
- How can you be contacted?

Finally — you are writing an exam answer, not the true story of your life. Don't be afraid to invent details where necessary.

Part 2: Discursive composition

Question

After a class discussion on wildlife, your teacher has asked you to write a composition giving your opinion on the following statement:

Zoos are part of the past and should be abolished.

Using 120-180 words, write your composition.

language points   structural points

Start by referring to the question, but keep this paragraph fairly short.

Learn the words for introducing an opposing argument...

...and for listing a number of points.

Refer to the opposite point of view again in the conclusion...

...but finish with your own opinions.

> Many people disagree today about the usefulness of zoos and whether they are cruel to animals.
>
> Some feel that the animals in zoos live in unnatural conditions and suffer from stress. They also say that zoos are unnecessary because people can travel more easily to see animals in the wild, and also that we can see films and TV programmes about animals.
>
> However, an important purpose of a zoo is to allow zoologists to study animals. Also, not many people, especially children, have the opportunity to travel round the world. Finally, if television and film are as good as the real thing, why do we never hear this argument in other areas of life?
>
> I agree that zoos do not provide a natural environment, but most of them are making improvements here. They also help to preserve species that would otherwise have died out. Finally, if we want to understand animal behaviour, I think people must have the chance to study animals close up. For these reasons I feel that zoos should not be abolished.

Decide which side you are on and present the opposite argument first.

In the next paragraph, give your own opinion.

You can also introduce a new argument here, to make things more interesting.

Part 2: Story

Question

An international magazine which you read is running a short story competition. You have decided to enter it. The rules say that the story must end with the following words:

I knew then that things were going to get better.

Write your story in 120-180 words.

The question will either ask you to end with a particular line or start with one – or you might have the choice.

language points   structural points

Start inside the main story, where something is happening.

You can fill in the background details later.

Use the Past Perfect for any previous events...

...but move to the Past Simple once you have fixed the earlier time.

Use participles to vary your style.

> The rain was falling steadily by then and the wind began to blow. There were still a couple of kilometres to the top of the valley. I was cold and my legs were tired now.
>
> It was the bike that had got me into this mess in the first place. Five days before, Alan, Mike and I had set off to cycle over the hills to the coast. But on the way, my bike had broken. So we left it at a repair shop and I hitch-hiked the rest of the way. Now, on the way back, I had no idea whether the other two were ahead of me or behind me.
>
> I came round a bend and saw a roadside café. There wasn't much for sale beyond coffee and biscuits, but they helped. I went back to my bike, dreading the next part of the journey, but then, in the distance, I saw two cyclists. As they came closer I saw they were Alan and Mike. I knew then that things were going to get better.

Use the Past Continuous for background events.

Help the reader to see the situation.

Give some idea of how the characters feel.

Use time expressions to make things clear.

Use the words in the question exactly as they are given.

Exam Writing Reference

Part 2: Article

Question

You have seen this announcement in an international young people's magazine:

> **Fashion is not an option!**
> If you don't look right you can't feel right.
> Dressing badly simply says that you don't care about yourself.
> Do you agree with these statements? Write and tell us how you feel about fashion. We will publish the best article and send you a £500 cash prize.

Write your article in 120-180 words.

Think of a title that will get the reader's attention.

Don't be afraid to make general statements, even controversial ones. This isn't an essay.

You can be ironic sometimes – especially if it puts you on the same side as most of your readers...

...and you can add to this by using 'we'.

Fashion – we're all victims!

Everybody cares about what they wear. Of course they do. It's just that not everybody wants to feel so very fashionable. If you pull on an old pair of jeans and a torn T-shirt, you are still saying, 'This is me. This is how I am.'

People who spend their time getting the latest look, who take an obsessive interest in what comes down the catwalk in Paris or Milan, are saying something else. It might be 'I'm up with what's happening,' or 'I am a successful person,' – or maybe just 'I've got money to burn.'

Somewhere in between these two extremes lie most of us. When we buy something we give a thought to whether this style is current or stone dead. We dress with some attention to the occasion: we don't turn up at work in open-toed sandals or go to a funeral in a multi-coloured shirt. But we don't think our appearance is the most important thing in the entire world.

Like everything else, fashion should be taken in moderation.

You don't need to use full sentences all the time.

Direct speech here and there provides variety.

Use specialist vocabulary where possible.

Use idiomatic language.

The last sentence is important. Make your point – and some humour is always welcome.

Part 2: Report

Question

Your school is going to accept a group of 20 British students for a month. They will live with local families and attend classes. The principal has asked you to write a report about what the students might do in their free time. Describe some possible activities and explain why you think these would be suitable.

language points   structural points

Use headings.

The number of paragraphs and their subjects will depend on the question. Make sure your layout is clear.

Number your points if the question allows it.

Don't be afraid to invent details, or use the names of real places where you live.

This particular question doesn't ask you to reach a for or against conclusion – but find some way of summing up.

Start by stating the reason for the report.

Say where you got the information from.

Don't use contractions.

Use formal vocabulary where there is a choice – e.g. *favour* rather than *like*.

Use impersonal language – e.g. passives where possible.

Introduction
The purpose of this report is to describe some suitable free-time activities for the group of 20 British students who will join our school for a month. I have reached these conclusions through discussion with current school students of the same age.

Recommendations

1   For general social mixing, the best places are the cafés. Most visitors favour those around the main square in the Old Town. However, younger people generally prefer to meet in the cheaper ones in the university quarter.
2   This area also provides the most suitable choice of discos and clubs. Currently the most popular are Club Astra and Dario's.
3   A full listing of events at the cinemas and theatres can be seen in the weekly What's On magazine.
4   A number of our students have volunteered to take our visitors to see either of the two local teams.

Conclusion
The general attitude among our students to the visitors is interested and positive and I am sure we can rely on them to make this stay a worthwhile experience for all.

Communication Activities

Loan words in English (p. 38)

Arabic

admiral, albatross, alchemy, alcohol, alcove, algebra, alkali, apricot, arsenal, aubergine, emir, gazelle, giraffe, harem, hashish, henna, hookah, Islam, jasmine, Koran, lemon, magazine, minaret, mohair, monsoon, Moslem, muezzin, mullah, Muslim, nadir, safari, saffron, sash, scarlet, sequin, sheik, sofa, syrup, talisman, zenith, zero

German

dachshund, fahrenheit, flak, frankfurter, hamburger, hamster, kindergarten, quartz, sauerkraut, schwa, strafe, waltz, yodel

Chinese languages

china, chopsticks, chopsuey, chow mein, ginseng, gung-ho, kowtow, kung fu, lychee, pekoe, sampan, tai chi, tea, yen

French, modern

aperitif, apres-ski, avant-garde, brasserie, café, camouflage, chateau, chef, croissant, cuisine, debacle, debut, dessert, elite, etiquette, fiancé(e), garage, gourmet, hotel, liaison, limousine, lingerie, marionette, morale, pastiche, patisserie, petite, pirouette, regime, risqué, silhouette, voyeur

Italian

alto, balcony, battalion, brigade, broccoli, cameo, confetti, contralto, cupola, design, frigate, ghetto, graffiti, granite, grotto, lasagne, libretto, mozzarella, pasta, piano(forte), piazza, piccolo, pizza, pizzeria, ravioli, risotto, seraglio, sonata, soprano, spaghetti, squadron, staccato, stanza

Japanese

aikido, bonsai, geisha, haiku, hara-kiri, judo, jujitsu, karaoke, karate, kimono, sake, samurai, sayonara, Shinto, shogun, , soy, soya, sushi, tofu, yen, Zen

Spanish

alligator, anchovy, armada, armadillo, barricade, bravado, cask, chinchilla, embargo, galleon, grenade, guerrilla, lariat, pronto, ranch, renegade, sherry, silo, sombrero, stampede, vigilante

Urban legends (p. 56)

Answers

1 Titanic

As far as anyone knows, this story is not true. It is usually told about a William T. Sloper, who left the *Titanic* on the first boat to be lowered into the water. However, at that time most passengers did not realise the ship was sinking and were reluctant to get into the boats. There was no panic and when the boat eventually left the ship it was less than half-full. The story of him dressing in women's clothing was written by a reporter for the New York Journal who was annoyed because Sloper wouldn't give him an interview.

2 Nike

This story is true. In 1989, Nike filmed an advert in Kenya using Samburu tribesmen. As one man spoke to the camera in his native Maa language, the Nike slogan 'Just do it' appeared on the screen. However, what he actually said was, 'I don't want these. Give me big shoes.' The problem appears to have been caused because the film crew's translator didn't speak Maa, only Swahili.

3 John F Kennedy

The legend has been repeated so many times that it has become accepted as fact. However, it simply isn't true. Throughout his inauguration day in 1961, Kennedy wore the traditional silk top hat, as many newspaper photographs of the time show. It is true that he rarely wore a hat normally, but hats for men were going out of fashion. The decline in sales of men's hats at the time wasn't caused by John F Kennedy.

4 Donald Duck

The best-known version of this story comes from 1977, when the city of Helsinki found itself short of money and decided to economise by stopping the purchase of Donald Duck comics for youth centres. A year later, during a parliamentary election campaign, the press started to print a story that one of the candidates had been responsible for banning Donald Duck from Helsinki. However, the decision was purely economic, and nobody opposed it at the time.

5 Nylon

Nylon (polyhexamethyleneadipamide) was invented in 1935 by an organic chemist called Wallace Carothers. He called his new invention Fiber 66. The company he worked for, Du Pont, chose nylon out of a list of 400 possible names, apparently because they liked the sound of it. Nylon stockings came on to the market in 1937, after they were introduced at the New York World's Fair. London was not involved in the development of the product.

Health and fitness quiz (p. 58)

Answers
Check your answers on the grid. Use a pencil to shade the correct squares to reveal your profile.

	questions	not so good	could be better	good
Diet	1	c	b	a
	5	a	b	c
	9	a	b	c
Health	2	b	a	c
	4	c	b	a
	7	c	b	a
Fitness	3	a	b	c
	6	c	b	a
	8	c	b	a

Quotations (p. 70)

1 Everywhere is walking distance if you have the time.
   Steven Wright

2 All good things in life are either immoral, fattening or overpriced.
   Rajavi Kejriwal

3 Happiness is having a large, close-knit family in another city.
   George Burns

4 The person who knows how to laugh at himself will never cease to be amused.
   Shirley Maclaine

5 It isn't necessary to be rich and famous to be happy. It's only necessary to be rich.
   Alan Alda

6 Happiness is not having what you want, but wanting what you have.
   Anonym

7 If everything is under control, you are going too slow.
   Mario Andretti

Happiness quiz (p. 70)

Answers
Circle your answers on the list below. Then decide which colour most applies to you — purple, blue or red.

1	c	a	b
2	a	b	c
3	b	c	a
4	c	a	b
5	c	a	b
6	a	b	c
7	b	c	a
8	a	b	c
9	b	c	a
10	c	a	b

Communication Activities

Now read the description of your main colour below.

Free and happy

You really understand how to be happy. You've got a brilliant approach to life.

At the centre of this is the understanding that if you're not happy, then it's up to you to sort it out. There are things you can do about it — changing the way you think, feel or the way you handle your problems. You have confidence and self-belief and won't accept misery as a way of life.

You believe in yourself and your ability to get through things. You're not smug, but at peace with the real you.

It could be, of course, that you aren't 100 per cent secure in all areas of your life — work, play and love — and that's natural. Or it could be that you lack some happiness skills, such as goal setting or managing your emotions.

It's not up to me!

You're not happy because you've never learned the skills to be happy. Not only do you not have these skills, but you don't feel you need them. You tend to think that your happiness or unhappiness is not up to you, that it comes from events beyond your control or from other people. You haven't fully realised that your happiness is in your own hands.

So maybe you need to make some changes to your lifestyle, to the way you handle events or your approach to other people. Or maybe you've become too focused on yourself — a bit 'me, me, me'. Remember that the basis of true happiness is finding the balance between considering yourself and giving to other people.

Your own worst critic

You're not very happy, are you? You try hard, you mean well, but inside you is that little voice that screams 'I'm not good enough'.

In short, your unhappiness comes from what's happening inside you — you never feel contented because you are always trying for maximum success and even if you reach it, you don't feel you deserve to enjoy it.

But happiness isn't something that you get just by hard work. Yes, reaching goals and getting where you want in life is important, but to be truly happy, you need to be at peace with yourself.

People who are at peace with themselves generally do much more, much better in life than those who try hard all the time. Learn to value what you do and you'll not only feel happier, you'll also be more effective.

Design and art direction: Nadia Maestri
Computer graphics and picture research: Sara Blasigh
Illustrations: Anna and Elena Balbusso, Eugène Collilieux, Franco Grazioli,
Simone Massoni, Fabio Visintin

The publisher and author(s) would like to thank the following people for their feedback
and comments during the development of the material:
Maria Carmela Lapetina Barozzi, Luigi Dodi, Justin Rainey, Patrizia Tambosi.
Some of the material in this book was piloted with students at Stevenson College
Edinburgh, to whom thanks is due.

David Maule would like to thank Zeynep, Harry and James for their patience while this
book was written.

We are grateful to the following for permission to reproduce copyright material:
NI Syndication for an extract adapted from 'A Life in the Day of Philip Tesha' by Ann
McFerran published in *The Sunday Times Magazine* on 8 April 2001; Trekforce Expeditions
for an extract adapted from their web site www.trekforce.org.uk; Guardian Newspapers
Limited for an extract adapted from 'Fined...' by Geoffrey Gibbs and Sally James Gregory
published on 7 November 2000 © GUARDIAN; Bryan Bennett for an extract adapted
from 'Lend me your words' published in MET Vol. 2, No. 3 April 1993; The Woolmark
Company for adapted information about their company and products; FriendsReunited
for an extract adapted from their web site www.friendsreunited.co.uk; Black Swan, a
division of Transworld Publishers for an adapted extract from *Notes From a Big Country*
by Bill Bryson, © Bill Bryson, all rights reserved.

In some instances we have been unable to trace the owners of copyright material and we
would appreciate any information that would enable us to do so.

Picture credits:
GeoAtlas - Graphi-ogre Europe vector 2 - World vector 2 / John Foxx Images Travel &
Transportation Today volume 21 / John Foxx Images Amazing Animals CD26 / Stockbyte
Entertainment & Leisure CD35 / Stockbyte - household CD 29 / Stockbyte - food CD 34 /
Stockbyte - business office CD 31 / Corbis Images - Secondary Education volume 198 -
Secondary Education 2 volume 223 / Stockbyte - World Business & Finance CD 84 /
Art Explosion, Nova development / Hulton Archive / Cideb Archives /© Doug Wilson/
Contrasto / www.cardiffphotolibrary.co.uk / www.liquidlibrary.com /
www.visibleearth.nasa.gov / www.esonet.org/pinacoteca/cropcircles /
www.friendsreunited.co.uk / www.sportwool.com

We would be happy to receive your comments and suggestions,
and give you any other information concerning our material.
editorial@blackcat-cideb.com
www.blackcat-cideb.com
www.cideb.it

ISBN   88-530-0181-X

Printed in Italy by Stige, Turin

CISQ

CISQ CERT
TEXTBOOKS AND
TEACHING MATERIALS
The quality of the publisher's
design, production and sales processes has
been certified to the standard of
UNI EN ISO 9001